SERBIAN PATERICON

Volume I

ST. SIMEON, FATHER OF THE SERBIAN SAINTS
surrounded by the hosts of the saints of the Church Triumphant.
A damaged fresco in the Pech Monastery, of 1345.

Serbian Patericon

Saints of the Serbian Orthodox Church

Volume I

JANUARY-APRIL

By FR. DANIEL M. ROGICH

Icon illustrations by Lillian Tintor

ST. HERMAN OF ALASKA BROTHERHOOD

ST. PAISIUS ABBEY PRESS

1994

Library of Congress Cataloging in Publication Data
    Rogich, Fr. Daniel M.
Serbian Patericon: The Saints of the Serbian Orthodox
    Church
Library of Congress Catalogue Number: 94-065-911
ISBN 0-938635-75-1

CONTENTS

MARCH

APRIL

Patericon of the Serbian Saints

GOD leaves the stamp of His own image upon each personality, which, after self-inflicted purification upon earth, will become an adornment to Paradise. So also the personality of a people, after the toil of developing the characteristics of Christ given to it by God, will have a place in Paradise as a host of saints. The saints, reflecting God's glory, praise Him in Paradise as deified earthly beings, beings who have been just like us here on earth. Thus, the mission of us earthly ones is to continue in that same divine calling and to sanctify earthly communities who call upon the saints.

Collections of accounts of these saints, these heavenly beings of earth or "earthly angels," are the primary source of information and at the same time models to instruct future generations. Prologues, Synaxarions, and Patericons and Matericons are indispensable in the formation of young souls.

Today, when universal Christianity is losing nobility of spirit through apostasy, the young generation is becoming spiritually impoverished. Yet Christians have to go on through the darkness resulting from the contemporary state of nonresistance to universal, nihilistic evil. People have to draw strength from their heavenly predecessors, and therefore it is timely that this work of Fr. Daniel appears as a supply of new energy from above to us here below.

This "heavenly energy," expressed in Serbian culture, was the result of the strong hesychastic influence planted by St. Sava, Enlightener of Serbia. According to the church historian I. M. Kontzevitch, St. Sava "was a hesychast in the true sense of the word: thoroughly imbued with the teaching of the ancient Fathers of the desert and the teaching of St. Simeon the New Theologian, he set the course which the spiritual life of Serbia has been following up to our days."

Hesychasm was passed on from Serbia to Russia through the general influence of Serbian Orthodox art and culture. Kontzevitch writes: "In the early 14th century, the Byzantine Empire experienced a renaissance of Byzantine Art, which lost its former abstract character and became more realistic: now evoking contrition, now dramatic or enchanting. Harmonious hues, cleverly used, imparted an almost impressionistic character to a painting. This school adorned the churches of Macedonia and old Serbia, and the ancient churches on Mt. Athos. While adhering to the Greek style, the masters of this school contributed something individual to their art: their religious world view and the spark of their own creative genius, thus leaving the mark of their national creativity in their paintings."[1]

This spark of creative genius, or "heavenly energy," the saints in the Church Triumphant give to us here below in the Church Militant, where we are to carry on the struggle in the daily task of existence.

By presenting this book, the editors offer help to contemporary converts who are new to the phenomenon of the heavenly intercessors. May the Serbian saints, from heaven, help to fortify our rapidly growing number of converts who are novices in the Christian faith, to help to sanctify the American land.

The editors ask the reader to accompany the reading of these lives with prayer and with fear of God, that the glory of God here upon earth will be multiplied, and that our creativity, or our Christian duty in creative existence, will reflect the otherworldly presence which we so badly need and which is the characteristic of the saints.

The purpose of this Patericon is to provide a link from the traditional, ancient Orthodox experience to the young generation in America, before it is too late. In the words of Fr. Seraphim Rose: "Let us hasten therefore to do the work of God."

Abbot Herman
St. Paisius Abbey
January 14, 1994
St. Sava, Enlightener of the Serbs

---

1. Kontzevitch, I.M., *The Acquisition of the Holy Spirit in Ancient Russia* (St. Herman Press, Platina, 1988) pp.129-30.

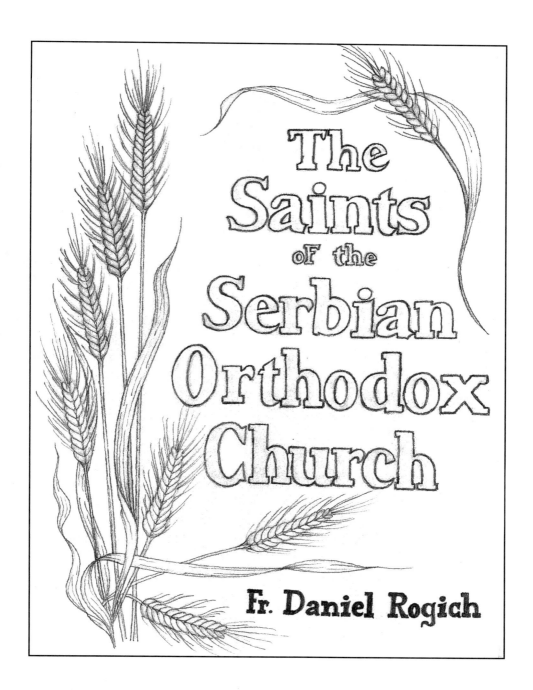

The Saints of the Serbian Orthodox Church

Fr. Daniel Rogich

In loving memory of my father,
Michael Rogich, Jr. (1920-1989),

WHOSE life above all other lives has been most inspiring to me, who while living on earth loved me with such a tenderness that words to express this love become stumblingblocks to our very living and eternal bond we will always share; whose care for his wife and children and grandchildren was marked by constant giving, total concern and unconditional love; whose service to others was unforgettable; who, like his Patron Saint "Sveti Nikola" (St. Nicholas), did so many things in secret for others, accepting nothing but only the reward from God above; whose life in Christ is still a source of guidance for me; who still speaks to me about the mysteries of eternal life, about the way I should go. I do not know which of his lives is more powerful to me: the one he lived on earth with us all or the one he now lives with the Lord in the eternal dimension of reality; but one thing is for certain—that I cherish my father Michael, as he is the reason I love God, my family, my Orthodox Church, my ethno-spiritual roots, and my fellow human beings!

May his memory be eternal!

Fr. Daniel Rogich

PREFACE

by Veselin Kesich

HOW DEEPLY has Christianity entered the minds and souls of Christians throughout the centuries? To find an answer, both concrete and illuminating, we cannot do better than to look at the lives of its saints. They are the purest fruits of the faith and of a life in Christ.

Father Daniel Rogich has assembled an impressive collection of the lives of Serbian saints throughout the history of their church, most of them available in English only here for the first time. After their ninth-century conversion, Serbs were rooted in Christianity. St. Sava and the Serbian Monastery at Hilandar on Mount Athos played a crucial role in the development of spirituality in the Serbian church.

The Serbian saints from medieval times to the present followed the models of sanctity that we meet throughout Christian history. They came from different strata of society and geographical regions. Some were medieval rulers and princes, whereas others were simple villagers. Yet they shared the same love of Christ in humility, and they have the same desire, in the words of St. Ignatius, to *be* Christians and not simply to be *called* Christians. Their lives have been influenced by those who preceded them, particularly by the Desert Fathers of the fourth century. And they in turn influenced and encouraged the people around them.

The author starts each life with a quotation from the Bible or the Fathers of the Church, which corresponds to the character and achievements of the saint, and he ends each chapter with a hymn to the saint. The life itself becomes a framed verbal icon. Through these lives, the author reveals the historical context of the times. We can learn about the circumstances in which the saints lived and through this about the history of the church. The struggle with the Islamic Turks and the Catholic Unia is vividly reflected in many of these lives. These saints, often of simple origin and background, empowered by the spirit of Christ and strengthened by their ascetic experience, overcame the threat of Turkish authority and also resisted the temptation to convert to Roman Catholicism. Dangers from outside never interrupted their inner effort: a constant examination of the soul, a cleansing of the mind and heart. The author skillfully presents their outward and inward activities.

We are fortunate that Father Rogich is the one who is introducing these saints to us. As a sensitive religious man who is well equipped with scholarly tools, he has a pastoral concern for the believer's spiritual needs, and he leads us to the heart of the matter. Not only Serbian Orthodox will profit from this collection, but all Christians concerned with the common spirituality of the Orthodox Church.

Here we meet exceptional human beings, brothers and sisters of Christ. *And looking around on those who sat about him, Jesus said: Whoever shall do the will of God is my brother, and my sister, and mother* (Mark 3:34-35).

Veselin Kesich
St. Vladimir's Seminary

Serbian
Patericon

January through April

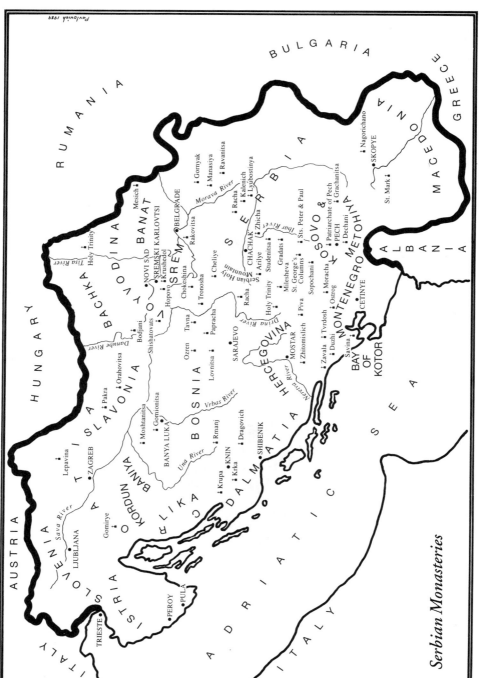

Pavlovich 1989

BULGARIA

RUMANIA

VOYVODINA

BANAT

HUNGARY

AUSTRIA

SLOVENIA

ISTRIA

ITALY

TRIESTE

PEROY • PULA •

GOMIRYE •

LJUBLJANA •

Sava River

KORDUN

BANIYA

† Lepavina

† ZAGREB

SLAVONIA

† Pakra

† Orahovitsa

Gomionitsa †

Moshtanitsa †

BANYA LUKA

† Dragovich

† Rmanj

† Krupa

KNIN •

† Krka

SHIBENIK •

LIKA

DALMATIA

ADRIATIC SEA

Una River

Vrbas River

BOSNIA

Lovnitsa †

Ozren †

Tavna †

Bodjani †

Shishatovats †

BACHKA

NOVI SAD •

Danube River

Tisa River

† Holy Trinity

Mesich †

SREMSKI KARLOVTSI •

Krushedol †

Hopovo †

SRÈM

BELGRADE

Chokeshina †

Tronosha †

Papracha †

Cheliye †

Rakovitsa †

Moravα River

Gornyak †

Manasiya †

Ravanitsa †

† Racha

† Kalenich

† Lyubostinya

SERBIA

Zhicha †

CHACHAK

Arilye †

Studenitsa †

Serbian Holy Mountain

Racha †

Holy Trinity †

Drina River

SARAJEVO

Milesheva †

Gradats †

Piva †

St. George's Columns †

Sopochani †

Sts. Peter & Paul †

KOSOVO & METOHIYA

Patriarchate of Pech

PECH †

Dechani †

Grachanitsa †

Moracha †

† Tvrdosh

† Zavala

Ostrog †

† Duzhi

Savina †

CETINYE •

MONTENEGRO

BAY OF KOTOR

† Zhitomislich

MOSTAR

HERCEGOVINA

Neretva River

ALBANIA

St. Mark †

SKOPYE †

Nagorichano †

MACEDONIA

GREECE

ITALY

Serbian Monasteries

Location of the most renowned monasteries which to this day are important centers of Serbian Orthodoxy (Map by Paul Pavlovich)

INTRODUCTION

by the Author

*Again we offer to Thee this rational service for
them that in faith have gone before to their rest,
forefathers, fathers, patriarchs, prophets, apostles,
preachers, evangelists, martyrs, confessors, ascetics,
and for every righteous spirit in faith made perfect.*
Divine Liturgy of St. John Chrysostom

THE LIVES of the saints," writes St. Justin Popovich, "are nothing more than the life according to Christ the Lord repeated in every
saint in greater or lesser degree, in this or that form, or more precisely:
it is the life of Christ the Lord continued through the saints, the life of
the incarnate Word of God, the God-man Jesus Christ, Who became a
human being so that as a human being He might give and grant us His
divine life; so that as God, by His life, He might illumine, deify and
sanctify our human life on earth, *for the One Who sanctifies and those
who are sanctified share a common origin* (Heb. 2:11)."[1] This definition
of the Lives of the Saints stresses the high level of importance the saints
should play in every Christian's life, as they are the human mediums
and instruments inviting us to partake of the salvific life in Christ on
earth. It is for this reason that the Orthodox Church has always treasured
the written Lives of the Saints and celebrates their memory in all her
Divine Services. In the Church's liturgical services we hear repeatedly

---

1. Justin Popovich, *Zhitije Svetih* (Belgrade, 1972), Vol. I: January, p. 9.

the petition, "With all the saints let us commend ourselves and one another, and all our lives unto Christ our God." As this prayer from the
Anaphora of the Divine Liturgy of St. John Chrysostom indicates, the
participation in the Eucharist is for the Orthodox Christian a unique
opportunity for union and communion with the very life and spirit of
the saints. Therefore the reading of the Lives of the Saints is not merely
a recounting of history, but more importantly an act of anamnestic
worship, a chance to place oneself in the very presence of God the Holy
Trinity.

Keeping this vision concerning the saints in mind, i.e., allowing it
to be the guiding principle and set the tone for understanding who the
saints are, I will touch upon three areas of importance in this short
introduction to *The Saints of the Serbian Orthodox Church:* 1) the history
of Serbian hagiographical literature; 2) the art of spiritual reading; and
3) an offering of several "uncanonized" Serbian Saints—in particular
some holy women. I will give some personal reflection within this
introduction, in order to preserve the unique spirit of the experience of
the Saints.

1. SERBIAN HAGIOGRAPHICAL LITERATURE

The first original literary work of any type written by Serbians was
the Lives of the Saints. The *Letopis* (Chronicle) of Pop Duklanin, an
anonymous priest of Diocletia, recounts the events surrounding the life
of St. John Vladimir.[2] The major work of St. Sava, the first real Serbian
author, was *Zhivot Svetoga Simeona (The Life of St. Simeon),* written
around 1200. This book in twelve chapters centered upon the events of
the life of Stephen Nemanja-St. Simeon, Sava's father, while Simeon
was a monk on the Holy Mountain. Sava's other well-known works are
the *Karejski Tipik,*[3] the *Hilandarski Tipik* and the *Kormchaja Kniga,*

---

2. Cf. Fedro Schischic, *Letopis popa Duklanina* (Belgrade, 1928).

3. For the only English translation, introduction and notes, see Daniel M. Rogich,
"St. Sava on Mount Athos: his monastic rule," *Sobornost: incorporating Eastern
Churches Review,* Vol. 11, nos. 1 & 2, 1989, pp. 69-81.

which all are basically translations of earlier Greek writings (and thus not truly original works). Besides Sava's *Life of St. Simeon,* two monks, Dometian and Theodosius, also each wrote a Life of St. Simeon. St. Simeon's son, St. Stephen "Prvovenchani" (the First-Crowned), also penned a life of his father (around 1216). The two aforementioned monks each wrote a Life of St. Sava, and Theodosius published the *Pohvale* (Praises) in honor of Sts. Simeon and Sava (around 1250). These *Vitae,* written by sons for fathers, may have been influenced by Byzantine secular biography, for example, the *Life of Emperor Basil I* by his grandson Constantine Porphyrogenitos, or the story of Alexios I's exploits by his daughter Anna Comnenos, which fostered a cult of the single native dynasty. Yet this Serbian style of royal biography, mixing a unique blend of family chronicle, hagiographical and monastic ideals and political concepts, served a more practical end, that of firmly rooting the fundamental aspect of Orthodox Christian ascetic life among the Serbian peasantry.

In the fourteenth century, the Serbian Archbishop Daniel II (1324-1337) wrote the famous book, *The Lives of the Serbian Kings and Archbishops* (around 1375). This work continued the hagiographical tradition among the Serbs. Archbishop Daniel's book reflects a warmth of style and creativity, granting us lively images of many saints of the Serbian nobility such as Dragutin, Urosh, Radoslav, Vladislav, Helen and Milutin, along with the archbishops Arsenius, Sava II, Daniel I, James, Eustathius II, and Sava III. D. Pavlovic believes that Daniel learned his art of writing from the translations of St. Clement of Ochrid.[4] Recognized as one of the principle contributions by Serbs to the literature of medieval Europe,[5] this text furthered "the cult of inheritance" *(dedina),* which in general created a unity and cohesion in

4. George A. Maloney, *A History of Orthodox Theology Since 1453,* (Nordland Publ. Co.: Belmont, MA, 1976), p. 248.
5. Nikola Radojchic, *O archiepiskopu Danilu II i njegovim nastavlachima* (Belgrade, 1935), XXIV; see also Dimitri Obolensky, *The Byzantine Commonwealth: Eastern Europe, 500-1453* (SVS Press: Crestwood, NY, 1971), pp. 400-401.

the Kingdom of Serbia and helped give rise to the development of monasticism in Serbia from the thirteenth to early fifteenth century. From 1220 to 1402 the princes and nobles of the kingdom of Serbia vied with each other to build monasteries. In this period, more monasteries were built in Serbia than in any other territory of the Balkans. Some of the more famous were Zhicha, Mileshevo, Pech, Sopochani, Gradach, Banja on the Drina, Ljevishka, Grachanitsa, Dechani, St. Nikita of Banja, St. George of Nagorichino, Ravanitsa, Kalenich, Ljubostinja and Manasia.

Two remaining hagiographers deserve mention. Gregory Camblak, born about 1364 in Trnovo, educated in Constantinople and on the Holy Mountain, became the Abbot of Visoki Dechani Monastery in Serbia. He is best known for his *Life of Prince Stephen of Dechani* and the liturgical service in his honor.[6] Constantine the Philosopher, also born in Trnovo, came to Serbia in 1402, and in 1431 wrote *The Life of Prince Stephen Lazarevich,*[7] a work that is also an extremely useful historical source for the period.

The very first literature among the Serbians—including all types of literature—was hagiographical. This meant that the formative Christian foundation of the Serbian people was that of the exquisite and powerful hagiographical tradition of Orthodox Christianity. For centuries, even up until the seventeenth century, almost all Serbian writing was done by monastics and centered primarily on translations of the necessary ecclesiastical books, with the emphasis on original biographies of their saints. The monastic ascetic tradition was for such a long period of time the major influence in the common life of the people. And in visiting the monasteries—although wars have destroyed many of them—the intimacy of this unique hagiographical tradition can still be felt.

It must be mentioned that a strong Serbian theological tradition never really developed during this early period of Serbian literary history.

---

6. Mateja Matejich and Dragan Milivojevich, *An Anthology of Medieval Serbian Literature in English,* (Slavica Publ. Inc.: Columbus, OH, 1978), pp. 134-139.

7. Ibid. pp. 167-168.

Schools of any quality were non-existent except for private tutoring in monasteries where a learned monk might be found who was educated outside of Serbia, chiefly in Bulgaria. The exception to this was the Serbian monastery of Hilandar on the Holy Mountain where many monks were trained in the best Byzantine spirituality, as well as hagiographies, liturgical books, and a few theological treatises, such as the *The Exact Exposition of the Orthodox Faith* by St. John of Damascus, translated into Serbian in the fourteenth century. Yet even Hilandar Monastery did not produce many great Serbian theologians. And it must be remembered that with the Turkish takeover of the Balkans in the late fourteenth century, virtually all theological writing came to a halt. Thus it was the Lives of the Saints and the Divine Liturgy which were the basic source of Christian training and influence among the Serbs for over four centuries. It was not until the early eighteenth century—after the migration of thousands of Serbs to the Austro-Hungarian empire— that Russia finally provided the Serbian bishops in Sremski Karlovac and in Serbia proper with books and even teachers, which resulted in the development of seminaries, academies and eventually in theological faculties (departments or schools of theology).

This historical evidence confirms that the earliest Christian writing and training among the Serbs stemmed from the hagiographical tradition; and that a Serbian theological tradition—original writings on scripture, dogma, canon law, iconography, etc.—developed later, being largely dependent upon the Orthodox Church of Russia (in Kiev).[8] One must appreciate, then, the work of two modern Serbian Orthodox spiritual geniuses, Bishop Nikolai Velimirovich (†1956) and Archimandrite Justin Popovich (†1979), for their primary message was a call to

---

8. Ibid. p. 253f; Interestingly, prior to the fourteenth century Russia was first influenced by southern Slavic literature and art, and only after the Turkish takeover of the Balkans in the early fifteenth century was this reversed, the Russian Orthodox Church then coming to the aid of the southern Slavic churches by providing literature and teachers. See I.M. Kontzevich, *The Acquisition of the Holy Spirit in Ancient Russia* (St. Herman of Alaska Brotherhood: Platina, California, 1988), p. 123f.

theological work, but also a living well and divine light to partake of in the formative personal Christian life. It is interesting to note that when Father Justin began his teaching career in Sremski Karlovac, there was no course offered on the Lives of the Saints! He had to create one, which in turn inspired him to translate the twelve volumes of the entire Orthodox *Lives of the Saints*. Thus it is to Sts. Nikolai and Justin that I am drawn, to the basic and fundamental love for the saints which was begun in earlier times by St. Sava. This love of the hagiographical tradition is perhaps the primary offering Serbian Orthodoxy grants to the entire Christian world. It is certainly my own most mature reason for humbly contributing to this legacy. Now let us turn to how we should actually delve into the reading of spiritual literature.

2. THE ART OF SPIRITUAL READING

As a cursory review of these volumes will show, I combined to a certain degree the two basic forms of hagiographical literature found in the Orthodox Church. On one hand, the full *Lives* from the various collections[9] are present; and on the other hand, the liturgical character

9. The following is a list of primary sources: *Mineja Cheti*, Sinodalnaja Tipografija (Moscow, 1897); *Synaxaristis, ipo tou markaria lixei Nikodimou Agioreitou, nin te triton epexargastheis ekditotai ipo Th. Nikolaito Filadelfeos, Athinisi*, 1868; *Mt. Athos Patericon*, 6th edition (Moscow, 1890); (St. Petersburg, 1894); *Zhitija svjatih*, Menaia of St. Dimitry of Rostov, Sinodalnaja Tipografija (Moscow, 1903); *Zhitija Svetih*, by Justin Popovich, (Belgrade, 1972) Vols. I-XIII; *The Prologue from Ochrid*, Bishop Nikolai Velimirovich, (Lazarica Press: Birmingham, England, 1986), Vols. 1-4. Also, a good source for English readers is the journal, *The Serbian Orthodox Church: Its Past and Present* (Belgrade); for the Life of Bishop Nikolai Velimirovich, see *Novi Zlatoust: Vladika Nikolaj (1880-1956)*, (Belgrade, 1986), and see the M. Div. thesis by Mirko Dobrijevic, from St. Vladimir's Seminary. For the Life of Archimandrite Justin Popovich, see Hieromonk Atanasije Jevtic, *Zhivotopis Otsa Justina, Na Bogochovechanskom Putu*, Otac Justin Popovich, (Belgrade, 1920), pp. 5-86. Also, the Life of St. Peter of Montenegro was published by Kosovo Publ. Co. (1980). For historical information and sources, the best is still Dr. Djoko Slijepcevic, *Istorija Srpske Pravoslavna Srkva* (Munich, 1962-1986), Vols. I-III. There one can also find a good bibliography on Serbian Church history.

of the *Prologue* (or *Synaxarion* in Greek) with various prayers, troparia and kontakia, and some short exhortations is apparent in the text. This "Lives/Prologue" format seemed to me to be more inclusive and practical, which could possibly facilitate a variety of readings—such as liturgically in a monastery "according to the typicon," or at a seminary in the refectory for example, or for the edification of a family or individual in a parish church. This is mentioned because we must come to grips with the content of the Lives of the Saints, and with what approach one is to take when reading spiritual (or soul-profiting) literature. At first glance, the reading of the Lives of the Saints may seem quite straightforward. One need only to open the book and begin reading. Yet I believe that in Orthodox tradition there is a certain approach and practical guideline in reading the Lives of the Saints as well as other types of soul-profiting literature. Spiritual literature in Orthodoxy is not considered "ordinary reading," like reading or perusing family magazines, or even a doctor's reading of medical journals, or a writer's research project or a teachers manual for preparation for classes. The reading of saints' lives and other soul-profiting literature is instead a special type of reading, done primarily outside of the time we spend on vocational or professional reading. Spiritual reading such as the Lives is the kind which "can console us in sorrow, deepen our joy, prompt a transformation, aid in growth in reflection, orient our whole being toward the Divine. It is the kind of reading, in other words, that nourishes the life of the spirit."[10]

Now, thanks be to God, there are plenty of modern translations of spiritual classics of the Orthodox faith, including some Lives of the Saints. But only a few practical guidelines exist in English for the general reader or for a parish priest, spiritual counselor, or retreat director who wants to know how to establish for himself, or for those under his care, a practical, workable program of spiritual reading. This is a very

---

10. Susan A. Muto, *A Practical Guide to Spiritual Reading* (Dimension Books: Denville, NJ, 1976), p. 11. Most of the ideas found in this portion of my introduction were received from reading her research in this area.

a practical, workable program of spiritual reading. This is a very important area in Orthodox ascetic living, developed through the centuries in the experience with spiritual elders, or in monasteries, or which has been formulated by serious-minded Christians. Before suggesting some practical guidelines, let me explain where the Lives of the Saints should be placed within the context of all Orthodox Christian literature.

Within Orthodoxy, there are several types of literature which must be approached in different ways when reading the various texts. This does not imply any formal "rationalistic" categorization of literature, as I am only suggesting this in order to better understand how one is to approach the reading of the Lives of the Saints. It must be remembered that Orthodoxy takes a more wholesome and integral approach to Christian reading—and to Christian living for that matter—than the departmentalized categorization of Christian literature and living often found in later Western Christian writings.

For our purposes, let me suggest five categories of Orthodox Christian literature.

1. FUNDAMENTAL. The *Bible* is the basic text for spiritual reading. How the Orthodox Church understands the Bible, its formation, doctrine and tradition, is essential to one's development as a Christian. Background reading (doctrinal, exegetical, historical) can inspire the Christian reader to learn more about spiritual living and the divine life of the Church.

2. CLASSICAL. These include in particular the doctrinal writings of the Fathers of the Church, such as the Cappadocians, John Chrysostom, Athanasius and Cyril of Alexandria, Maximus the Confessor, John of Damascus, Symeon the New Theologian and Gregory Palamas. The credal statements of the Ecumenical Councils are included here. In this regard, understanding the definition of the personal Christian life as an interplay between dogma and spirituality (human experience) is integral to one's appropriation and actualization of the beliefs of the Church.

3. PATRISTIC. These include the writings of the *Philokalia* or the many spiritual writings of the saints of Russia which deal with, for example, particular themes in the Christian ascetic life such as silence, obedience, hesychasm, suffering and death, discipline, detachment, freedom, and so forth. Liturgical poetry may be included here. These texts are to edify and inspire the reader to "rid himself of passions" and to prepare himself for the contemplative life.

4. HAGIOGRAPHICAL. These include Lives of the Saints, Prologues, Patericons, Matericons, Synaxarions, biographies of un-canonized righteous men and women, and literature related to the psychological state of men and women who through ascetic, self-inflicted labors have become a reflection of divinity in the traditional Orthodox understanding of saints.

5. SOUL-PROFITING READING. These include works that do not directly deal with spritual life but that "enlarge" the heart and refine the soul, such as those of the Montenegrin Peter Njegosh, St. Nikolai Velimirovich, ecclesiastical writers such as St. Ignatius Brianchaninov, St. Theophan the Recluse, St. John of Kronstadt, the epistology of the Optina Elders, Theophan of Poltava, and writers of Mt. Athos such as the Russian Seraphim the Hagiorite (his letters), or secular writers of world literature who contributed to the formation of the Orthodox way of life as opposed to the anti-Christian growth of secular values of the modern man of the post-French Revolution: Charles Dickens, Victor Hugo, Dostoevsky, Leskov and Gogol.

I have delineated the above categories in order to point out that not every piece of Christian literature is approached in the same way, read the same way, and understood with the same mentality. One may be able to read in one sitting an entire set of short stories by Nikolai Gogol, but to read more than two pages of the *Philokalia* at one sitting would certainly be difficult, if not inadvisable. One would not read the great dogmas of the faith in the same spirit as one would the life of a saint. The dogmas call for a highly analytical eye trained in ancient languages,

the origin and meaning of words and phrases, in reflective contemplation, whereas the Lives of the Saints require one to be more attuned to
self-examination, the active pursuit of virtue and spiritual motivation.
In sum, each type of Christian literature was written under different
presuppositions, with a direct purpose and goal in mind, in order to
address various and certain aspects of Christian life in the Church. As
the "mind of the Church" is multi-faceted, so too is Christian literature.

3. "UNCANONIZED" SERBIAN SAINTS

In these volumes, there are several Lives I have written of what I
term "uncanonized" saints. These include Archimandrite Sebastian
Dabovich, Metropolitan Michael of Belgrade, and others. Perhaps
someone may accuse me of "jumping the gun," but I have entitled each
of these "of Blessed Memory," reserving of course the right of canonization to the Holy Synod of Bishops. These righteous people have
withstood the test of time, being venerated by pious Christians not only
for their holy life on earth, but also for their prayers and visitations from
Heaven! I simply wish to offer several short Lives of Serbian Saints—in
particular some holy women—who have been so inspiring to and
prayerfully sought by the pious faithful who know them to be Saints of
the Orthodox Church.

1. KATERINA OF PECH. Sister Katerina was truly a holy woman
from the area of Pech who lived in the second half of the nineteenth
century. All women, and especially women monastics, were subject to
slavery and great harassment by the Turks in Serbia during this time.
As a result, monasteries for women did not flourish during the Turkish
occupation of the Balkans. (Besides, in the areas beyond the Sava and
Danube Rivers, where Serbs settled in so-called "free" territories within
the Austro-Hungarian empire, Orthodoxy—including monasticism—
was not favorably received.) Among her many Christian *podvigs* (labors),
Sister Katerina founded a children's school in Pech (1855), in which
girls learned to read and write, as well as other skills. In 1860 there were

24 girls enrolled, and around 1865 there were 40. The famous British travellers Erby and MacKenzie met Sister Katerina in Pech in 1863 and regarded her as the most significant person they met in the entire Turkish empire.[11] Two of her disciples, *Sisters Vana* and *Csana*, continued her work among children and became highly esteemed Orthodox Christian teachers as well.

2. STAKA SKENDEROVA. Sister Staka, known as "Hadji Gospoja" (Lady Pilgrim), due to her travels to the Middle East as well as for her sojourns in many territories of the Balkans, lived approximately at the same time as Sister Katerina of Pech. Staka founded a school in Sarajevo for girls of all religious backgrounds, including the Turkish Pasha's daughters. She taught literacy skills as well as the fundamentals of Orthodox spirituality. She formed a choir of Orthodox students who traveled to various churches in Bosnia to sing at liturgical services. Her great Christian compassion earned Staka respect from the Pasha of Sarajevo, to the extent that she exerted great influence upon the Turkish court in Sarajevo. As a result, she saved many people from death. It was said the "Lady Pilgrim Staka takes men down from the gallows and brings up innocents out of prison."[12] She courageously traveled to Belgrade and Serbian Voyvodina to purchase Christian books and materials for her school and beloved disciples. The Russian historian and consul to Sarajevo titled her "the greatest woman of the Balkans." Her pure life, educational endeavors and readiness to help all Christians, granted Staka after her repose in the Lord tremendous veneration from the pious Serbians in Sarajevo and throughout Bosnia. She was not a monastic in the formal sense, yet she lived "like a Christian woman of ancient times."[13]

---

11. Heiromonk Amphilocius Radovich, "The Significance of Serbian Woman's Monasticism for Our Spiritual Life and Education," *The Serbian Orthodox Church: Its Past and Present* (Belgrade, 1983), vol. 6, p. 63.

12. *Spomenica Povodom Osamdesetogodishnjice Okupacije Bosne i Hercergovine (1878-1958)*, (Belgrade) p. 69.

13. Ibid., p. 70.

3. VENERABLE STOJNA (†1890). Her life was written by Bishop Nikolai Velimirovich in 1924 (Belgrade). Beloved Stojna—Euphemia as a monastic—performed miracles in the late nineteenth century. She lived for many years in Devich Monastery, in Kosovo, and built there an *Ispostnica* (House of Silence) in 1895. She even had a profound effect upon the Moslems in Kosovo. She spread the "Good News" through word and holy living in areas outside Kosovo, as far as Novi Pazar. A devoted disciple of St. Ioannikios of Devich (see Vol. I, April 26th), Blessed Stojna was a committed Christian servant, miracle-worker, renewer of the monastic life and beloved preacher of the Gospel of Christ.

4. VENERABLE EUPHEMIA OF RAVANITSA. Sister Euphemia is considered a "new Myrrh-bearing woman" among zealous Orthodox Christians who know her life and eternal presence. She was initially known as Sister Bogina as a newly tonsured monastic of Ravanitsa Monastery (1920), where she later became Schema-Abbess Euphemia (1945). As a young woman she was one of the founders of the Prayer Movement Community of Chukojevac and became an ardent lay missionary for about twenty years. She traveled from village to village, "preaching the Gospel, healing the sick, and exhibiting a truly Orthodox manner of ascetic living, attracting many souls to faith in Christ the Lord." Following this missionary period, Euphemia lived in Divian Monastery (under the guidance of the Russian Abbess Theodora of Blessed Memory), then entered the monastic ranks and for a while took 12 other women monastics to renew Temska Monastery. She then transferred to Kovil Monastery in Bachka where the first Prayer Movement of Bogomolci Convention was held in 1933. Under the supervision of Bishop Nikolai Velimirovich, Blessed Euphemia began translating writings of the Holy Fathers from Russian. She also wrote numerous prayers and instructional epistles.

Venerable Abbess Euphemia suffered bitterly during World War II. The 48 sisters of Kovil Monastery in Bachka—where Euphemia was the

Abbess—along with those in Hopovo and Kuvezdin (in Bachka as well) were exiled to Belgrade by the marauding Croatian Ustashi. From Belgrade, these Holy Confessors went to the Monastery of St. Petka in Paracin, taking with them 30 refugee children, war orphans. After the war, these children were placed in loving families. It was said of Euphemia that she was a "great and zealous God-given teacher."[14] As Abbess of Ravanitsa after the war, she instituted a strict monastic rule, emphasizing the reading of the New Testament and the teaching of the Holy Fathers and Mothers on the ascetic life. After her repose in the Lord, she left 53 sisters in the Monasteries of St. Petka and Ravanitsa who to this day venerate her as a saint who took great care of suffering children and led a life truly pleasing to God.

5. MOTHER ANNA OF VRACHEVSHINA. At baptism Mother Anna was named Nada Adjic, the daughter of Sreten Adjic, the founder of the famous Jagodin Teachers School. Highly educated and skilled in the arts and literature, she gave her entire life to Christ and the education of children. While still a lay person, Nada ran a children's orphanage called "Bogdaj" (God gives) in Bitola under the administration of Bishop Nikolai. When the Bulgarians invaded Bitola in 1941, she moved to Kraljevo and Trstenik where she continued, under harsh conditions, her social and educational work among the refugee children from Bosnia, Voyvodina and other territories. After the war, the governmental takeover of all orphanages propelled Nada to think more seriously about entering the monastic ranks, which she did at Sretenje Monastery in Serbia in 1945. She then transferred to Vrachevshina Monastery, located at the foot of Mt. Rudnik not far from the Kragujevac-Gornji Milanovac highway. After several years of monastic labor in the Lord, Sister Anna became the Abbess of Vrachevshina. She was a "spiritual light" to the community of sisters there, as she led by example more than words, stressing ascetical effort, spiritual perfection and missionary spirit. She even led many young men to the seminary

14. *Zhivotopis Schi-Igumanije Euphemije* (Belgrade, 1966), p. 92.

to prepare for the priesthood. Mother Anna is truly a modern saint to all who continue to receive her maternal guidance through veneration in faith, hope and love.

6. STEPHANIDA OF KOSOVO (†1945). At baptism this beloved child of God was named Stevka Djurchevich. She was born in 1887 in the village of Vraka, near the town of Skadar, Albania. When she was still a child, the Albanians expelled Stevka and her family, forcing them to move to the village of Drenovac in Kosovo. Upon maturity, Stevka lived alone in a little house in Drenovac, dedicating herself to the Lord and Saviour Jesus Christ through prayer, fasting and silence. She went regularly to confession and communion at Dechani Monastery, where she was discovered by Bishop Nikolai, who asked her to move to Zhicha Monastery in order to make her an example to all the monastics there. Due to a leg ailment from standing at the long liturgical services, she could no longer make the grueling walk to Dechani Monastery and therefore accepted Bishop Nikolai's bidding. Desiring prayerful isolation, Stevka then accepted the invitation of Nada Adjic—later Mother Anna—and traveled to Bitola, where she spent the last years of her life in an isolated little house in the garden of the "Bogdaj" nursery. The end of her life witnessed a two-fold martyrdom. She patiently withstood the pain of the open sores in her legs from the many hours of personal prayer in her little house; moreover, the German soldiers aggravated her health condition when they beat her for not extinguishing the icon lamp which burned continuously in her room, at a time when a total black-out was ordered in the town. Eyewitnesses said that during the beatings the blood from her sores was splattered over the floor and walls of her room. She died as a martyr in 1945. Just prior to her death, a Bulgarian bishop received Stevka into the monastic ranks, giving her the name Stephanida, which comes from the Greek word "Stephanos" meaning Crowned. Sister Stephanida the New Martyr was honorably buried in the Monastery of St. Christopher, near Bitola.

Sister Stephanida left us an Orthodox spiritual classic of our times— her *Confessions*. These 92 confessional letters, composed due to her vow of silence, were compiled by her father confessor, Victor, the Serbian Orthodox Bishop of Skadar. The letters contain, in the words of Bishop Amphilocius Radovich, "the bright effulgence as well as the simple spiritual experience of this Saint of our time. In them we notice that, with her burning faith for Christ and love for God, she partook of the Eucharist every week and sometimes twice a week. She fasted strictly throughout the entire year, using oil mainly for her icon lamp, and eating fish only on the Nativity of Christ and Pascha, out of love for others. Her *Confessions* are saturated with a deep traditional sorrow, characteristic of our people in general, but with an even deeper joy, which was born in her by her continual union with Christ."[15] Truly considered soul-profiting for all Serbian Orthodox zealots, these confessional letters, when translated, will become a source of living water for all.

---

15. A. Radovich, ibid., p. 69; for her letters, see Stevka Djurchevich (Monahinja Stephanida), *Ispovedna Pisma Svome Duhovniku,* Biblioteka Monastira Dechana, no. 878, pp. 1-328.

ACKNOWLEDGEMENTS

I want to express my gratitude to several people for their contributions to these volumes.

The iconographic sketches were done by Miss Lillian Tintor, one of the finest iconographers in the Serbian Orthodox Church in America.

His Eminence Amphilocius (Radovich), Metropolitan of Montenegro and the Coastlands, helped inspire me to see this work to fruition.

In the area of texts I am grateful to the Very Reverend Father Mateja Matejich, who provided me with his then unpublished manuscript of several of the troparia and kontakia of the Serbian saints; the Very Reverend Father Dragan Filipovich for allowing me access to his library; and the Reverend Father Rastko Trbuhovich, for his advice and encouragement as well as for providing me with several troparia and kontakia (in English) of the Serbian Saints.

I am thankful to have met, been taught by, and become friends with Dr. Veselin Kesich, who is one of the most remarkable persons I have ever met. Moreover, his own life story, which very few know, is a remarkable testament to "living out the Gospel message."

Finally, all that is useful and edifying in these volumes is due to the saints, and any mistakes which remain are my own. My only recourse is to ask the Blessed Lord to forgive me, by the prayers of all the saints, and by your prayers, Christ-loving readers.

Fr. Daniel M. Rogich
Belle Vernon, Pennsylvania
June 15, 1991
Vidovdan

VOLUME ONE

January –April

St. Eustathius I

Archbishop of Serbia

TROPARION, Tone 4
Thou wast elected by God and beloved of men,*
O divine beauty of hierarchs, Father Eustathius;* thou wast
a fellow-minister with the Angels,* and a preacher of divine
mysteries;* therefore, entreat Christ God to deliver us from
every evil,* and may thy prayers, O Blessed One,*
save us who venerate thy memory with love.

OUR HOLY FATHER

EUSTATHIUS I

ARCHBISHOP OF SERBIA

(†1286)

*Love is a good disposition of the soul
by which one prefers no being
to the love of God.*
St. Maximus the Confessor

OUR HOLY FATHER EUSTATHIUS I was born in 1230 to God-fearing Orthodox parents in the Diocese of Budimlje (inland Montenegro). From his youth he truly obeyed and honored his parents, and also had a tremendous love for the Church's liturgical life, especially the chanting and reading, always concentrating on the deeper meaning of the words of prayer. One day, at age ten, Eustathius came to his parents and said, "I really want to learn more about our faith and love of God; please, my dear parents, provide me with books so that I may learn." His parents, praising and blessing the Lord God for implanting such a beautiful desire in their young son's heart, sent Eustathius to the local priest so that he might learn and experience the faith more fully. Being enthralled and illumined by the Lives of the Saints, the teachings of the Scriptures and great Fathers and Mothers of the Church, and being transformed by the life of prayer, fasting and the sacraments, the young boy began to lose all interest in the things of this world, and at times even skipped meals and sleep. He also began to love the Lord Jesus Christ over and above his parents (cf. Matt. 10:37; Lk. 14:26).

As a result, at age fourteen, Eustathius decided to leave his parents' home and travel to Zeta (coastal Montenegro) to become a monk. He traveled to the Monastery of Archangel Michael in Prevlac, near Kotor, the episcopal center of the Diocese of Zeta. After being introduced to Bishop Neophat, Eustathius petitioned him for entrance into the monastic community. He then gave away all his earthly possessions to the poor (cf Lk 18:22), and entered the daily life of the monastery, which included the liturgical as well as the ascetical and contemplative Christian life. Spending his days and nights in prayer, fasting and vigil, the young *izkushenik* (novice, or literally "one who is being tested") rapidly became known as a virtuous ascetic and devout Christian. As a matter of fact, within a short period of time he was received into the monastic ranks and, due to his great ascetic feats, was allowed to live in hesychia[1] and silence in a cell away from the monastic community. Eustathius' humility and gentle spirit preceded him, as he was known throughout all of Serbia as a true follower of St. Sava and the prayerful way of the ancient desert Fathers.

Just prior to his twentieth birthday, the Lord God placed a burning desire within Eustathius' heart: to visit the Holy City of Jerusalem in order to venerate the Tomb of the Lord and the other Holy Places. Not revealing this desire to anyone, Eustathius unceasingly prayed to the Lord Jesus Christ to provide a way for him to visit the place where He had shed His blood for the life of the world and where He had performed so many miracles. And the Lord heard Eustathius' fervent and committed prayer. One night while praying, to his surprise, Eustathius was visited by two monks he had never met. These two Messengers of the Lord informed Eustathius that the Lord had truly heard his supplication

---

1. "Hesychia" is a Greek word meaning "silence," "solitude" or "quietude," and in Orthodox spiritual tradition is considered the highest form or art of prayer. It has often been associated with the Jesus Prayer: "Lord Jesus Christ, Son of the Living God, have mercy on me, a sinner."

34

and that they were sent to accompany him on his way to the Holy Land. Thus, after receiving Bishop Neophat's blessing and venerating the Holy Icons of the Lord Christ and His Chief Messenger, Michael the Leader of the Bodiless Hosts, Eustathius and the two monks set off for Jerusalem. By the grace of God they arrived safely in Jerusalem and straightway went and piously venerated Golgotha, the Tomb of Christ, and the other Holy Places. Besides this, Eustathius, not in any hurry, ventured to visit the venerable and God-fearing ascetics living in the areas outside Jerusalem. Here he learned of their spiritual rules and ascetic triumphs, and of the radically devoted life in Christ fighting the demons.

After spending more than a year in the Holy Land, Eustathius, now twenty-one years old, decided to return home; but instead of returning to his beloved Serbia, he went to the Holy Mountain,[2] seeking to further train himself in the cleansing of his body and soul of all earthly passions,[3] necessities and cares. There he entered the Serbian Orthodox Hilandar Monastery , consecrated to the Most Holy and Ever-Virgin Mary the Theotokos, the true Abbess of the entire Holy Mountain. Eustathius came as a humble and quiet monk, always practicing mental silence and prayer of the heart; however, in a relatively short time, even the eldest, most experienced and wisest of the ascetics on the Holy Mountain could be found seeking entrance into Eustathius' cell in order to receive the grace and love of the Lord God from the lips of this twenty-one-year-old monastic. And after several years at Hilandar, the entire brotherhood

---

2. The Holy Mountain or Mount Athos (in Greece) is the citadel of Orthodox monasticism, begun officially in 963 by St. Athanasius of the Great Lavra, and still continuing today.

3. "Passions," a Greek word ("Patheia"), has essentially two definitions in Orthodox Christian spiritual literature: 1) appetites or impulses, such as anger, inordinate desire or jealousy, that violently dominate and corrupt the soul; 2) impulses originally placed in humans by God, and so fundamentally good, although at present distorted by sin. In both cases, passions must be controlled and either eradicated or transformed into good.

unanimously elected Eustathius as the Igumen (Abbot) of the Hilandar community.

Leading the Hilandar Monastery, Eustathius increased his spiritual warfare against the pollutions of the flesh, preferring to lead more by example than by words. He was not only loved and respected by the monks of all the twenty monastic communities on the Holy Mountain, but was also held in high regard and esteem by the kings, queens and lay people of all Orthodox countries. Quite often Serbian princes as well as rulers of various Orthodox countries could be seen knocking on the door of his cell, seeking advice, comfort and blessings. Therefore it came as no surprise when the virtuous Venerable Eustathius was chosen and consecrated, against his humble will, in 1270, as the Bishop of Zeta, residing in the same monastery in which he began his spiritual journey twenty-six years before as a fourteen-year-old novice—at the Monastery of the Holy Archangel Michael. Furthermore, when the Serbian Archbishop Ioannikios fell asleep in the Lord in 1278, King Milutin, having called together all the bishops and leaders of the Serbian Orthodox Church, heard only one nomination for the successor to the archiepiscopal throne of St. Sava. The assembly, with one voice, chose Bishop Eustathius as the new Archbishop of Serbia.

Residing in Zhicha Monastery in Kraljevo, Archbishop Eustathius lead his flock, as always, by being an image of prayer, giving, and unconditional love. He was especially loved by the lay people of the Serbian Church, for he was constantly concerned with not only their spiritual condition, but also their material needs. Many times he called upon both ecclesiastical and civil leaders to give greater attention to the most needy in the Church's dioceses.

St. Eustathius did not lead the Serbian Church for a long time (1279-1286). Only seven years after he ascended the archiepiscopal throne at Zhicha, he became grievously ill. Thus he began to prepare for his departure from this world to enter the Heavenly Chambers. Although physically ill, his soul was nevertheless always ascending spiritually to the heights, expressing to all the transfigured and hallowed life of blessed suffering on earth. Just prior to his departure from this world, around his bed the entire episcopacy of the Serbian Orthodox Church gathered, along with many monks from the Holy Mountain and leaders from all other Orthodox countries. Bishops, clergy, monastics and lay people were visibly shaken and in great sorrow over the thought of the impending loss of their great teacher, ascetic, and archpastor. Yet Eustathius would have none of this, as he rose from his bed and repeated the words of Psalm 33:3: "O magnify the Lord with me, and let us exalt His name together!" Then all received the Holy Eucharist from his pure hands, as each came as a spiritual child to the venerable Holy Father for a final blessing and forgiveness of sins. Finally, Blessed Eustathius raised his hands towards Heaven and said: "You alone, O God of gods and Lord of lords, know the end of my life; into Your hands I commend my spirit!" Uttering these final words, the blessed Holy Father Eustathius divinely and gloriously entered the Mansions of the Lord, on January 4, 1286. He was 56 years old.

A sweet smell encompassed the funeral procession into the Church of the Savior in Zhicha, where Eustathius was laid to rest in a marble crypt he had previously made with his own hands. Many miracles occurred after the funeral. Often the gravesite was surrounded by a bright light; often a sweet smell fragranced the tomb; and often a voice saying prayers was heard coming from his crypt. One man, terminally ill, after spending all his life's earnings on cures, finally gave up on earthly means and came to the Church of the Savior to ask the Lord for help. Each time he prayed in the Church he stood next to the crypt of St. Eustathius. One night, in a dream, the man saw himself standing next to this crypt in the Church. Appearing to him was a gentle and humble-looking man arrayed in the vestments of an archbishop. The sick man cried out to the Archbishop and received a reply: "The Lord sent me to heal you; only do not sin anymore or your condition may worsen."

"And who are you?" the terminally ill man asked the Archbishop, making the Sign of the Cross.

"I am a servant of Christ. I am a monk and my name is Eustathius, and I rest in the Lord here in this Monastery."

After this, the sick man awoke and at once, with blessed fear, went to the new Archbishop of Serbia, James, informing him and the entire episcopacy what had exactly taken place in his dream. After this confession, the man was completely healed, and all glorified the Lord and His saint, Eustathius.

Also, inexplicably, three beautiful flowers grew out of the marble at the head of the crypt of St. Eustathius. The crypt was made totally of stone with no earth nearby. Some thought this to be a sign from God revealing Eustathius' immortality and incorruptibility; furthermore, matters intensified when the monk ecclesiarch[4] saw in a dream a terrifying youth with a fiery shovel in his hand, saying, "Don't you understand this sign of the flowers; don't you understand the eternal beauty and blossoming immortality of the Lord's saints?" With this news, King Milutin, with the blessing of Archbishop James, ordered the casket of Eustathius to be opened. There lay Eustathius completely intact, fragrant, his body aglow, looking very much alive. He was venerated by all as his body was placed in the center of Zhicha Monastery's Catholicon (main church) of the Savior. As a result, the day of Eustathius' entrance into Heaven—January 4th—was declared an official feast day of the Orthodox Church of Serbia.

Shortly thereafter, due to the danger from Serbia's foreign enemies, the life-giving body and relics of Eustathius, by the command of Archbishop James, were taken from Zhicha to Pech, where they remained in the Church of the Patriarchate until 1737, when they were transferred to the Monastery of the Archangel.

"O Holy Father Eustathius, thou didst demonstrate and express by thy love and zeal for our Lord and Savior Jesus Christ that all of life is to be consecrated and offered to God as a sweet-smelling sacrifice. We

---

4. The ecclesiarch is the liturgical specialist of the worshipping community. This person knows the divine services by heart and also prepares everyone and the church proper for all the Divine Services which are to take place.

The ancient monastery of Zhicha as it looks today.

beg thee O loving One, pray to Christ our true God for us miserable sinners, that our souls may be illumined and sanctified by that very same love of Christ, to Whom belongs glory, honor and worship, together with His Unoriginate Father, and Life-giving Spirit, now and ever and unto ages of ages. Amen.

KONTAKION TO ST. EUSTATHIUS I
Tone 2

Receiving grace from God on High, Father Eustathius,* thou wast robed in the likeness of holy hierarchs;* with thy lips thou piously didst teach all* to worship the Consubstantial Trinity;* therefore, as we venerate thy memory,* we glorify God Who hath glorified thee.

Holy Martyr
Onuphrius
of Hilandar

TROPARION, Tone 1

Having fought the good fight with humility and courage,*
Most Righteous and Glorious Martyr of Christ, Onuphrius,*
thou didst receive a double crown from the Lord God,* for
thou wast united with the choirs of ascetics and martyrs;*
therefore, pray unceasingly to Christ our true God*
for us who celebrate thy memory with faith.

Bless My Enemies

Bless my enemies, O Lord. Even I bless them and do not curse them.[1]

Enemies have driven me into Thine embrace more than friends have.

Friends have bound me to earth, enemies have loosed me from earth and have demolished all my aspirations in the world.

Enemies have made me a stranger in worldly realms as an extraneous inhabitant of the world.

Just as a hunted animal finds safer shelter than an unhunted animal, so have I, persecuted by enemies, found the safest sanctuary, having ensconced myself beneath Thy tabernacle, where neither friends nor enemies can slay my soul.

Bless my enemies, O Lord, Even I bless them and do not curse them.

They, rather than I, have confessed my sins before the world.

They have punished me, whenever I have hesitated to punish myself.

They have tormented me, whenever I have tried to flee torments.

They have scolded me, whenever I have flattered myself.

They have spat upon me, whenever I have filled myself with arrogance.

Bless my enemies, O Lord. Even I bless them and do not curse them.

Whenever I have made myself wise, they have called me foolish.

Whenever I have made myself mighty, they have mocked me as though I were a dwarf.

Whenever I have wanted to lead people, they have shoved me into the background.

Whenever I have rushed to enrich myself, they have prevented me with an iron hand.

Whenever I thought that I would sleep peacefully, they have wakened me from sleep.

Whenever I have tried to build a home for a long and tranquil life, they have demolished it and driven me out.

Truly, enemies have cut me loose from the world and have stretched out my hands to the hem of Thy garment.

Bless my enemies, O Lord. Even I bless them and do not curse them.

Bless them and multiply them; multiply them and make them even more bitterly against me—

So that my fleeing to Thee may have no return;
So that all hope in men may be scattered like cobwebs;
So that absolute serenity may begin to reign in my soul;
So that my heart may become the grave of my to evil twins: arrogance and anger;
So that I might amass all my treasure in heaven;[2]
Ah, so that I may for once be freed from self-deception, which has entangled me in the dreadful web of illusory life.

Enemies have taught me to know—what hardly anyone knows—that a person has no enemies in the world except himself. One hates his enemies only when he fails to realize that they are not enemies, but cruel friends.

It is truly difficult for me to say who has done me more good and who has done me more evil in the world: friends or enemies.

Therefore, bless, O Lord, both my friends and my enemies. A slave curses enemies, for he does not understand. But a son blesses them, for he understands. For a son knows that his enemies can not touch his life. Therefore, he freely steps among them and prays to God for them.

Bless my enemies, O Lord. Even I bless them and do not curse them.

—St. Nikolai of Ochrid,
from *Prayers By The Lake*, Ch. LXXV.

[1] Cf. Matt. 5:43-48. [2] Matt. 6:19-21.

Christ of the Hills Monastery
New Sarov
Blanco, Texas 78606-1049
USA

January 4th

LIFE AND SUFFERING OF
NEW MARTYR

ONUPHRIUS

OF HILANDAR, MT. ATHOS

(†1818)

> *So that we will not think*
> *that we are doing something great*
> *through our ascetic efforts*
> *and our many sighs and tears,*
> *we are given knowledge of the*
> *sufferings of Christ and His saints.*
> St. Peter Damascene

OUR HOLY NEW MARTYR ONUPHRIUS was born in 1785 in the village of Gabrovo, in the Diocese of Trnovo, Bulgaria. His parents, God-loving Christians, had their child baptized, giving him the name Matthew. When Matthew reached schooling age, his parents provided for his education, in which he showed great promise and success.

On one occasion after school in his early teens, Matthew was accused of causing some trouble. Quite naturally, his parents disciplined him; but Matthew, being of a youthful and sometimes rebellious spirit, felt insulted and hurt by his parents' punishment. As a result, he rebelled against his parents and began to be seen in the company of some Turkish youths in Trnovo and even hinted to one that he was contemplating accepting the Muslim faith. This kind of desire was unheard of and also could be easily accommodated, for the Turkish authorities protected and even gave political rights to any Christian who converted to their religion. Yet, despite his spiritual fall he was raised up again by the constant intercessions of his parents on behalf of their son Matthew; and glory and honor was given, in the end, to our Lord and God and Savior Jesus Christ and Holy Orthodoxy.

As Matthew grew to maturity, he mellowed in his spirit and once again honored his father and mother and the Holy Orthodox faith in Jesus Christ; yet he never forgot this incident of rejecting his parents and Christ Jesus. As a result, he decided, after finishing school, to travel to the Holy Mountain, to the Serbian Hilandar Monastery in order to become a monk. He received the monastic tonsure and the name Manasia, and within a short period of time, due to his zeal and ascetic efforts, was ordained deacon. He completely fulfilled the duties of a deacon, acquiring virtue while serving the brotherhood like a God-loving mother serves her children. But, according to the experiential teaching of the Holy Fathers, the closer one approaches the Lord, the more one sees his own sins; and, to the God-fearing ascetic, the most minute sin or flaw in character is as a huge abyss between him and his Lord. Thus, Manasia, constantly examining and guarding his soul, was pierced by his past youthful fall, that is, his rejection of Christ the Lord when he was a teenager. His heart was convicted each time he heard the words of the Savior, "So everyone who acknowledges me before men, I also will acknowledge before my Father who is in Heaven; but whoever rejects me before men, I also will reject before my Father who is in Heaven" (Matt 10:32-33). Manasia struggled with these words and was filled with fear each time he heard them. "How can it be," he thought, "that I have no peace in my heart even after I have repented? Am I a slave to my own repentance? What will become of me on the Great Judgment Day of Christ when He will have to reject me before our Heavenly Father since I rejected Him before men?" Desiring to be completely cleansed of his sins, Manasia fervently sought the Lord in prayer. In his heart stirred the notion that he would only be purified when he acknowledged and confessed his faith in the Lord Jesus before unbelievers. Thus, Manasia decided to vindicate his rejection of Christ by going before the Turkish authorities and confessing Him; and he understood that for him this would result in nothing less than death!

This desire never left him. It was on his mind night and day. Not having faith in himself, he once again humbly and lovingly petitioned the Lord to reveal to him "what is the will of God, what is good and acceptable and perfect" (Rom. 12:2). Furthermore, he asked for the grace of God to strengthen him and to grant him sufficient heroic courage in order to fulfill a task which would mean certain martyrdom. And "since the reasoning of mortals is worthless, and our designs are likely to fail, for a perishable body weighs down the mortal soul and this earthly tent burdens the thoughtful mind" (Wisdom of Solomon 9:14), Manasia began to fast and pray, and to consult the God-inspired advice of the Holy Fathers.

Manasia received the counsel of these God-bearing ascetics with great joy, honor, and humility, as it incited him to greater vigilance over his soul and body. The thought of suffering for Christ warmed his soul, especially since he heard of the sufferings and martyrdom of three of his contemporaries, the New Martyrs Ignatius (Oct. 20th), Acacius (May 1st), and Artemius (Oct. 20th), which took place in 1814. Manasia visited his spiritual father Nicephorus who resided in the Hilandarian Skete of St. John the Baptist, located in the woods outside the Monastery grounds. As Manasia explained his plans to suffer as did his three contemporaries, Nicephorus advised him, "My dear child, I accept and laud your plans and intentions; only do not tell anyone of your desire to suffer for Christ, and spend the time of your preparation for martyrdom in constant battle and warfare against your own passions and inordinate desires."

Manasia replied, "I will carry out, Holy Father, your instructions and command." Manasia returned to Hilandar Monastery and there divided his earthly possessions and money, giving one-half to the poor and the other half to the Monastery, to be used as a means to provide for his natural father who, at this time, was so touched by his son's commitment to Christ the Lord and the Holy Orthodox faith that he too entered Hilandar to live as a monk.

Shortly thereafter, under the pretense of traveling to Jerusalem to visit the Holy Places, Manasia hid from all and came to his spiritual father's cell. There he was completely alone, speaking to no one. He spent his nights and days in prayer and vigil, purifying his soul and body by performing 3500 prostrations and countless full-body "metanoias"[1] per day; also, he ate only on Saturday and Sunday, and only once a day at that. He then received, by God's grace, the gifts of tears and of unceasing prayer in his mind, which was now firmly rooted in his heart. After four months, his spiritual father Nicephorus returned to his cell and tonsured him to the Great Angelic Schema,[2] giving him the name Onuphrius. And, by the decision of the entire brotherhood, Onuphrius was allowed to travel to the Greek isle of Chios in order to accomplish his spiritual task—to die for Christ. With the prayers and blessings of the Hilandar community, the brave soldier for Christ, Onuphrius, left the Holy Mountain with Monk Gregory, the same Elder who led the three martyred saints, Ignatius, Acacius and Artemius, to their most blessed witness to the Cross and Resurrection of our Lord and God and Savior Jesus Christ.

Arriving safely in Chios, by the grace of God, the two monks lodged in the home of a hospitable Christian. Onuphrius spent the next seven days in prayer, fasting and in preparation for partaking of the Holy Eucharist. After communing, being filled with the Holy Spirit and

---

1. A "metanoia," from the Greek word "metanoein" meaning "to change one's mind," or "to repent," is a penitential form used in both Orthodox communal and personal worship, whereby the believer fully prostrates his body to floor in worship offered to the Lord Jesus Christ.

2. The Great Angelic Schema is the highest devotion and tonsure a monastic can be given. It corresponds to the angelic life in which a person is thought to be living a life in continual glorification and unceasing meditation on the Divine Trinity.

The towers of Hilandar Monastery, seen from inside.

strengthened by the medicine of the Lord, Onuphrius decided that on the following Friday, the weekday dedicated to the Cross and sufferings of Christ, he would spill his own blood as a vindication for past transgressions as well as a witness to the glorious and victorious life in Christ. One night, exhausted from prayer, Onuphrius fell into a deep sleep. He was given a vision in a dream in which he saw standing before him an Archpriest, a Priest and a Soldier who with one voice said to him, "Arise and go to the King who wishes to see you."

"For what reason?" Blessed Onuphrius asked. "Why does the King want to see me, a worthless and sinful man? I beg you, let me be."

"That is impossible," replied the Heavenly Visitors. "You must rise and come with us."

Onuphrius arose and followed these Blessed Men to a place filled with amazingly bright light and suprasensual warmth. In the center was the throne of the King. Onuphrius prostrated himself fully before the King. The King, raising him by His hand, pointed to one of the areas filled with light, saying, "There, My son, I have prepared a place for you in My Heavenly Mansion."

With these words, Onuphrius awoke from his dream with heavenly joy which captivated his heart and soul. Blessing the Lord God for this miraculous vision, he resumed his prayer to St. Basil the Great, as it was the eve of his feast day (Jan 1, 1818). However, the following night, Onuphrius experienced a cooling of this heavenly joy and was saddened and even frightened. In this condition, he rushed with tears to his companion, Elder Gregory, crying, "O Father, the divine fire which had warmed my heart and soul has been extinguished! Why has this happened?"

"This is because of pride," the Elder said, "for you imagined yourself as now being great in God's eyes; actually, my son, you have hidden the grace of God."

"My Lord and my God! What has happened to me?!" cried Onuphrius. "How will my Athonite brothers accept me, I who am to be a brave witness to the Cross of Christ!"

At this, Monk Gregory was filled with compassion for this simple soul, instructing Onuphrius to stand fixed in prayer and to guard his soul by repeating the Jesus prayer; "Lord Jesus Christ, Son of the Living God, have mercy on me, a sinner." Within a short period of time, tears of rejoicing came once again to Onuphrius as he was restored to spiritual vitality and health. "O blessed Father Gregory, bless the Lord God, I am fine now," he said.

The following day, Elder Gregory closely monitored the spiritual state of Onuphrius in order to protect him from falling again. He instructed him to perform a virtuous task which would enable Onuphrius not to be self-centered or concentrate too much on his own spiritual condition. Gregory ordered him to pray for each member of the household in which they were staying and then to prostrate himself before each of them, kissing their feet. After carrying out this task, Onuphrius was sent to the local church to pray alone. Onuphrius began to pray in a loud voice, sighing and expressing openly to God his most inward fears and problems. Elder Gregory, not wanting to cut off Onuphrius' desire for prayer, let him finish. But when he concluded, Gregory, out of love, said to Onuphrius, "Do you not know the evangelical words of the Lord: 'Do not let your left hand know what your right hand is doing' (Matt. 6:3). Why were you praying so loudly? Everyone heard you. Oh, again you have fallen into *prelest* (spiritual deception or pride)."

Listening to these words of Elder Gregory, the Blessed Saint answered, "I have sinned, Holy Father! Forgive me and pray to God for me, that I may be delivered from the snares of the devil."

Gregory, seeing this tremendous humility on the part of Onuphrius, rejoiced in the Lord for him, for he now knew that the devil would be overthrown by Onuphrius' humility and meekness. Onuphrius was, in Gregory's thinking, now ready to become a sign and witness to his Lord and Savior, the Christ, "the Lamb of God who takes away the sin of the world." Following this, Onuphrius spent the entire evening in prayer and partook of the Holy Eucharist during Divine Liturgy the next morning. Gregory then dressed him in Turkish civilian clothing and cut Onuphrius' hair and shaved his beard, sending him on his way to accomplish his heroic Christian task.

On his way, Onuphrius met a faithful Christian to whom he disclosed his desire—to die for Christ. The young man rejoiced, but noticed that Onuphrius' dress, although completely Turkish in style, nonetheless still lacked one item: red shoes. The Christian then bought Onuphrius a pair of red shoes and directed him to the Turkish High Court. Upon arriving at the Court, Onuphrius asked the court officer to see the Judge. "What does he want with you?" the officer asked in reply.

"I have a complaint," answered Onuphrius.

"Then why didn't you first petition the lower court?"

The confused Onuphrius had no answer.

"In that case, then, you cannot see the Judge," said the officer.

Unsuccessful, Onuphrius returned to the home of the young Christian who had befriended him and bought him the red shoes. The Christian advised him to return to the High Court, only this time not to appear before the court officer; instead, Onuphrius was simply to ring the bell which summoned the Court itself, and then enter.

Onuphrius carried out these instructions and found himself before the Court. He said the following words: "Fifteen years ago I contracted a most dangerous and deadly disease, and I have been to numerous doctors in various cities, but no one has been able to cure me. All of them have told me that my affliction can only be remedied by a reversal of the manner in which I contracted it. Therefore, I have come before you to be healed."

"And what is your affliction?" asked the Judge. "What do you desire from us?"

"My affliction," replied Onuphrius, "is of this kind: As a youth, in my lack of understanding, I rejected the Orthodox Christian faith before your fellow Moslems. But I never followed the Muslim religion at any time, as I have kept the faith of the Orthodox Church and have fulfilled her commandments. Yet, upon growing to maturity, this fall of mine pricked my heart and has constantly afflicted my soul with deep pain and sorrow. I have visited many places in the world hoping to heal my soul, but to no avail, as my repentance has never granted me total peace. Therefore, I curse your religion with your false prophet Mohammed, and confess before all of you that I am an Orthodox Christian." Saying this, Onuphrius threw before them the green turban he was wearing, one end of which hit the face of the Judge and the other end the warden.

The entire court was outraged and astonished by such audacity (and courage) on the part of Onuphrius. One of the officials then indignantly said, "What are you doing, you idiot?! Raise your head and put on this holy garment!" Yet the Martyr took courage and refused, once again confessing his faith in the Lord Jesus Christ.

Listening to this blasphemy of their religion, the Judge pronounced sentence: "Death to this man!", and he ordered that Onuphrius be placed in chains and sent to prison.

In prison, the Saint met several other Christians who asked him his name and background; but the warrior for Christ, unwilling to fall into spiritual pride once more, only revealed that he was from Trnovo and that his name was Matthew. Blessed Onuphrius did not stay long in prison, as the court officials, upon examining him, found that he would not reject his faith in Christ Jesus. Thus he was sentenced to be beheaded and his body cast into the sea.

After public pronouncement of the sentence, Onuphrius was taken to the exact spot where the New Martyr, Venerable Mark (June 5th), was murdered. There Onuphrius fell to his knees and was beheaded as a meek lamb of God, and his pure and undefiled soul ascended to the Heavenly Mansions where a place of honor had been prepared for him. This took place on Friday, January 4, 1818, at three o'clock in the afternoon, the same hour and week day on which his Lord was crucified. New Martyr Onuphrius was 33 years old, also the same age as his Savior, the Lord Jesus Christ, when He was crucified "for the life of the world."

With this task completed, the suffering servant of our Lord and Savior Jesus Christ, Onuphrius the Venerable New Martyr, was freed of his rejection of Christ as a youth; and, going beyond this, the Saint became a witness to the saving grace of our Lord's Cross and Resurrection. The Turkish authorities would not permit the Christians to bury the body and relics of Onuphrius, for fear of the Christian belief in the miraculous and life-giving properties of the bodies of the Lord's saints. Instead, his body was placed in a burlap sack and secretly cast into the sea. His body has never been recovered, yet the Lord God protects it, according to the words of Scripture: *"Many are the tribulations of the righteous, and the Lord shall deliver them out of them all. The Lord keepeth all their bones, not one of them shall be broken. The death of sinners is evil, and they that hate the righteous shall do wrong. The Lord will redeem the souls of His servants, and none of them will do wrong that hope in Him"* (Ps. 33:19-22).

O Holy Venerable Martyr Onuphrius, thou wast privileged to demonstrate and reveal that true martyrdom begins at "home," with the slaying of our own passions and inordinate desires. We beg thee, All-Virtuous one, pray to Christ our true God that we, most miserable sinners, may also witness to His Saving Passion and Bounteous Resurrection by our humility of mind and meekness of heart, being made worthy to inherit His Eternal Crown of Glory, to Whom belongs glory, honor and worship, together with His Unoriginate Father and His Life-giving Spirit, now and ever and unto ages of ages. Amen.

KONTAKION
Tone 8

To Thee, O Lord and Author of all creation,* the universe offers as first fruits of nature the God-bearing Onuphrius;* therefore, by his prayers, preserve Thy Church in perfect safety,* for the sake of the Theotokos, O Most Merciful One.

Mt. Athos looming over Karakallou Monastery, with other sketes nearby.

Russian 19th-century engraving of the Synaxis of all Athonite Saints

St. Gregory

Archbishop of Ochrid

TROPARION, Tone 8

Thou hast shown thyself, O God-inspired Gregory,* to be a
guide of the Orthodox Faith,* and a teacher of true
worship and purity,* O Star of the Universe and companion
of hierarchs, O All-wise One;* through thy light thou
hast enlightened all, O Harp of the Spirit;* therefore,
intercede with Christ God to save our souls.

January 8th

OUR HOLY FATHER

GREGORY

ARCHBISHOP OF OCHRID

(†1012)

An all-embracing and intense longing for God
binds those who experience it
both to God and to one another.
St. Maximus the Confessor

VERY LITTLE is known of the life of our Holy Father Gregory of Ochrid. The only remembrance of him is that he was the Archbishop of Ochrid in the early eleventh century. On the dyptik[1] on the Table of Preparation[2] in the Church of "Sveta Mudrost" (Holy Wisdom) in Ochrid are written the following words: "The All-wise Gregory, who instructed the people in the commandments of the Lord." He fell asleep in the Lord in the year 1012. Yet the memory of Archbishop Gregory

---

1. A dyptik is a double-framed apparatus with a center hinge (like a double picture frame) which sits on the Table of Preparation in the Holy Altar. On one side are the names of the departed souls and on the other are the names of the living to be remembered (prayed for) during the various Divine Services of that particular Orthodox Church.
2. The Table of Preparation is located in the northeast section of the Holy Altar area where is completed the Proskomedia (Preparation Service) prior to Divine Liturgy.

has truly become quite powerful, for he has inspired both clergy and laity of the Serbian Orthodox Church for almost a millennium!

If, then, we desire to understand what our Lord God accomplished through this wonderful hierarch, we must read and study the era in which he lived. History tells us that Archbishop Gregory pastored the faithful from his throne in Ochrid during one of the most tumultuous and difficult periods in the history of Balkan Christianity. The Serbs, although they had officially accepted Orthodoxy over two hundred years before Gregory's episcopacy, were nonetheless still quite unorganized and uneducated in the Orthodox faith.[3] The internal workings of the Serbian Church were constantly upset and assaulted by the infighting of various tribes and clans located in the two main regions inhabited by Serbs, namely the territories of Zeta and Rashka. Archbishop Gregory, consecrated by the Imperial Patriarch in Constantinople, the capital of the Byzantine Empire, was given the task of organizing and administering this still fledgling Orthodox Church of the Serbs. To make matters worse for Gregory, during his archiepiscopacy the warlike Bulgars continually raided and ravaged the Serbian villages and countryside. Therefore, under these circumstances, it is easy to understand and proclaim that the "All-wise" Gregory was truly a blessed Archshepherd to his flock, guiding them in virtue and leading them to the salvific life in Christ which is able to overcome any human obstacle. His memory is truly worth keeping alive!

On a slate tablet in the Church of Holy Wisdom, in Ochrid, are inscribed the words: "Wash your sins, not just your face." This short saying expresses a fundamental teaching of the Orthodox Christian faith, for the personal acquisition of virtue has always been considered a necessary requirement for the followers of Jesus Christ. This is a task

---

3. We must note that it was not until 1219, over two hundred years after St. Gregory's episcopacy, under the blessed guidance of St. Sava, the Eternal Enlightener of Orthodox Serbia, that the Serbs were able to unite and finally secede from the Archdiocese of Ochrid, establishing, by the consent of all Orthodox sister Churches, their own autonomous Orthodox Church.

Ochrid Lake and the Church of St. John
the Divine Kaneo.

The city of Ochrid, Church of
Holy Wisdom-Sophia.

which can only be accomplished by the daily examination of the soul, the constant guarding of the mind, and the sincere cleansing of the heart. Yet many Christians, even in our own day, believe this is a task only required of monks, nuns and the clergy. Many say, for example, that Apostle Paul's commandment to "pray without ceasing" (I Thess. 5:17) can only be accomplished by (and hence required of) those living in monasteries, huts or caves. To this notion, the Orthodox Christian faith and practice replies very loudly and emphatically: NO!

Just listen to a few exhortations from the Fathers of the Church on this matter.

St. Symeon the New Theologian (949-1022; honored March 12th): "One who has wife and children, many servants, much property, and a prominent position in the world" can attain the "vision of God"; and it is altogether possible to live "a heavenly life here on earth ... not just in caves or mountains or monastic cells, but in the midst of cities."

From the Life of St. Gregory Palamas (1296-1360; honored Nov. 14th and the Second Sunday of Great Lent):

"Let no one think, my fellow Christians, that it is the duty only of priests and monastics to pray without ceasing, and not of lay people. No, no; it is the duty of all of us Christians to remain always in prayer. For look what the Most Holy Patriarch of Constantinople, Philotheos, writes in his *Life of St. Gregory Palamas.* This saint had a beloved friend by the name of Job, a very simple but most virtuous man. Once, while conversing with him, His Eminence said of prayer that every Christian in general should strive to pray always, and to pray without ceasing, as Apostle Paul commands all Christians, 'Pray without ceasing' (I Thess. 5:17), and as the prophet David says of himself, although he was a king and had to concern himself with the whole kingdom: 'I foresaw the Lord always before my face' (Ps. 15:8)—that is, in my prayer I always mentally see the Lord before me. Gregory the Theologian also teaches all Christians to say God's name in prayer more often than they breathe."

In sum, life in the Church—participation in her liturgical and sacramental worship—can only be realized, actualized and incarnated in our own personal lives when we begin to pray constantly, examine ourselves and consciously attempt to rid ourselves of sins and passions, hence acquiring virtue.

Therefore, begin today. Find an experienced and wise elder in the faith and practice of virtue, and learn how to travel the "narrow and hard path" which leads to salvation. This is the only way which offers us the everlasting peace and joy of the Holy Spirit of God.

And along the way, St. Gregory of Ochrid will be discovered as a "Pillar of Truth" and "Champion of Virtue" for our own benefit and salvation.

" O Holy Father Gregory, O All-wise and All-virtuous One, pray to Christ our true God that we, too, most sinful servants, may be granted the knowledge of our own sins and the need for His love, mercy, peace and healing, which is sufficient alone to wash not only our faces, but our sins as well, so that we may offer eternally clean and pure glory to Christ Who is Virtue Incarnate, to Whom belongs glory, honor and worship, together with His Unoriginate Father, and Life-giving Spirit, now and ever and unto ages of ages. Amen"

KONTAKION TO ST. GREGORY

Tone 3

Thou didst appear in Ochrid, O holy One,* and fulfill the Gospel of Christ, O righteous One,* by laying down thy life for thy people,* rescuing the innocent from death;* therefore, thou wast deified as a great initiate of the grace of God.

The Byzantine Church of St. Mark in Belgrade.

January 13th

HOLY MARTYRS

Hermylus and Stratonicus

OF BELGRADE

(†315)

I venerate your life, O friends, for it is valiant.
And I weep over my life , for it is worthless!
Ancient Serbliak

DURING the reign of Lycinius (executed in 324), who co-reigned in the Eastern provinces with Emperor Maximian Valerius, the fate of all Christians was threatened. They were sought out in all countries, cities and villages. Anyone who found Christians had to inform the rulers about them, and they would receive favors for this, as a reward. Therefore, all people sought the whereabouts of Christians for the king, who was a severe idol-worshipper. One of these was Hermylus, a young zealous Christian. He was brought to Lycinius, and admitted that he was not only a Christian, but was even in the rank of deacon. He said that he served Christ for quite some time, and even laughed at the gods of the king.

Hearing this, Lycinius asked him: "Being a deacon, that is a server (of the altar), that means you're also serving the gods." To this, the martyr answered that he serves the unseen God, and not the mute idols who do not see, know, or understand anything. The ruler, seeing the freedom in the speech of the martyr, ordered that he be punished by

59

being beaten with a specially prepared whip, stating the if he would submit, he would avoid these tortures. But the martyr warned that [the king] himself will endure many terrible wounds because he abandoned his Creator and pays homage to idols (which took place in 324). To all the inquisitions the martyr answered quoting the psalms and singing to God aloud. He was thrown into prison and there the Lord consoled him by sending an angel who said to him: "Hermylus, be manly, speak, do not be silenced and do not fear, for thou wilt soon be victorious over the schemes of the torturer, and thou wilt receive for thy suffering a most luminous crown from above."

After three days the king again summoned Hermylus to the tribunal and asked whether he repented and agreed to bring sacrifice to the gods in order to free himself from future torments. But the Saint with valor responded that he had the heavenly God, and to Him alone would he bow down and bring sacrifice. Again he was tortured, but the Saint endured all suffering as if he was not beaten, and prayed aloud: "O Lord my God, Thou didst suffer, endure wounds and beatings by Pontius Pilate; strengthen me too, in my suffering for Thee, send me strength to endure these tortures, so that through participation in Thy suffering I may become a worthy participant in Thy eternal glory." When the Saint prayed thus, there was suddenly heard a voice from heaven which said: "Amen, amen, Hermylus, in three days thou wilt be delivered from these sufferings and wilt receive great reward for thy suffering." This voice gave great courage and strength to the martyr, and to the torturers brought fear and trembling and they fell on the ground and could do nothing. And they quickly threw him into the prison.

One of the guards, called Stratonicus, was a secret Christian and a friend of Hermylus. His heart was crushed seeing the suffering, but at the same time in his soul he rejoiced seeing such manliness and firmness, but he hesitated to follow. When Hermylus was entering the prison, he sang psalms and a light came from above and a voice was heard, promising that in three days all would be finished. The next day the interrogation continued and the Saint answered, quoting psalms and scripture. Stratonicus, seeing the inhuman suffering of Hermylus, that his intestines were crushed, began to cry. Bystanders noticed this and reported it to the king, who summoned Stratonicus and asked if he was a friend of Hermylas. Stratonicus, as a disciple of the Truth, did not wish to tell lies. Seeing that the time had come for him to perform his spiritual exploit, he called himself Hermylus' friend and a Christian, and fearlessly accused those who worshipped idols as madmen, and glorified the one God, Creator of heaven and earth. The king became furious and ordered that Stratonicus be stripped naked, and that his body be beaten with sticks. In his suffering Stratonicus raised his eyes to his friend Hermylus and said: "Pray for me to Christ, Hermylus, so that He will help me to be firm and unwavering and to preserve my faith and to rise above my tormentors," and he at the same time begged Lycinius to stop worshipping the soulless idols and to fear the true God, into Whose hands it is a fearful thing to fall (Heb. 10:31).

After thus suffering, they were thrown into a dungeon, and they both sang psalms and encouraged each other with great love. Then they were interrogated again and Hermylus was hung on a tree and his body was cut into strips. As the Saint prayed to God he heard a voice that said: "Do not fear, I am with thee, Thy God." After that the king condemned Hermylus to be drowned in the Danube river. Then the king turned to Stratonicus and said that such will be his fate too if he will not bring sacrifice to the gods, adding: "Thou wilt suffer just as thy friend did." Blessed Stratonicus answered: "Truly, how can I choose earthly life when my friend will die for Christ? I want to join him. True friends must endure together both tribulations and the enjoyment of grace. What is more joyful to us than suffering and death for Christ?" And he was condemned to be drowned in the Danube river together with Hermylus. And while walking to the river they sang: *Glory to God in the highest, and peace on earth and to men good will* (Luke 2:14). Then the soldiers brought them to the place, put them in a net and threw it in a deep spot, and thus the Danube river took in the holy martyrs and the heavens accepted both their souls. This took place around the year

315. On the third day Christians found their bodies on the shore, and with honor buried them 18 stadia from the city of Belgrade. They were placed together in one coffin so that they would have everything in common: common confession of Christ, common prison, common suffering, common drowning, common burial of their bodies, and common glory in Heaven, through the grace of our man-loving Lord Jesus Christ, to Whom belongs glory and honor, together with the Father and the Holy Spirit, both now and ever and to the ages of ages, Amen![1]

TROPARION
Tone 3
O holy Martyrs who have faithfully confessed the transcendent Trinity,* renowned and invincible Hermylus* and steadfast, godly Stratonicus:* since you partake of the glory that surpasses understanding,* pray that we may be granted great mercy.

KONTAKION
Tone 1
You drowned the enemy in the depths of your contests* by your steadfastness, O noble Prize-winners.* You received your end in the streams of the river,* hence were brought to the waters of incorruption. * You magnified Christ, O divine Hermylus* and Stratonicus.

---

1. Condensed from *The Lives of the Saints* by St. Dimitry of Rostov, Volume for January, Moscow, 1904. Also *Saints of South Slavonic Countries* by Philaret, Archbishop of Chernigov, Petersburg, 1882, pp. 24-25.

A fresco of 1265, in the monastery church at Sopochani, of St. John the Apostle, depicting him the same way ancient martyrs were.

St. Sava

Archbishop
of Serbia

TROPARION, Tone 3

Thou wast the way leading to life,* guide and
first-enthroned hierarch and teacher;* thou camest first, Holy
Sava,* to enlighten thy homeland and race,* regenerating
them by the Holy Spirit;* thou didst plant thy most holy children* like olive trees in a spiritual paradise;* therefore, honor-
ing thee as co-equal to the Apostles and saints,* we ask thee,
pray to Christ God to grant us great mercy.

January 14th

LIFE OF OUR HOLY FATHER

SAVA I

ENLIGHTENER AND FIRST
ARCHBISHOP OF THE SERBS

(✝1235)

Seek ye first the kingdom of God, and His righteousness;
and all these things shall be added unto you.
Matthew 6:33

THE SERBIAN Grand Zhupan (Patriarchal leader) Stephen
Nemanja had two sons, Stephen and Vukan; yet, he and his wife Anna
desired, if it be God's will, to have another child. Their pious prayers
ascended before God, Who heard their petition and blessed them with
their last child, a son who was born in the year of our Lord 1175. At
baptism the child was given the name Rastko, a name derived from the
Old Slavonic verb "rasti" which means "to grow." And grow divinely
he did. There were many special things about Rastko: he was a lovely
child, with pronounced features and smooth skin, and possessed, already
in his childhood, an unusually alert and pious demeanor. Little did
Rastko's parents and all those of the Royal Court (and even the entire
Serb nation) realize that his birth and baptism into Orthodoxy would
providentially set in motion their own historical and spiritual journey,
which would result in the blossoming of their Christian faith, nation-

hood and total Christian cultural orientation. This young child, Rastko, whose monastic name later was Sava, became and still remains the most beloved of all Serbian Orthodox saints, considered by all Serbs everywhere and at all times as the ultimate expression and example of what it means to be fully human, that is, what it means to be a devout and committed follower of Jesus Christ.

Rastko was provided the best education of his day. He succeeded in all subjects as he was a quiet and introspective boy, preferring to read and to probe into the meaning and nature of things than to find passing pleasure in mundane children's games. Being of royal lineage, Prince Rastko was given, at age 15, the territory of Zahumlje (later called "the Hercegovina of St. Sava") to rule as his own. When he was 17, his parents arranged for Rastko to be married; but Rastko's innate disposition towards the quiet solitary life led him to never even consider such an event taking place. According to St. Sava's biographers Dometian and Theodosius, when Rastko Nemanjich was 18 years old, a Russian Orthodox monk from the Monastery of St. Panteleimon on the Holy Mountain came to visit the Royal Court of Grand Zhupan Stephen Nemanja to ask for alms for his monastery. After meeting the monk, Prince Rastko went into a private room with him and questioned him about the way of life on the Holy Mountain. As the monk spoke about the peace of God exhibited by the ascetics, and about the hope of eternity and the priceless treasure of salvation found in the monastic way of life, Rastko seemed to have been baptized once again. The Holy Spirit filled Rastko's heart with internal stirring and commotion, sensitizing him to a deep desire which the Lord God had implanted within him: *That I may dwell in the house of the Lord all the days of my life, that I may behold the delight of the Lord, and that I may visit His holy temple* (Ps. 26:4). Rastko knew at that very moment that in order to fulfill this desire he had to travel to the Holy Mountain. God was calling him there. Yet little did Rastko realize that this rebirth experience would prove to be the first step of a more encompassing and profound journey, one which entailed eternal ramifications, that is, a spiritual movement toward the

Main icon of Christ the Savior in the Hilandar Monastery
Catholicon, 13th century.

sanctification of an entire race—the Serbian people. To Rastko, marriage and all worldly knowledge, authority or possessions could not compare to what he had experienced while in conversation with this unknown and simple monk from the Holy Mountain.

"But how can I face my parents?" thought Rastko to himself. "How will I ever make such a journey to the Holy Mountain?" Pondering this dilemma, Rastko, by the grace of the Holy Spirit, came up with a solution. He organized a hunting trip and at an opportune time fled his homeland with the monk to make the long journey to the Holy Mountain.

Discovering his flight, Rastko's father, Zhupan Stephen Nemanja, quickly assembled his best soldiers of the Royal Court and ordered them to the seaport city of Thessalonica, where he hoped they would catch up with Rastko. Stephen also sent a letter with his troops which they presented to the military governor of the city; in it the Grand Zhupan threatened violence to the city if his son was not safely returned. However, these efforts were unfruitful, as Rastko traveled quickly through Thessalonica and arrived by boat at the Russian Monastery of St. Panteleimon on the Holy Mountain.

When the soldiers arrived at the monastery, the all-night vigil had just begun. The soldiers, not wishing to disturb the Divine Service, entered the Catholikon (main church) and sat in the stalls along the inner walls of the church. Spotting Rastko, they decided to wait patiently until the end of the vigil service and then order Rastko back to his father. However, the soldiers never expected the all-night vigil to last over six hours! As time passed, due to their being physically and mentally exhausted from the grueling journey from Serbia to the Holy Mountain, each of the soldiers fell fast asleep in his stall.

Taking advantage of the situation, Rastko and an elder hieromonk (priest monk) quickly left the church and climbed to the top of the bell tower in the monastery courtyard. During the rest of the night and early morning, the blessed elder instructed Rastko concerning the monastic life and, just prior to the completion of Divine Liturgy (as Divine

St. Sava's portrait, painted from his actual likeness in the fresco of
Mileshevo Monastery, 1235.

Liturgy follows every vigil service) the elder received Rastko into monasticism, tonsuring him and giving him the name of Sava, after the great ascetic and holy man of Jerusalem, St. Sava the Sanctified (†532; honored Dec. 5th). When the soldiers awoke from their sleep in the morning, they quickly went to search for Sava. High up in the air from the window of the bell tower, Sava revealed himself, and then went on to explain to them that his monastic tonsure was completed and that they should not harm any of the monks. Then he threw down his shorn hair and civilian clothes, saying, "Please take this to my parents as a remembrance of my youth." This took place in 1193, when Sava was just 18 years old.

Sava was not the first Serb to become a monk on the Holy Mountain, as there were Serbs there prior to his arrival. However, there was no Serbian monastery. Serbian monks found shelter and lived in the existing Greek, Russian, Bulgarian or Georgian monasteries, or eventually lived in caves, leading the life of a solitary or hermit. Only a few months after his tonsure, Sava was invited to the Greek Monastery Vatopedi for the celebration of its patronal feast, the Annunciation of the Theotokos (March 25th). It was here that Sava first began his true entrance into the profound spiritual life of monasticism. In leaving the Panteleimon Monastery, Prince Rastko was no more; now only Sava the monk was alive in Christ by the power of the Holy Spirit.

Sava quickly proved to be a relentless warrior and ascetic for Christ. He kept constant vigil over his body, thoughts and passions—his total person. At times, the abbot of Vatopedi had to restrain Sava from excessive ascetic practices, for fear that he might harm his health. Also, as time passed, Sava's parents and brothers began to accept his new life and provided him with abundant financial support, which he unselfishly distributed to the various monasteries on the Holy Mountain. He had especial love for Vatopedi, providing it with assistance for both a new roof for the main Church of the Annunciation and for the building of three small chapels. Vatopedi at this time was a kind of Byzantine university, as the monastery was lavishly supported by the Byzantine

St. Sava Nemanja and his father St. Simeon.
Fresco of 1314 in Studenitsa Monastery.

St. Sava's flight to the holy mountain.
Icon from Moracha monastery, 1645

emperors as well. It possessed a large library full of all the ancient writings of the Fathers of the Church on the various theological topics of Christian life: Scripture, liturgy, asceticism, doctrine, sacraments, Lives of Saints, icons and architecture, and canon law. At Vatopedi Sava learned the ancient Greek language perfectly. (He had previously learned the contemporary Greek language from his mother Anna—named Anatasia as a monastic later in her life [see June 21st]—for she was Greek by birth, the daughter of the Greek Byzantine Emperor Romanos IV Diogenes [1068-1081].) Studying the writings of the Fathers of the Church, along with practicing the strict ascetic life and participating fully in the communal liturgical/sacramental life of the monastery, the image of God in Sava began to slowly shine forth, transforming him into a spiritual man of God, whose sole longing was to be with the Lord Jesus Christ in the bosom of God the Father, enlivened by the Holy and Gracious and Life-creating Spirit.

In 1196, when Sava was 21 years of age, he received the greatest gift of his life: his father, Stephen Nemanja, decided to abdicate the throne of the Kingdom of Serbia and become a monk in Studenitsa Monastery on Mt. Radochelo in Rashka. He took the name Simeon. To replace him on the Royal Throne, the Grand Zhupan appointed his second oldest son, Stephen, as the heir. This news thrilled Sava, as it was for him a spiritual blessing for his many prayers, ascetic efforts and even letters he had sent to his father urging him towards monastic life. Along with his father, Sava's mother Anna, on the same day—the Feast of the Annunciation, March 25, 1196—also received the monastic tonsure and was given the name Anastasia, retiring to the Monastery of the Holy Virgin in Kurshumlija near Toplica.

At his son's request, the monk Simeon-Stephen Nemanja, only a few months after his monastic tonsure, left Serbia and traveled to Vatopedi Monastery. There for the first time in three years he met his favorite child, Sava, who by this time was an experienced and well-respected monk. The reunion was incredible. The biographer Theodosius writes: "They were both speechless; and, had not someone supported

72

Vatopedi Monastery on Mt. Athos.

St. Sava's mother, Nun Anastasia, fresco in the Church of the Virgin. The scripture above her says, "O Most Holy Virgin and Mother of our God, accept the prayer of Thy slave, Nun Anastasia."

his father, he would have fallen. After he regained his composure, he poured many tears over the much longed-for and saintly head of his beloved son, embracing and kissing it and pressing it to his chest." Thus Sava's dream was coming true. Simeon's "conversion" and total acceptance of the monastic life marked a beginning once again, not only for the two saints, but perhaps more importantly, for the entire Serbian race. By this act, Simeon, the most powerful and influential man of the Serbian kingdom, was solidifying Serbia's ties with the treasury of spirituality of the Holy Mountain, as well as paving the way for all future royalty—rulers of the Kingdom of Serbia—to accept and acknowledge Orthodoxy as the way and ultimate criterion for the total christianization of the Serbian people. Simeon was like the Holy Byzantine Emperor of old, Constantine the Great (†337), paving the way for Orthodoxy to be the foundation and basis for all Serbian culture, history and civilization.

The most wonderful element in the legacy of the monks Sava and Simeon—son and father—was their joint effort to bring to the Serbian nation a spiritual center in which prayer and committed Christian life would be the eternal flame and vigil lamp guiding the Serbian people to the Kingdom of God. This eternal torch and divine light was Hilandar Monastery. Hilandar Monastery was once a small monastic settlement which had fallen into ruin for many years. The property was owned by Vatopedi Monastery. Due to Sava's virtuous life and his representation of the Vatopedi brotherhood at the Imperial Court in Constantinople, and also because of Simeon's generous material support of the Monastery, the ruins of Hilandar, by Imperial decree, were given to the Serbs as an independent and self-governing property to be used as a monastery. This was made official by two foundational charters: the chrysobull of Byzantine Emperor Alexis III Angelos of Constantinople in June 1198, and the charter of Hilandar Monastery's co-founder, Zhupan Stephen Nemanja—monk Simeon—in late 1198. Hence, the idea of a Serbian monastery on the Holy Mountain became a reality when father became obedient to son, when both of these spiritual pillars

Fr. Simeon Nemanja, father of St. Simeon in the fresco of Studenitsa Monastery, holding the symbol of the Studenitsa Monastery, and the inscription says, "The founder of this place." Fresco from 1209 in the Holy Virgin Church in Studenitsa.

of the Serbian race became totally dedicated to our Lord and Savior Jesus Christ and Holy Orthodoxy.

In May 1199, the main church, dedicated to the Feast of the Presentation of the Theotokos in the Temple (November 21st), along with several other buildings necessary for the Monastery to function properly, were completed and consecrated. The Typikon of Hilandar (rules and regulations governing the communal prayer life of the monastery) was based upon the Greek Typikon of the Monastery of the Theotokos the Grace-giver in Constantinople, St. Sava's favorite Imperial monastery. St. Sava himself translated the Greek text of this typikon into Old Slavonic for use at Hilandar. When monastic life at Hilandar began, there were only fifteen monks, but within a short period of time the number grew to ninety. There was no doubt that the Hilandar community would be successful as long as the great Sava and Simeon were leading the way: that is, by being totally dedicated to Jesus Christ they were able to attract many candidates to the radically devoted monastic life in Christ led by the Holy Spirit. Hence, Sava saw another blessing and miracle develop before his very own eyes: the arrival of many young Serbian ascetics desirous, as he was in his youth, of the totally committed life in Christ.

To any normal Christian ascetic, these accomplishments would have been enough to perfect his own life or even make one consider himself great in God's eyes; but Sava never considered himself complete or perfect. He always sought "to get away from it all," to serve the Lord in the solitude of his heart, in order to *be perfect as* [his] *Father in Heaven is perfect* (Matt. 5:48). Therefore, to fulfill this desire placed within his soul by the creative and energetic grace of God, Sava traveled to the capital of the peninsula of the Holy Mountain, Karyes, in order to seek a piece of property there for the purpose of building a monastic cell for the solitary life in the Lord.

From September to December 1199, Sava, only 24 years old (but with the wisdom of Solomon), built in Karyes, the capital of the Holy Mountain, a monastic cell and small chapel dedicated to his namesake,

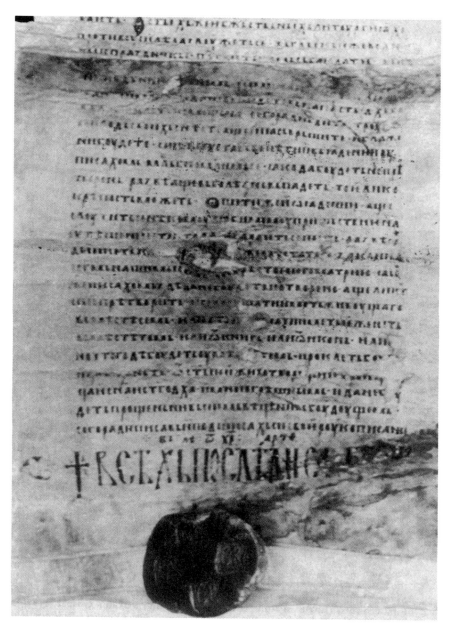

The original text of St. Sava's Typicon Rule (Karejski Tipik) including signature and seal.

St. Sava the Sanctified of Jerusalem. To provide a liturgical rule of prayer for himself and for those who would live in the cell after him, Sava wrote his famous Karejski Typikon (Typicarnica).

The Karejski Typikon is one of the most important documents in the history of Serbian spiritual literature.[1] In 115 lines Sava detailed the rules for prayer, fasting and liturgical worship to be carried out by the kelliote (monk who lives in a cell) residing in Karyes. The Karejski Typikon was patterned after the ancient rules of prayer of the early ascetics who strived in the Lord in the deserts of Egypt, Sinai, Palestine and Syria. The Karejski Typikon expressed a most fundamental under-standing and belief concerning human beings held to this day by all pious Orthodox Christians: the truth that all human beings are origi-nally made and therefore destined to know and be friends with their Creator—God the Holy Trinity—and to be personally and intimately known by Him, which is a flowing and most powerful relationship of love, peace and joy. And this is totally possible for those who are seriously committed to "the Way, the Truth, and the Life," our Lord Jesus Christ who rests in the bosom of God the Father, and for those who are animated by the Holy Spirit. And if there is one clear message revealed in the life of St. Sava, it is precisely this: that the Christian life consists primarily in seeking and finding God, in searching and discovering His will, and in hungering and thirsting for His righteousness—*Seek ye first the Kingdom of God, and His righteousness, and all these things shall be added unto you* (Matt. 6:33). Sava's sojourn in his cell in Karyes built him into a pillar of Orthodoxy, as it was here that he *prayed without ceasing* (I Thess. 5:17) and also wrote many hymns, treatises and prayers to the glory of God the Holy Trinity.

---

1. For a more detailed historical and theological analysis, with a full first-ever English translation of the Slavonic text of the Karejski Typikon of St. Sava, see the article by Fr. Daniel Rogich, "The Karejski Typikon of St. Sava," found in two scholarly journals: *Sobornost*, Vol. 11, nos. 1 & 2, 1989, pp 69-81, and *Serbian Studies*, University of Illinois at Chicago, Vol. 5, no 2, fall 1989.

View from above of the Monastery of Hilandar built by St. Sava,
as it looks today.

Only a few months after the completion of his cell, Sava's father, monk Simeon, became grievously ill. On February 13, 1200, Blessed Simeon fell asleep in the Lord. He was 86 years old. (And only four months later, on June 21, 1200, Princess Anna-St. Anastasia, Sava's mother, fell asleep in the Lord at age 75 in the Monastery of the Holy Virgin in Kurshumlja near Toplica.) In Sava's biography of his father which he wrote in his cell in Karyes, he described the tremendous sorrow he experienced over the loss of his father, as well as the holy and divine way in which Blessed Simeon died. After Simeon's death, Sava asked the Lord God to reveal to him concerning the judgment of his father. One night, in a dream, Simeon appeared to Sava with a luminous countenance, and delivered a most powerful message to him. Simeon told Sava that Serbia needed him, that there was much work to be done there. Although Sava did not desire, after entering monastic life on the Holy Mountain, ever to return to Serbia, this message of Simeon made him realize that it was now time for the son to be obedient to the father.

The state of affairs in Serbia had been quite poor ever since Simeon's departure in 1196: there was little religious leadership, and the brothers Stephen and Vukan were locked in a terrible fratricidal struggle for political rule of the kingdom. In response to the supplication of Simeon—whose appearance to Sava also demonstrated Simeon's own saintliness—and to the numerous pleadings for Sava to return on the part of his younger brother, the newly coronated King Stephen (1196-1228), Sava decided to travel back to his birthplace in the cause of peace, and in order to comfort and guide his Serbian people. Thus, in 1204, at age 29, after eleven years of monastic life on the Holy Mountain, Sava began his journey homeward. His departure was mourned by the monks, but they knew Sava's departing was the will of the Lord. Sava did not leave without honor bestowed upon him, as he was elevated to the rank of Archimandrite in Thessalonica by four bishops of the nearby dioceses.

When Sava entered his native land in 1204, he unfortunately found the country just as Simeon had informed him in his dream—in total

Bird's-eye view of Studenitsa Monastery, as it looks today,
preserving its medieval authenticity.

disarray. The Serbian state was split in two. By secret negotiations with Hungary and Pope Innocent III, Vukan, the eldest of the three brothers, who was bitter over the appointment of his younger brother Stephen as heir to the throne, was able to amass troops and capture Zeta; he then was set to launch a campaign against Rashka, King Stephen's portion of the divided kingdom. This civil war was only a microcosm of a larger conflict instigated by the West—that is, the hostilities initiated by the Great Crusades of the Latin church. In 1204, the soldiers of the Fourth Crusade captured Constantinople and much of the territory of Byzantium, including the Holy Mountain. In 1205, the Holy Mountain was officially placed under the authority and jurisdiction of a Roman Catholic bishop. It is believed that this occurrence was the most influential factor in Sava's decision to return to Serbia. Hence, the Saint returned home with his work cut out for him.

When he returned, Sava brought with him the medicine to heal the entire situation: the relics of his father, the Grand Zhupan and saint, Stephen Nemanja-Simeon the Myrrh-bearer and co-founder of Hilandar. Upon entering Studenitsa Monastery, St. Simeon's foundational monastery, Sava invited his two brothers to a proper and rightful Memorial Service for their father. As the casket was opened, before their eyes the body of their father was found to be sweet-smelling, exuding a fragrant oil and myrrh, warm and aglow, looking very much alive, as if he were only restfully sleeping. This act of veneration of their father was the first step in healing the fraternal schism between Vukan and King Stephen. Shortly thereafter, the civil war was halted and a peace agreement was drawn up, once again restoring the kingdom of Serbia as it was under the reign of the great King Stephen Nemanja-St. Simeon the Myrrh-bearer. In discussions with his reunited brothers, Sava also designed plans for an immediate, systematic and far-reaching missionary program to save the Orthodox soul of the Serbian people. Studenitsa Monastery, with St. Simeon's relics making it a national shrine, was chosen as the outreach station for all activities. St. Sava wrote the Monastery's Typikon, which strengthened Studenitsa's monastic life.

ST. SAVA'S UPPER POSTNICA

The most striking place near Studenitsa, but to the north of it, is called "Nemanja's [Nehemiah's] Tower." To reach it you must walk up the rapid, murmuring Studenitsa River. On your left you will see springs of water and the quarry of white marble which Nemanja used to build his great church. A little further, as you pass through the forest, you may step down to the brink of the river to drink the sparkling mineral water, which is very healthful and refreshing. After about an hour of walking, you cross the river over a narrow wooden bridge and turn to your left to climb a hill. You proceed first through bushes with a few small trees until you get to a boundary of a sacred ground with a fine shade forest, where the trees are safe from a stranger's ax and it would be a sacrilege to eat meat. Such is the rule of St. Sava, everyone will tell you. For that forest and ground belong to his House of Silence, or Postnica. For another hour you walk through the forest until suddenly an inviting green glen appears before you. You cross a tiny silvery brook—there you are in Lower Postnica—from which you have to climb for about half an hour to Upper Postnica. In Lower Postnica you will be welcomed by two or three monks of Studenitsa brotherhood. In their simple quarters they will show you a beautiful small chapel, in which they strictly keep the prayer rule prescribed by St. Sava. The brothers will receive you very kindly, but only one of them will answer your questions. The questions exhibiting too much curiosity, however, they will pass over in silence.

Now you walk up a steep mount through a forest of fir trees. Suddenly you find yourself over a precipice. On your right hand stands a high wall of monolithic rock, through which a path has been cut no wider in places than half a yard. On your left you will see an almost perpendicular slope covered with slabs of rocks as big as huts, lying in disorder, cast there as if by some titans in battle. At the bottom of this terrific panorama roars the Studenitsa River. Those with weak nerves turn back to avoid dizziness and loss of balance. At the end you reach a narrow opening in a half-circle. And there you find St. Sava's Upper Postnica. As a swallow's nest perches on a cliff, there stands a structure of stone and oak beams, now half in ruins. Under that structure there is a well with a little water, which is taken to the sick.

Who could ever foresee that a royal prince of Serbia would choose this frightening precipice for his abode in preference to court life? Sava chose it for his periodic retreats while in Serbia, and this not only while he was a monk or the superior of a monastery, but later also when he was archbishop. After the end of his retreat Sava, transfigured as it were, would return to Studenitsa to gladden and fortify the whole brotherhood with his presence. Then again he would proceed on his journeys all over the country to preach, teach, build, and work among the Serbian people as before.

The Church of the Mother of God in Studenitsa Monastery, frescoed in the
eastern part of the church in 1209, during the time of St. Sava's life there.

As newly elected abbot of Studenitsa, Archimandrite Sava personally went on several missions throughout the territories, preaching and teaching the Word of God in the churches as well as renewing and creating monasteries, building many churches, opening iconography schools, and in general establishing and confirming the populace in the Orthodox faith. Sava was concerned not only with the spiritual welfare of the kingdom, but also with the material condition of the people, as he constantly advised his two older brothers, especially King Stephen, on how to better feed, clothe and administer the people. It is believed that through the monasteries in Serbia at this time, Sava was able to put the kingdom's economy in order by raising to the highest level the production of food, wine, honey, fish, vegetables and livestock, not only sustaining the monastics but also benefitting thousands of Serbs: pilgrims, visitors, and especially the sick and aged. Truly St. Sava carried out and actualized the great commandment of Christ: *Thou shalt love the Lord thy God with all thy heart, and with all thy soul, and with all thy strength, and with all thy mind; and thy neighbor as thyself.* These missionary efforts were for Sava, as always, ascetic exercises allowing him to be more fully immersed in the eternal grace, love and beauty of the Holy Spirit of God. These acts demonstrated his tremendous love for his people. Sava was fast becoming a great Serbian ecclesiastical leader; and in the ensuing years his continual wise leadership would enable him to become a well-respected international ecclesiastical figure as well.

The international situation, as mentioned, was also in disarray. The increasing papal power in the East could no longer be ignored. Byzantium was fighting a losing battle. The Byzantine Empire, like Serbia, was divided in two, with one political center at Constantinople and the other at Thessalonica; with the two rival factions, the Niceans and the Epirotes, fighting for political control over the Empire. The Patriarchate of Constantinople, the ultimate ecclesiastical administrative overseer of Serbia, was split in three, with centers at Nicea, Trebizond and Ochrid. As a result of this confusion and turmoil, King Stephen, at the advice of his wife, Queen Anna, decided to ally Serbia with the Pope of Rome in order to stem the tide against the attacks of the Hungarian King Andreas III and those of the Latinophiles in Constantinople. This decision on the part of Stephen angered his brother Sava, who, due to his loyalty to Orthodoxy and the Byzantine State, decided to return to the Holy Mountain. Hence, in 1217, at age 42, after thirteen years of missionary activity in his homeland, Sava traveled once again to his true spiritual home, Hilandar Monastery on the Holy Mountain, in order to be alone with his Lord and Savior Jesus Christ. And, like his Savior so often did, Sava too "departed from his flock for a little while" in order to rest in the bosom of the Father, and to retreat from the world and its passing struggles and desires. Yet this was only for a short while, for the Lord had many tasks still ahead for Blessed Sava to fulfill.

Sava spent a little less than two years at Hilandar after his departure from Serbia (1217-1219). The moment he left, Serbia's situation worsened both domestically and internationally. The miracle-working oil exuding from the holy relics of his father Simeon stopped flowing. The people were outraged at King Stephen for driving Sava away. Under no terms would they accept the Pope's support and disavow Orthodoxy. As a result, Stephen wrote to Sava imploring him to return. Stephen also renounced his western ties and attempted to reconcile with the Byzantine emperor in Nicea, Theodore Laskaris (1204-1222). Spending his days and nights in prayer and vigil, guarding his soul from all passions, and incessantly petitioning the Lord in behalf of his Serbian people, Sava was elated to receive his brother Stephen's repentant letter. When he heard from Stephen, Sava immediately went to his cell and prayed tearfully to his father Simeon: "O Saint, having been commanded by God and implored by us, please disregard our transgressions. For whatever we are, we are still your children. Allow, therefore, the myrrh to flow again from your body in the tomb as before, to bring joy and relief to your people now in mourning." This prayer, which Sava sent to King Stephen in a letter, was read aloud before the tomb of Simeon in Studenitsa Monastery and was then published throughout the land. The letter also disclosed plans Sava had received in a dream from Almighty God: to obtain from Nicea the independence of the Serbian Orthodox Church. When the letter was read aloud in Studenitsa, immediately the miraculous myrrh from the relics of the holy patriarchal leader Simeon began to flow once again. Thus, by the will of the Lord, Sava set out to journey homeward for a second time from Hilandar in order to heal his people and to bring them glad tidings of salvation, faith and unity.

Prior to his return, Sava traveled eastward to Nicea, the city where the Imperial Patriarch Manuel Sarantenos (1215-1222) resided, the highest ecclesiastical authority permitted to grant independence to a local Church. Sava, who also brought with him several monks of Hilandar, discussed his vision with the Patriarch and Emperor Theodore. At first, the Patriarch was reluctant to grant Sava's request. Why hadn't Sava, he thought, petitioned through the Archbishop of Ochrid, who was the immediate jurisdictional authority over the Church of Serbia? But after a careful review of the political and ecclesiastical difficulties in the Balkans—not only in Serbia but also between Nicea and Epirus—this request on the part of Sava began to make perfect sense to both the Patriarch and the Emperor. By granting autonomy to the Church of Serbia, Rome and the West's attempts to capture the Balkans could be thwarted. Also, the Archbishop of Ochrid was becoming too powerful; with independence granted to the Serbs, his power would diminish. The Serbian Orthodox Church, now independent, would remain under the direct jurisdiction of the Patriarchate. (As is well known, the Serbian Orthodox Church did not receive her own Patriarch until over one hundred years later, becoming autocephalous on Palm Sunday, April 9, 1346.) Thus, the situation was quite favorable to all involved. At Patriarch Manuel's request, Sava was selected to be elevated to Archbishop. At first, Sava vehemently refused this offer on the grounds that he felt he was truly unworthy for such a position and calling. He offered several of the monks from Hilandar who were present as potential candidates for the position. In the end, Sava accepted and was consecrated in Nicea on the Feast of St. Nicholas, December 6,

St. Sava, fresco from the 13th-century Church of the Holy Apostles
in Pech Monastery.

1219, becoming the first Archbishop of the newly autonomous Orthodox Church of Serbia. He was 44 years old at the time. The following are the exact words of the Greek text of Patriarch Manuel's decree elevating Sava to Archbishop, thus granting autonomy to the Serbian Church:

> I, Manuel, the Ecumenical Patriarch and the Archbishop of the City of Constantinople, New Rome, in the name of our Lord Jesus Christ, have consecrated Sava, Archbishop of all the Serbian lands, and have given him in God's name the authority to consecrate bishops, priests, and deacons within his country; to bind and loose sins of men, and to teach all and to baptize in the name of the Father, and the Son, and the Holy Spirit. Therefore, all you Orthodox Christians, obey him as you have obeyed me.

After his consecration, Sava returned to the Holy Mountain in order to say farewell to Hilandar and to receive the blessing and prayers of the entire monastic community of the Holy Mountain. This was the most emotional moment in Sava's life. To the Holy Mountain (and Hilandar in particular), his true spiritual home, the holy place where he had spent over twenty-five years of his life and which he thought he would never leave, Sava now had to bid farewell. Although the monks welcomed him and treated him with the highest dignity and respect accorded his ecclesiastical position, they all nevertheless were saddened by the loss of their beloved brother and friend, the simple monk Sava. And if there is anything that shines forth and is easily ascertained from Sava's personality and character, it is precisely this: no matter what position or accolade or accomplishment Sava attained or achieved, he never forgot his spiritual core and roots, which were to love and live with Christ in simplicity, in common friendship and in humble love.

The newly consecrated Archbishop Sava then traveled by boat to Thessalonica, where he tarried awhile at Philokalos Monastery. At Philokalos, he, along with a few others, made a translation from Greek into Slavonic of the Byzantine ecclesiastical law book *The Rudder* or *Nomocanon* of St. Photios the Great (9th century). Called *Kormchaja*

Knjiga (Book of the Pilot) in Slavonic, this translation contained not only the ecclesiastical canons—including the dogmatic decrees of the Seven Ecumenical Councils—with commentaries by the best medieval Greek canonists, but also numerous precepts of the Fathers of the Church along with several of the imperial edicts of the great Byzantine Emperor Justinian (6th century). This work was one of Sava's greatest literary and political feats, for it enabled the kingdom of Serbia to be greatly influenced by the highly cultured and civilized Byzantine state, whose vision of society and human life was primarily motivated and governed by the Orthodox faith. For example, Sava divided the kingdom into nine dioceses according to the civil boundaries of the land, which was the Byzantine way of ecclesiastical division. Each episcopal seat was located in the capital of the said territory, which enabled both the civil and ecclesiastical leaders to work harmoniously for the material and spiritual benefit of the Serbian people. Each diocese residence was established in a monastery, with the headquarters of the Archbishop at Zhicha Monastery. (Also, it is worthy to note that this Slavonic translation, St. Sava's Nomocanon, became the basis of the civil and ecclesiastical constitution of the kingdoms of Bulgaria and Russia throughout the entire Middle Ages.)

When he arrived in Serbia, Sava, the first Archbishop of the Serbs, was greeted with open arms by his brother King Stephen and his nephews (Stephen's sons), Princes Radislav (1228-1233) and Vladislav (1233-1243). Sava went straightway to Studenitsa to venerate his father Simeon's myrrh-flowing relics. After a short stay there, he left in order to ascend his archiepiscopal throne in the newly consecrated Zhicha Monastery, the foundational monastery of King Stephen, located on the right bank of the Ibar river only five miles southwest of Kraljevo. The architectural style of Zhicha Monastery was of the school of Rashka, or the Serbo-Byzantine style, characterized by the semi-circular apse at the eastern end of the main church, a separated narthex (entrance area or vestibule on the west end where in the monasteries the Divine Services of Compline, Midnight Office, Hours and the Litya on the eve of Great

Feasts are said), along with a large dome joining the two ends to focus the worshippers to the center of the church. A unique feature of the main church of Christ the Savior in Zhicha was the brick and stone construction of the church which was plastered over and colored red, after the model of the Holy Mountain monasteries, symbolizing the blood which our Savior and His beloved followers, the holy Martyrs, shed "for the life of the world."

As the spiritual center of Serbian Orthodoxy, Zhicha Monastery would once again lead the efforts toward the total enculturation of the Serbian people into the Orthodox vision and way of life. To establish Zhicha as the religious and political center of the kingdom of Serbia, Sava decided that on the first day of his archiepiscopacy in Zhicha, the Feast of the Ascension, 1220, he would, as the newly consecrated Archbishop of Serbia, coronate his brother Stephen as the first Serbian King. Even though Stephen had previously assumed the throne in 1196 after his father Stephen Nemanja-St. Simeon had abdicated, nonetheless his coronation at this time officially proclaimed him, before all countries, as the rightful Orthodox King of Serbia. This coronation marked the end to any western ties by the Nemanja dynasty. Accordingly, Stephen received the title "Kralj Stephen Prvovenchani" (King Stephen the First-Crowned).

As during his earlier stay in Serbia, Sava met with difficulties. The Roman Pope Callistus III as well as Archbishop Demetrius Homatian of Ochrid were not pleased, to say the least, with the elevation of Sava to Archbishop and the new status of the Serbian Church. Sava spent the first ten years of his archiepiscopacy (1219-1229) primarily in organizing the Church, setting up dioceses, renewing monasteries and strengthening the populace against all pressures from both the Greeks and the Latins. It must be noted that never once did Sava call for any retaliation or hostilities against the Greek or Roman dioceses in Serbia. Also, during this time, Sava experienced another setback. His brother, King Stephen the First-Crowned, fell asleep in the Lord in late 1228. Prior to his death, Stephen received the monastic tonsure and the name Simon. After the

King's death, his son Radislav came into power. Unfortunately for the Serbs, Radislav favored his Greek mother Eudokia's side. As a result, the newly coronated King Radislav, against the wishes of Sava, called for a return of the fledgling Serbian Church to the protectorate of the Greek Archbishop of Ochrid. This political maneuver was too much for Sava, and he once again had thoughts of fleeing his homeland. But where could he go? He was now their permanent Archbishop and could not possibly go back to Hilandar. After some deliberation, Venerable Sava decided to visit Jerusalem and the Holy Land. Thus, in 1229, after ten years of dedicated hard work and fruitful labor in the vineyard of the Lord in his homeland, Sava decided to renew his own spirit by pilgrimaging to the cradle of Christianity itself, Jerusalem, where the Lord first brought salvation to the world.

In Jerusalem, Sava purchased the house in which, according to some records, Jesus Christ and His disciples celebrated the Passover in the year he was crucified. He bought it from a Moslem and returned it safely into the hands of the Orthodox Church in Jerusalem. Also, Sava made arrangements which facilitated visitations by Serbian pilgrims to the Holy Land. He paved the way for Serbian monastic colonies to settle and flourish in Palestine and the surrounding desert areas during the time of the Serbian Medieval State (early 13th to mid 15th centuries). Sava also built new churches, renewed existing ones, financed monasteries, and spent many hours in conversation with the great ascetics of the deserts of the Middle East, learning more of the art of prayer, fasting, and the taming of the passions of the flesh. In particular, Sava visited the monastery of his namesake, St. Sava the Sanctified of Jerusalem, where his episcopal ministry was confirmed by his fulfilling a seven hundred-year-old prophecy whereby he received two famous miraculous icons, the Miraculous Icon of the Theotokos "With Three Hands" (called "Troiruchica" in Slavonic; see July 12th) and the Miraculous Icon of the Theotokos "The Nursing Virgin" (see July 3rd), and brought it to Hilandar and placed it in his typicaria.

When it was time for Sava to leave the Holy Land for Serbia, he decided to go by way of Nicea. He did this to further solidify the promise made by Patriarch Manuel in 1219 to keep the Serbian Church autonomous. There he met with John, the new Emperor of Byzantium (1222-1254) now residing in Nicea, who succeeded Theodore Laskaris. He also met Germanus, the new Patriarch who succeeded the late Patriarch Manuel. Irene, Emperor John's wife and the daughter of the deceased Theodore Laskaris, was present at these meetings, and she recalled memories of Sava's first visit to Nicea. Sava at this time petitioned for autocephaly, i.e., the right of the Serbian bishops to select and consecrate their own Patriarch. This promise was made to Sava in 1219, and he was in Nicea to renew this pledge. Although this latter request was not granted, Sava nevertheless confirmed the independence of the Serbian Church from the Archbishop of Ochrid. Hence, the plans of the new King Radislav were thwarted. Also, unfortunately for Radislav, his military prowess waned as well, for in a fratricidal civil war against his younger brother Vladislav during the summer of 1233, he was defeated and exiled to Durazzo, Albania. Although Sava was unsuccessful in reconciling these brothers—who were both disloyal to their grandfather St. Simeon's call for unity—nevertheless he knew it was better for the country to be ruled by Vladislav. Several years later, as a result of his negotiations with King Vladislav, Sava was able to obtain safe conduct for Radislav, who was allowed to return to Serbia. Unfortunately again for Radislav, his wife had eloped with a French duke during his exile in Albania. Radislav then decided to become a monk, and Sava tonsured him, giving him the name John.

In the spring of 1234, Archbishop Sava, age 59, only five years after his first trip to the Holy Land, decided to make a second pilgrimage to Jerusalem. This time he had particular goals in mind. He wanted to garner support for the Bulgarians who were seeking the ecclesiastical status of autocephaly. Previously, the Imperial Patriarch residing in Nicea had recognized this new situation in Bulgaria, but the Patriarchs of Jerusalem, Alexandria and Antioch had not followed suit. Sava also

Holy Icon of the Three Hands, brought by St. Sava from St. Sava's Monastery in the Holy Land, and placed in the main catholicon of Hilandar.

Mount Sinai, Monastery of St. Catherine, which looks today almost the same as it did at the time of St. Sava's visit.

Monastery of St. Sava the Sanctified, in the Holy Land.

Monastery Mileshevo, where the relics of St. Sava of Serbia were deposited.

hoped to seek this same type of support from these Patriarchs in behalf of his own autonomous Serbian Orthodox Church. His mission was to promote the federation of Orthodox sister churches with Jerusalem as the eternal mother Church. There is no doubt that these ecclesiastical missions demonstrated a far-reaching and even prophetic insight on the part of Sava. For the Serbs, he was setting in motion something which would come about only one hundred years later—the autocephaly of the Serbian Church. Sava was a man of his times with a clear vision of the future! Yet there was something even more special about Sava which was personally exhibited by him just prior to his second trip to the Middle East. For no apparent reason, Sava decided to abdicate his archiepiscopal throne. He appointed one of his younger disciples, Arsenius, to be the Archbishop of Serbia. In accordance with the canons of the Orthodox Church, Arsenius was then elevated by the assembly of bishops gathered at Zhicha. This was confirmed by the Imperial Patriarch in Nicea. Sava, like the saints of old, displayed prophetic insight far beyond human wisdom and reason, as no one at this time realized that when they escorted their beloved Saint to the Serbian kingdom's border so that he could begin his trek to Palestine, they would never again see him alive in this world. Sava knew the Lord would soon call him home to the Heavenly Mansions of the righteous, and thus, as a good archpastor, he lovingly prepared his spiritual children for their own future.

Upon arrival in Jerusalem, Sava lodged at the St. George Monastery in Akre, a monastery he had purchased from the Latins during his first pilgrimage. Sava visited Patriarch Athanasius of Jerusalem and then went by boat to Alexandria, Egypt, to meet with Pope Nicholas, "Patriarch of Alexandria and all Africa." He then went to St. Catherine's Monastery on Mt. Sinai, where he spent Great Lent of 1234. This was a most blessed Paschal journey for Sava, for he climbed the heights where the great man of God, Moses the God-seer and Deliverer of his people, had spent many hours speaking to the Lord God face to face as a friend converses with a friend. Sava, too, had been a "Moses" to his people, pastoring, leading and organizing them into a community of God. After the Paschal celebration of 1234, Sava returned to Jerusalem and then traveled to Antioch. After visiting Constantinople, Sava intended to visit the Holy Mountain and Hilandar, but "it did not please the Holy Spirit." Instead, he left for Trnovo, Bulgaria, the capital of King Ivan Asen II's Bulgarian kingdom.

Sava arrived in Trnovo on January 1, 1235. He was received with great honor and dignity, not only because of his efforts on behalf of the Bulgarian ecclesiastical authorities while in the Middle East, but more importantly because he was truly the most respected and venerated person of his era. At the request of King Ivan Asen II, Sava stayed at the Royal Palace in Trnovo. Many state dignitaries, monastics, clergy and pious faithful came to venerate this holy pastor and to receive his blessing. Sava officiated at the Divine Liturgy on Epiphany, January 6, 1235, in the Royal Cathedral of the Holy Forty Martyrs in Trnovo. As was the custom, he participated in the service of the Blessing of the Waters held outside the Cathedral, at the nearby Jantra River. After the Divine Service, the Saint caught a cold which developed into pneumonia, eventually causing his death during the night between Saturday and Sunday, January 14, 1235. He was 60 years of age.

The news of St. Sava's death was a shock for both the Serbian and Bulgarian nations, as well as for the entire Byzantine commonwealth. The saint received a most honorable Christian burial and was laid to rest in the Cathedral of the Holy Forty Martyrs in Trnovo. He remained in Trnovo for over two years, until May 6, 1237 when, after the personal visit of the Serbian King Vladislav, a solemn procession from Trnovo to Mileshevo Monastery returned the Saint to his rightful homeland. Mileshevo Monastery, located only a few miles east of the Lim River near Prijepolje, was founded by King Vladislav (1234-1243). Although renowned for its beautiful icons and frescoes—the Angel at the Tomb of Christ for example—the Monastery could never have imagined the attention it would receive after the placing of the body of Sava in the main church. Upon opening the casket, Sava's body was found completely intact, fragrant, exuding myrrh, looking simply as if he was comfortably sleeping. Thousands of pilgrims—Serbs, Roman Catholics, and even Jews—came to venerate the divine Sava. To all, he was a source of unity, healing, wisdom, joy, and spiritual strength, uniting the various tribes of Serbs into a cohesive nation of Orthodox believers. As a result, only eighteen years later, in 1253, the Orthodox Church of Serbia officially canonized their beloved St. Sava (see April 27th and May 6th).

As time passed, the tremendous legacy of holy leadership on the part of the great Sava kept the Serbian people united under one flag: the royal kingdom of Serbia which avowed Orthodoxy and the way of Christ. He was the sole person who was responsible for the transformation of the Serbian people into a people of God. And their allegiance to the way in which he lived was to the Serbs the only true model and expression of religious, political and cultural life. Hence, as in the case of every great human being who inspires generations after him to even greater heights of civilized life, so too was it with Sava, for his ideal motivated the people of Orthodox Serbia to become, in the thirteenth and fourteenth centuries, one of the most resplendent kingdoms the world has ever known. Religious life peaked as the monasteries in Serbia, the most beautiful being based upon the Byzantine style, were crowded with monastics who led an austere life, inspiring the Serbian people to greater heights of humility, while also leading them to exhibit the trait they were (and are to this day) most recognized for —hospitality. And, as mentioned, due to the astute ecclesiastical wisdom on the part of Sava in 1219 in Nicea, the Serbian Church was able, in 1346, to obtain her own autocephaly, i.e., her own Patriarch. Political and economic life also flourished, following the example of the Christ-like Sava, in the centuries following his repose in the Lord. A unity among the Serbs, based on their adherence to Orthodoxy and maintenance of the political ideals of their beloved St. Sava, allowed them to develop into a Balkan power to the point that in 1346 the Serbian King Dushan the Powerful was given the title of "Emperor of the Serbs, Greeks, Bulgars and Albanians."

In sum, after his death St. Sava was to the Serbs a type of ideal and measuring rod of what it meant to be a true Serb, which is, to be fully committed to Jesus Christ and the way of Orthodoxy. Religiously, Sava was thought of as an equal to St. Nicholas, the ideal and standard of bishops; as a humane politician, Sava was considered an equal to St. Constantine the Great, the founder of the Byzantine Empire; and, as a Great Martyr later in 1595, Sava was considered an equal to the humble St. Polycarp of Smyrna, the first Great Martyr to be burned to death (see April 27th, Burning of the Relics of St. Sava). Bless the Lord God! All these Christian traits and attainments manifested in one person! During the two centuries following his death, the person of St. Sava became the brightest star ever known to the Serbs, inspiring them to a way of life which succeeding generations have as yet been unable to recapture or match.

This love for Sava continued unabated even during the time of the barbaric Turkish occupation of the Serbian lands, beginning with the Battle of Kosovo on June 15, 1389. On that day, the Serbs chose to remain faithful to Christ, Orthodoxy, and the embodiment of their faith, St. Sava. After receiving the Precious Body and Blood of our Lord and Savior Jesus Christ on the eve of the Battle on the Field of Blackbirds, the Serbian armies went on victoriously to their martyrdom and "crucifixion" at the hands of the ungodly Turks, proving to history (and of course to themselves) that it is better to die for Christ, *the way and the truth and the life,* than to live for any earthly cause or dominion. This martyrdom on Kosovo Polje, more than any other event in the history of the Serbian race, proved their allegiance to the way of life that St. Sava taught them, that is, living with Christ the Lord in His Heavenly Kingdom. It was this vision of life which sustained the Orthodox Serbs during the oppressive times to follow. It was this vision given to them by St. Sava which was their hope. Not a vanquished hope or a defeated one, but a hope that was alive, hallowing, sustaining, unifying, strengthening, abiding, and truly a hope worth living for, no matter what the costs. This vision was salvation to the Serb!

No wonder the Turks, on Orthodox Holy Friday in 1595, could not withstand this unifying force, the force of committed life in Christ led by the example of St. Sava, for they once again "cracked" under this pressure and, to their eternal folly and damnation, incinerated the life-giving body and relics of St. Sava (see April 27th). They believed they could kill the spirit along with the body—something the unbelieving Jews thought they could also do with Jesus on Golgotha—on that glorious day on Savinac Hill in the district of Vrachar in Belgrade. However, to their dismay, the Serbian Orthodox spirit was only made stronger by this ungodly act, for all pious Serbs at that time and to this day believe in a Lord and Master, the Savior Christ, who was savagely and brutally crucified and martyred *for the life of the world;* and Who rose from the dead, trampling down death by death, Whose victory and Kingdom will have no end. This Great Martyrdom of St. Sava was not an end for the Saint, but a beginning, for along with the title of "Venerable Holy Father and First Archbishop and Eternal Enlightener to the Serbs," he was granted, by Divine Providence, the most wonderful title of "Great Martyr," thus fulfilling a legacy that certainly will last forever! And to his glory, on that very Savinac Hill in Vrachar, a glorious Cathedral is being erected to once and for all confirm his steadfast love and example of unity, strength and piety that every Orthodox Christian everywhere must follow in order to inherit eternal life!

> Holy Father Sava, we thy sinful servants ask:
> Lead us to give our hearts to God first,
> Lead us to live for Christ the Lord first,
> Lead us to seek His righteousness first,
> Lead us to desire Orthodox truth first,
> Lead us to remember the Saints first,
> Lead us to cherish the Church first,
> Lead us to love one another first,
> Lead us to seek unity of all first;
> Holy Father Sava, pray to God to save us.

St. Sava Memorial Church in Vrachar, Belgrade.

TROPARION
Tone 8

O guide of Orthodoxy and blessed teacher of virtues,* purifier and enlightener of thy homeland,* beauty of monastics,* most wise Father, Holy Sava,* by thy teaching thou didst enlighten thy people,* O flute of the Spirit, pray to Christ God for our souls.

KONTAKION
Tone 8

As the first great hierarch and co-worker with the Apostles,* the Church of thy people magnifies thee;* and since thou hast found favor with Christ,* save us by thy prayers from every calamity,* so that we may proclaim to thee: Rejoice, God-wise Father Sava.

Venerable Gabriel

of Lesnovo

TROPARION, Tone 8

Loving Christ wholeheartedly above all things,* thou hast adorned thy entire life on earth* by meekness, humility and endurance;* therefore, thou hast inherited a heavenly mansion,* and have been granted the honor accorded the righteous ones:* Pray with them to save our souls.

January 15th

LIFE OF OUR FATHER

GABRIEL

OF LESNOVO

(†980)

Worldly virtues promote human glory,
spiritual virtues the glory of God.
Abba Thalassios the Libyan

OUR HOLY FATHER GABRIEL was born around 910 to Serbian parents in the village of Osechka Polje near the town of Kriva Palanka (40 miles northeast of Skoplje). His parents were very wealthy and well-known, both being advisors to the Zhupan (Patriarchal leader) at the time. Prior to his birth, his parents, being barren throughout their marriage, prayed to the Lord Jesus Christ with heartfelt tears that they might be granted a child to honor them in their old age. God, who abundantly blesses those who sincerely pray to Him and do His will, heard their petition and provided them with a son, who of course was a great joy and divine gift for their entire household. As the child developed, his parents never forgot this eternal blessing bestowed upon them by Almighty God. They provided their son with the best education as he "grew in grace and wisdom" by the power of the Holy Spirit before God and all people. Young Gabriel excelled in all subjects; his crowning achievement was the memorization, while in the fourth grade, of the entire four Gospels, which he carried in his pocket at all times.

When Gabriel grew to maturity, around 18 years old, and marriage seemed imminent, his parents chose a young maiden of a noble Serbian Orthodox family for him to marry. However, the young lover of Christ had other ideas concerning marriage. Praying constantly and keeping vigil over his total person—as he was accustomed from his youth—Gabriel, with the aid and counsel of his guardian, Archangel Michael, the Leader of the Bodiless Hosts, was able to persuade his parents otherwise. Reminding them that he was God's gift to them, Gabriel humbly refused their offer; moreover, he sought their permission to leave home and to begin sojourning in order to seek the Lord's will more fully. After some serious consideration, his parents granted Gabriel their blessing.

In his early travels, Gabriel met a deacon named Thomas with whom he had many conversations concerning the ascetic life. One night, while staying with Deacon Thomas, Gabriel was given, in a dream, a message from an Angel of the Lord, who said to him, "Arise and return home to Osechka Polje where I will reveal to you exact instructions concerning the building of a chapel to be dedicated to the Nativity of the Most Holy Theotokos." Awaking from sleep, as if rising from the dead, the Saint returned home to Osechka Polje and told his parents of his dream. His parents, fervent Christians, obeyed the dream and provided Gabriel with the necessary materials to construct the Chapel in their home town. This Chapel, quite beautiful and divine, still exists in Osechka Polje to this very day.

As the grace of God began to take over his life more and more each day, Blessed Gabriel became fervently devoted to the Christian ascetic life. He decided to leave home once again and to ascend the mountain of Lesnovo to the Monastery of Archangel Michael (25 miles east of Skoplje), in order to seek entrance into the monastic life. Arriving at the Monastery, Gabriel prostrated himself before the abbot of the Monastery and detailed to him all the events of his life. The abbot and brotherhood then accepted Gabriel as an *izkushenik* (initiate or novice), putting him to test so as to develop within him the salvific traits of the Lord: humility, mercy, courage and perseverance. Within a short period

St. Gabriel of Lesnovo.
Fresco in Holy Archangels Monastery Church.

of time, the young *izkushenik* was received into the monastic ranks, and was even tonsured with the Angelic Schema, signifying his great humility and contriteness of heart, mind and spirit. Gabriel was also given the abbot's blessing to reside in a cell outside the Monastery walls in the countryside near Zletovo. Immersed in the constant prayer life of worship, purifying his soul of all defilements of flesh and spirit, Kelliote Gabriel was transformed, by the grace of the Most Holy Spirit, into a healer and deliverer of people from the snares of demons. Many Christians traveled to his cell in the woods to be healed of various diseases and to be cleansed of their spiritual maladies. Due to this outpouring of visitors and the fame acquired therefrom, the healing Saint desired to flee the follies of human glory. He fled to a place called Lukovo, travelling deep into the woods where no human being had ever trodden—and no one knew of his whereabouts.

One day a shepherd, while grazing his flock, happened upon the venerable father, who was at this time standing on a small rock in a huge field in fervent prayer. The prayer which flowed incessantly from Holy Gabriel's heart was the prayer of the righteous Publican: "God be merciful to me, a sinner" (Lk 18:13). The shepherd fell before Gabriel's feet, seeking his blessing. The Saint then asked, "What do you want, my son?"

The lowly shepherd cried, "Holy Father, as a result of my sinful nature, all of the wool of my sheep has dried up and fallen off. Please, I beg you, pray to Christ our God for them."

"Fear not, my son, God will turn your sorrow into great joy," replied the Saint to the distraught shepherd, comforting him with the knowledge that God desires every living being (which includes animals, of course) to be whole and sound.

Near the place where Gabriel was praying there was a large hole, filled with water from an early morning rain. The Saint raised his eyes and hands towards Heaven and prayed to God the Pantocrator (Creator of all), making the Sign of the Cross over the water. Drawing some of this blessed water, the Saint gave it to the shepherd, saying, "Take this, my son, and sprinkle it on your flock." After doing this, to the amazement of the shepherd, the wool of his sheep instantly began to grow. The shepherd joyously thanked Gabriel for bringing life once again to his flock. The venerable father told the shepherd to give thanks instead to Almighty God, Who shows mercy upon the repentant and desires that all of creation be saved.

Not desiring the plaudits and praise of humans, Gabriel once again decided to leave his cell in the woods in Lukovo. He returned closer to Lesnovo, near the Monastery of Archangel Michael, and climbed to the top of a nearby mountain called "Obli Vrh" ("Round Top" in Serbian, or in Greek "Strongilos," as that place was also called). Here the Saint was completely isolated from all human life. Unknown to all, St. Gabriel spent thirty years in unceasing prayer on Round Top, fighting and defeating the devil by the power in the name of our Lord and Savior Jesus Christ. This tremendous striving in the Lord formed Gabriel into a pillar of Truth, and his salvific prayers "for the life of the world" delivered many, unbeknownst to them, from various diseases and calamities.

St. Gabriel fell asleep in the Lord around the year 980, unknown to anyone except the Lord God. As time passed, this fact saddened many monastics and pious Christians, who greatly feared that Gabriel had died in a foreign land or had been eaten by savage wolves.

Many years after his repose, Venerable Father Gabriel appeared in Sophia, Bulgaria, to a Serbian monk from Bachka named Joseph. Joseph, a God-fearing ascetic, very humble and of a discerning spirit, did not wish to fall into *prelest* (spiritual pride), and thus did not accept this apparition. Venerable Gabriel appeared a second time to Joseph, saying to him, "Listen! Go to Round Top and there you will find my relics which you must take to the Monastery of Archangel Michael in Lesnovo." The monk again feared human vanity and did not heed these instructions. Then St. Gabriel appeared a third time, saying, "God has ordered me to tell you what I have said. Go to Round Top and recover my relics." After this, the virtuous monk went to the Metropolitan of

Sophia and told him of these apparitions. The Metropolitan questioned the nearby dioceses to learn if indeed Round Top was a mountain located in one of their jurisdictions. He also consulted several other bishops outside his metropolitanate concerning the location of Lesnovo and also about the truth of such an apparition. A letter then arrived from the Bishop of Zletovo which stated that Round Top was actually near the Monastery of Archangel Michael in Lesnovo.

The Metropolitan himself, with Father Joseph, several priests, monastics, state officials, and some pious faithful, then traveled to Lesnovo to the Monastery of Archangel Michael. After the vigil service that evening, the party ascended the mountain of Lesnovo to the peak and, reaching the top, began to pray. As darkness set in, each took rest. Then St. Gabriel appeared once more to pious Joseph, saying to him, "Look there, to your left." Joseph immediately arose and began to pray. When it was dawn, he went to the indicated place and found the relics of St. Gabriel. All were amazed, praising the Lord God for such a wonderful miracle. Everyone present—the Metropolitan, clergy, monastics, and pious faithful—venerated the completely intact, sweet-smelling and myrrh-bearing body and relics of St. Gabriel. Descending the mountain, they placed his holy body in the Catholicon (main church) of the Monastery of Archangel Michael in Lesnovo. Many who came in faith to venerate the life-giving relics of St. Gabriel were healed of their physical sicknesses and all manner of spiritual diseases. One wealthy man from the nearby town of Kratovo, whose only child, a daughter named Hermenina, was sorely afflicted with a withered arm, came one day to venerate the body of St. Gabriel. At the very moment he prostrated himself before the relics of St. Gabriel, his daughter's arm was completely healed and restored to full strength.

Almost four centuries after the discovery and return of the relics of St. Gabriel to the Monastery in Lesnovo, John Oliver, the adviser and chronicler of the Royal Serbian Court under King Dushan the Powerful (1331-1355), founded a church in Lesnovo to the glory of St. Gabriel. Prince John, handsome in physical appearance, yet more beautiful in his soul and spirit, had a tremendous love for St. Gabriel, to whom he attributed much of the peace and prosperity of the Serbian Kingdom at the time. However, the ugly head of satan rose up against the Serbs at the end of the fourteenth century in the form of the Turkish hordes under Sultan Murad I. Realizing the upcoming onslaught, the Bulgarian Patriarch in Trnovo feared the burning of the relics of St. Gabriel; thus he, along with Bulgaria's King John Shishman (1371-1391), went to Lesnovo and, with full permission of the Serbian ecclesiastical authorities, took the relics of the Saint and had them transported to the Church of the Holy Apostles in Trapezir, Bulgaria, where they remain whole and intact to this very hour, granting healing and spiritual blessings to all who venerate them in faith, hope and love.

"O Holy Father Gabriel, thou didst demonstrate that our Lord reveals Himself to those who seek His purity, His healing, His life and His love; come, O Holy Father, and reveal thyself to us, miserable and decrepit sinners; pray to Christ our true God to visit us by His Most Holy Spirit, in order to pacify our flesh, free us from all human vanity, and heal our hearts of every infirmity, so that we may constantly seek and flee to Him, to Whom belongs glory, honor and worship, together with His Unoriginate Father, and Life-giving Spirit, now and ever and unto ages of ages. Amen."

KONTAKION
Tone 6

Taking up the angelic life on earth,* thou didst live by the power of the Gospel;* thy mind meditated on heavenly things,* as thou didst bless all by thy teachings;* therefore, we magnify thee:* Rejoice, Venerable Gabriel, the pride of Lesnovo.

Holy Martyr Damascene

of Gabrovo

TROPARION, Tone 4

As a righteous ascetic thou didst prove thyself * to be worthy of the throne of Hilandar, O Holy Father Damascene,* and as a Holy Confessor thou didst lay down thy life for the cause of Christ,* defending the faith in eloquence of word and deed;* therefore, O Holy Martyr Damascene,* the Heavens open for thee today,* enter into the glory of the Everlasting Kingdom of the Lord.

January 16th

SUFFERING OF OUR HOLY MARTYR
DAMASCENE
OF GABROVO
(✝1771)

> *Those who wish to follow the Lord Jesus*
> *wholeheartedly in all things and at all times,*
> *must be willing, at a moment's notice,*
> *to shed life and limb for the cause*
> *of truth, justice, faith and holiness.*
> *For in this, eternal salvation is received.*
> Fr. Daniel Rogich

HOLY MARTYR DAMASCENE was born in the early eighteenth century in Gabrovo, Bulgaria (100 miles east of Sophia). From his youth, he loved and sought the quiet contemplative life. In his early teens, he left his family and traveled to the Holy Mountain, seeking to become a monk in the Serbian Hilandar Monastery. At Hilandar he was received into monasticism, and shortly thereafter, due to his piety and strict ascetic life, was ordained deacon and then priest. After spending many years in ascetic labor and the practice of prayer of the heart, Damascene was unanimously selected as the abbot of the Hilandar community. On one occasion, Abbot Damascene decided to represent the brotherhood in order to recover a debt owed the Monastery by several Turks. Little did he know that this confrontation with these

113

obscure Turks would lead to his everlasting glory as a witness to the Cross and Resurrection of our Lord and God and Saviour Jesus Christ.

Damascene journeyed from the Holy Mountain and lodged in the home of a pious Orthodox Christian family in Svishtovo, Bulgaria (on the south bank of the Danube River, about 80 miles north of Gabrovo), where he petitioned the Turks to repay their debt. After confronting these debtors concerning repayment, Damascene was told by them that he should return to his house and that during the evening they would come to make restitution. However, being viciously shrewd and fiendish, these Turks persuaded a Moslem woman to go into the house where Damascene was staying. The Turks then came and found the woman and, after falsely accusing Damascene of wrongdoing, forcibly brought him to trial before the Turkish authorities. Damascene was given no right of defense; he only had two choices: conversion to Islam or hanging. To this he gloriously replied: "I was born an Orthodox Christian, and in this belief I will die. For me, to reject Jesus Christ is the same as rejecting eternal life. Without Him, there is no salvation for sinners, as we all are, both you and I. He is the Reconciler of the Truth of God with sinful humanity. He is the Gift-giver of the grace of God, indispensable for the fulfilling of the will of the Lord. I am saddened for you, if you do not understand this. It certainly would be foolish for me were I for temporal life to buy eternal peril."

After this defense of the Christian faith, the judge passed sentence: hanging. Bound hand and foot, Damascene was taken to the gallows. Ascending the steps and arriving at the top of the gallows, Damascene turned and asked the Turkish hangmen if he could pray to God. Receiving permission, Damascene faced the East, raised his holy head and hands toward the Lord, and then sealed himself with the Sign of the Cross. Then he said, "I am ready for death."

Holy Martyr Damascene was hanged to death on January 16th, 1771, in Svishtovo, Bulgaria. As an eternal witness to Jesus Christ and His Life-giving Cross, the eternal Damascene entered the Heavenly Mansions of the Righteous. He demonstrated the Christian belief that

The inside view of Hilandar Monastery court with hagmiasma for blessing.

to die for Christ is better than to live for any human security, let alone evil. And, as the God of justice always prevails, his murderers, trying to cross the Danube River, met an unusually violent storm which capsized the boat, drowning them all.

"O Holy Father Damascene, thou wast privileged to witness to our Lord's life, trial, death and resurrection; pray to Christ, the only true God, for us miserable sinners, that our spirits may be quickened to that very same courage, strength and commitment, so that we may respond faithfully to His call, His sacrifice and His love, to Whom belongs glory, honor and worship, together with His Unoriginate Father, and Life-giving Spirit, now and ever and unto the ages of ages. Amen."

KONTAKION TO
ST. DAMASCENE
Tone 4

Thy suffering has been redeemed, O meek lamb of Jesus,* and thy confession of Christ has gained thee victory* over the godless heathen, O Holy Martyr Damascene;* therefore, thou art worthy of veneration, * as we ask of thee:* Pray to Christ God to save our souls.

Hilandar chapel of St. Nicholas,
frescoes painted by pop Danilo, 1667.

Hodigitria, the Mother of God with Christ.
Icon, 2nd half of the 14th century.
Tradition claims that the original was painted by St. Luke.
Preserved as Serbia's great holy object.

Venerable Romilos

of Ravanica

TROPARION, Tone 8

The streams of thy tears made fertile the barren wilderness,*
and thy deep sighing from thy struggles produced fruit a
hundred-fold,* as thou becamest a Star of the universe
sparkling with miracles, O our Father Romilos;*
therefore, pray to Christ God to save our souls.

January 16th

LIFE OF OUR FATHER

ROMILOS
OF RAVANITSA
(✝1376)

*The great tidings which Christianity proclaims
daily to the world is that nothing is assessed
at its face value, but by its essence; that things
are not assessed by their color and shape,
but by their meaning; that a human being
is not assessed by his status and possessions,
but by his heart, in which are united
his feelings, his mind and his will.*
St. Nikolai Velimirovich

THE LIFE of our Venerable Holy Father Romilos, written in
Greek by his disciple Gregory, tells us that he was born in 1300, in
Vidin, Bulgaria, into a God-fearing pan-Orthodox family; his mother
was Bulgarian and his father Greek. Given the name Rajko ("Man of
Paradise") at baptism, he grew "in grace and in wisdom" before God
and humankind. As a child, Rajko spurned mundane children's games.
Once, as a grade-schooler, he remarked to a student who mocked him

119

for not playing the usual games: "It is much better, my dear friend, to sit at home and study your lessons with attention and concentration." This love of learning was not a result of parental coercion; nor was his developing piety, wisdom and love of God something contrived. His parents, teachers, and the townsfolk were constantly amazed by Rajko's intelligence, zeal for God and practical wisdom. Yet, when he finished gymnasium (high school) and revealed to all his desire to enter the monastic life, Rajko met with disapproval, shock and downright rejection! Oh, how so-called Christian people, even the closest of relatives, try to extinguish the flaming love of God in their pious youths!

To his dismay, after Rajko finished school, his parents selected a young maiden of a wealthy family for him to marry. Discovering these marriage plans, Rajko fled to Trnovo, Bulgaria, in the Diocese of Zagoro, to one of the local monasteries, dedicated to the Theotokos Odigitria ("the Directress"). The abbot of the Monastery, according to standard Orthodox practice, asked him about his prior life, saying, "Who are you, my child, where do you come from, and what are your desires?"

Rajko answered and spoke about his entire past life, adding, "I have come, Holy Father, in order to enter the monastic life."

After a short period of preparation, Rajko was given the monastic tonsure and the name Romanos; and, due to his highly developed piety and love for the liturgical services of the Church, he was given the responsibility of being the monastery's ecclesiarch.[1] The abbot, watching young Romanos grow spiritually in the Lord, decided to test him: "I know he possesses great love and zeal for God and the liturgical life of the Church," the abbot thought, "but does he have this same love for his neighbor?" Without even putting him to the test, the abbot was answered. Shortly thereafter, Romanos gave away all his possessions, knowing *it is better to give than to receive* (Acts 20:35). Romanos was

---

1. The ecclesiarch is the liturgical specialist of the local church community. See note 4 of St. Eustathius, January 4th.

Christ our Saviour. Ancient fresco from Ravanitsa Monastery,
detail from Christ's healing of the blind man.

then granted, by the grace of God, the gift of *umilenje* [2] coupled with tears, following the words of Scripture: *I toiled in my groaning; every night I will wash my bed, with tears will I water my couch* (Ps. 6:5), and *My tears have been my bread by day and by night* (Ps. 41:3). These gifts were not a result of human emotions which come and go, but rather were truly a gift from God, the gift which comes from contrition of heart achieved by prayer, fasting and constant supplication to the Lord God.

While the Abbot rejoiced over his obedience, humility and love for neighbor, he knew, nonetheless, that Romanos was headed for even greater feats. So it came as no surprise to the abbot when the young holy monk asked permission to leave the Monastery in order to travel to Paroria, a monastic settlement on the border between the kingdom of Bulgaria and the Byzantine State at the time, so as to meet and venerate the great hesychast and teacher of piety, Gregory of Sinai.

St. Gregory, a Greek monk of Mt. Sinai, came to the Balkan peninsula in the early 1300's. He was the founder of the hesychast movement in the Balkans. This prayer movement which transformed monasticism, particularly in the Middle Ages (10th -14th centuries), had ancient roots. It was tied to the commandment of the great Apostle Paul: *Pray without ceasing* (I Thess. 5:17). Developed in the deserts of Egypt, Sinai, Palestine and Syria, the hesychast movement arrived on the Holy Mountain in the early tenth century. Its basic message was that monastic life and indeed all of Christian life consists not only of ascetic labor (giving alms, feeding the poor, visiting the sick, reading the Scriptures, etc.), but also can be expressed in the life of solitude, contemplation and meditative prayer. A hesychast is a person who

---

2. Umilenije is an Old Slavonic term which is very difficult to translate by one word in other languages. It means tenderly loving God, and in turn being intimately loved by Him, similar to the spiritual state of John the Evangelist, *the disciple whom Jesus loved, who also leaned on his breast at supper* "(John 21:20). This gift of God makes a believer soft-hearted, peaceful, humble, enabling him to see the shining uncreated grace of the Lord in every person, place, thing or event. This gift of God often fills the believer with tears of compassion for all of creation.

Above: St. Gregory of Sinai
An engraving by Photios
Kontoglou.

Left: St. Romilos, fresco from
Ravanitsa Monastery.

Below: Magoula Hermitage of
St. Gregory.

123

practices "hesychia," which is a Greek word meaning "quietude," "calmness" or "solitude." This prayer movement was bolstered by the development of the Jesus Prayer: "Lord Jesus Christ, Son of the living God, have mercy on me, a sinner." To make of life one continual prayer to God in ever more intimate union with Christ by the power of the Holy Spirit was the task, example, and revelation of the hesychast movement. Christian life, to them, was made up of "faith and works" (prayer and ascetic labor) or "prayer and fasting" (prayer and good deeds), whereby these two interpenetrate one another to form the Christian into a loving and deified person of God, a person who is simultaneously "calm" (hesychastic) and "active" in the world. This prayer movement was not a separate or sectarian movement in the Church, but really grew out of and was a by-product of the Church's liturgical and sacramental life, which is based primarily on the Eucharist, the Precious Body and Blood of our Lord, Who Himself prayed and fasted, shed His Blood "for the life of the world." It was this profound life that young Romanos, not yet 21 years of age, sought from Gregory of Sinai.

Venerable Romanos spent over twenty years as the disciple of Gregory of Sinai. His nights and days he spent in vigil, making himself a strong warrior for Christ the Lord. His humility and quiet manner always preceded him, as he was known as "Kalo Romanos" (Greek for "Good Romanos"). His prayer life was the basis for his good deeds, obedience, and zeal for Christ. As he grew in faith and in obedience to Christ through God's servant Gregory, Romanos enfleshed and exemplified the words of St. John Climacus: "As much faith as one possesses, so too is one's body urged into obedience" (Ladder of Divine Ascent, Rung #4); as well as the words of St Mark the Ascetic: "The Lord is hidden in His commandments, and he who desires to find Him, let him keep the commandments. In fulfilling them he will find the Lord" (ch. 191, *Philokalia*). It was these thoughts ever present in his mind, which was now firmly rooted in his heart, that enabled Romanos to serve the sick, the poor and the hungry. Yet, there was another test and tribulation in store for him: his spiritual father, Gregory of Sinai, fell asleep in the Lord on November 27, 1346, when Romanos was 46 years old. With Gregory's passing, Romanos almost fell into despair. Only by the grace of God given him by the comfort of his life-long companion, Monk Hilary, was Romanos able to continue his struggle against death and the demons.

After Gregory's glorified death, Romanos and Hilary returned to the Diocese of Zagora, to the Monastery in Mokren, a day's journey from Trnovo, Bulgaria. Romanos stayed only several months in Mokren, where he spent Great Lent of 1347 in order to renew his spirit and mind. During Great Lent of that year, Romanos only came to the Monastery on the first Saturday—"Teodorova Subota" (the Saturday of St. Theodore; see St. Theodore Sladich). The rest of the fasting period he spent in complete silence and hesychastic contemplation of God the Holy Trinity. When asked of his whereabouts, as the brothers sat in discussion in the refectory of the Monastery, one brother said to the rest, "We, Holy Fathers, eat earthly food, but Romanos heavenly." After the Glorious and Divine Pascha of the Lord Jesus Christ that year, Romanos once again returned to the Monastery of the Theotokos in Paroria, to the cell of his blessed spiritual father, the newly departed Holy Gregory of Sinai.

During the reign of King John Alexander of Bulgaria (1331-1337), the area around Paroria was besieged by marauding Turks. As a result, Venerable Romanos returned to the Mokren Monastery in the Diocese of Zagora, where he spent five years in complete silence in a cell he made in the woods outside the Monastery walls. Afterwards, Romanos was found to possess the gift of casting out demons. Opening his cell to visitors, Romanos became a font of healing and a vessel of grace. Exhibiting this gift of God, Good Romanos was consecrated with the Angelic Schema by the abbot and brotherhood of the Monastery of Mokren. His name was changed at this time to Father Romilos.

In the late 1360's, when the Turks drew near the Balkan peninsula, Father Romilos was advised to flee the territory and to travel to the Holy

Ravanitsa Monastery, general view of the main church.

Mountain, where he could continue to be a source of prayer, healing, and holiness. He arrived on the Holy Mountain at age 70 and was received with great joy and honor, as many there had known and heard of his ascetic life, miracles, and especially his discipleship under Gregory of Sinai. Romilos felt uncomfortable with such "glory before men" and once more fled to an unknown cell near the Monastery of the Great Lavra on the tip of the Holy Mountain. However, he could not be kept a secret for long. He was discovered once again, as his cell was flooded by visitors hoping to receive a blessing, healing, or spiritual counsel.

The following are two of his messages translated from the Greek text of his life written by his biographer, Gregory the Younger:

My fathers and brothers, maintain a pure conscience with your neighbors; keep your hearts pure from unclean thoughts, which too often defile the wretched soul. We will not succeed in the ascetic life if we do not preserve in their natural state the three parts of our soul:

126

the mind, the will, and the affections. These three the All-loving God has placed within the human soul as fortresses, so that the human being, preserving them in their natural state, as it pleases God, will be able to spend life in peace and in comfort. This is what our Holy Fathers have taught us by their divine teachings and even more by their God-inspired experience. Let the wrath of your mind be unified against the demons, because of whom we fell in the beginning. Let your will be directed fully towards God, not upon something else which will deceive and corrupt it. Let your mind stand above all things, and let that which is lower not be desired over that which is above. When, therefore, in the will, we savagely fight against our spiritual enemies, i.e., against demons and passions, and against all who are against our salvation, then we are preserving that part of our soul in its natural state, for then we can correctly love God with our entire soul and our neighbor as well. When, therefore, we preserve the affectionate part of the soul in its natural state, as God has given it to us, then we are desiring the eternal blessing which *Eye hath not seen, nor ear heard, neither have entered into the heart of man, the things which God hath prepared for them that love him.* (I Cor 2:9), because of which goodness we toil with joy at every labor of the body and soul, creating virtues, which are: fasting, vigil, love of the poor, a pure body, unceasing prayer. In one word: day and night creating that which is sufficient for salvation....

On spiritual obedience, Romilos wrote this to a disciple:

My beloved brother, the way which we journey is the apostolic way. Such is the piety and reverence the Apostles possessed toward our Lord and God Jesus Christ; and each of us must practice this reverence toward our own spiritual father, rejecting at once our entire will, as the Lord Himself taught: *For I came down from heaven, not to do mine own will, but the will of him that sent me (John 6:38). Learning this from Him, the Apostles did not answer back, nor say otherwise; they did not desire their own will or thoughts, but rather they persevered in the commandments of their Teacher, and thus in truth heard from Him these words: Where I am, there shall also my servant be* (John 12:26). And truly, they did not turn back from this hope. Therefore, I can say to you with assurance that each of us who rightly forsakes the desires of his will, and bears with humility, forbearance and unfailingness the commands and directives of his spiritual father, not disrespecting him in the least, will live eternally with the Holy Apostles and will rejoice in and with Christ in the eternal age.

It was words such as these that revealed St. Romilos to be truly holy, a blessed follower of the ancient Desert Fathers, and a treasured jewel of the Holy Mountain.

It was another military event which had a tremendous impact on Romilos' life, eventually leading him to his final resting place in the kingdom of Serbia. On September 26, 1371, Serbia's Despot John Uglesha, who had been ruling the territory of Macedonia (from the city of Serres), was killed in the famous Battle of Marica. This battle signaled the end of the benevolent Serbian rule of the Balkans, and was a severe blow not only to the Orthodox Churches in Serbia and throughout the Balkans, but also to the monasteries on the Holy Mountain. Many monks were threatened with violence; and discovering their homelands now under Turkish domination, they were heartbroken. As a result of this persecution, St. Romilos had to flee once more, this time leaving the Holy Mountain and traveling to Valon, Albania, the mountainous region on the southern Adriatic coast.

St. Romilos did not desire to live in Albania, and thus sent a letter to his spiritual father who resided in Constantinople. In it he asked, "Since I believe, Holy Father, that I cannot stay here for long, what is your directive for me? Where should I go, to the Holy Mountain once again?"

The answer came from his spiritual father, who wrote, "Since you ask me in faith, I advise you to go to another place, where God will comfort you, and not to the Holy Mountain."

With this advice, Venerable Father Romilos left Albania, and with his disciples came to Serbia, to the territory known as Ravanitsa, where there was built a new monastery dedicated to the Most Holy and

Ever-Virgin Mary the Theotokos. Ravanitsa Monastery, near the town of Chuprije, was built from 1375-1381 under the direction of Holy Prince Lazar (1371-1389; see June 15th). It was here that Romilos spent the last five years of his earthly life. While at Ravanitsa, St. Romilos renewed the hesychastic prayer movement, and thus traditionally, even to this day, the monastics of Ravanitsa Monastery have been called "Sinaites," after the great hesychast, St. Gregory of Sinai, the true spiritual father of St. Romilos, as well as the institutional founder of hesychasm in the entire Balkan peninsula.

Our Holy Father Romilos died peacefully in the Lord on January 16, 1376, in Ravanitsa Monastery. He was 76 years old. To this day, on the south side of the main Church of Ravanitsa Monastery lie the relics of St. Romilos. Several times throughout the centuries his relics have exuded a fragrant myrrh. The records of Ravanitsa reveal that many who have been anointed with this myrrh have been healed of both physical and spiritual afflictions. Above all, St. Romilos has remained for the pious Serbs of Ravanitsa a divine example of piety, of the love of the ascetic and contemplative life, and of the relentless warfare necessary to overcome all obstacles in life in order to serve the Lord God *in spirit and in truth.*

Finally, St. Romilos was able, in his lifetime, to actualize and exhibit a fundamental Christian truth concerning God and human beings. This truth is most aptly revealed in what is called "the communion of Saints" in the Orthodox Church. As is known, St. Romilos was not a Serbian by birth, and all but five years of his life were spent outside of Serbia. Nonetheless, he was and still is highly venerated by all pious Serbs everywhere primarily because he was able, following the principle of unconditional love—called "the divine image" God has implanted in all human beings—to transcend his own human nature, particularly his own nationality and human origin, as he was, in Christ, *born not of blood nor of the will of the flesh nor of the will of man, but of God* (John 1:13). St. Romilos loved all of God's creatures, regardless of human origin or background. This "principle of unconditional love" the saints in Heaven continually draw to our attention, for the Glorified Body of the Risen Lord in Heaven is made up of various saints from completely different cultures, eras, earthly languages and origins; yet each of them, while on earth, exhibited a commonality: each lived (and even died) for the personal salvific life in Christ. Many of them still appear to peoples of diverse backgrounds, nationalities and languages. And each time they appear, they speak in the vernacular of those they are engaging in conversation! Glory be to God! This proves that language, nationality, and human origin, though essential to our human identity, are nonetheless not essential to our eternal identity and destiny. What is essential is our quest for God, our ascetic struggle for eternal truth, and our ability to transcend especially our human nature, our passions, and our inordinate desires in order to lay hold of that which is above, *what no eye has seen, nor heart of man conceived, what blessing God has in store for those who love Him.*

Therefore, let "the communion of Saints," and particularly the example of St. Romilos, be our method of understanding and actualizing the unity of the Church; and let us strive, though we be "in" the world, not to be "of" the world, which means to live by the grace, love and divine energies of the Lord Jesus Christ, transcending and going beyond not only our own nationality, but most assuredly our own passions, senses, and mind—our total being.

"O Holy Father Romilos, thou didst live an angelic life on earth, and thus thou hast been found worthy to continue thy praise of the Lord in Heaven with all the angels and saints; pray, therefore, O Prayerful One, that our Lord's Spirit may fill us with His grace and love, so as to hallow us and purify us from all iniquity, so that we too may attain a measure of that same sanctification which knows no limits of its glorification of Christ, to Whom belongs glory, honor and worship, together with His Unoriginate Father, and Life-giving Spirit, now and ever and unto ages of ages. Amen."

St. John the Baptist, fresco from Ravanitsa Monastery.

KONTAKION, Tone 1

O Holy Father Romilos,* Jewel of the Holy Mountain,* Pillar of true Orthodoxy,* divine follower of Righteous Gregory,* and glory of Ravanitsa,* come and heal us who in faith run to thee,* for we celebrate thy memory in love.

St. Maxim

Archbishop
of Wallachia

TROPARION, Tone 3

Thou wast born and raised in a foreign land, O Holy
Father,* yet thou didst return to the dominion of thy kingdom;* desiring the Heavenly Kingdom,* thou didst abandon
the earthly;* by humility thou didst receive heavenly
blessings,* O Most Blessed Maxim;* therefore,
we beg thee to pray for our souls.

January 18th

OUR HOLY FATHER
MAXIM
ARCHBISHOP OF WALLACHIA
(†1516)

If you want to be freed from all vices simultaneously,
renounce self-love, the mother of evils.
St. Thalassios the Libyan

OUR HOLY Father Maxim was born in 1462 to the Serbian Despot Stephen the Blind Brankovich (1458-1485) and his wife Angelina, after the Despot was forced to flee from Serbia to Albania. Despot Stephen married Angelina, the daughter of King George Arianet, the ruler of Albania at the time, during his exile (in 1461). They had two other children, Prince John and Princess Maria. At baptism, the divine child was given the name George. A pious, studious, and quiet boy during his formative years, Prince George was given the best education of the time: not only did he receive the usual religious catechism (from his personal tutor, Monk Marko), but he also benefitted greatly from the experience of the royal court of Albania, for quite often artists, writers, and sculptors from Italy, France, and Hungary would give lectures and display their works before King Arianet. This experiential knowledge was a great blessing to Prince George when he became the Serbian Despot and, later, Archbishop of Wallachia.

When Prince George was 23 years old, his father, Stephen, died (April 16, 1485) in exile in Udine, Republic of Venetia (Italy), leaving Serbian rulership to him and his younger brother John. Along with his mother Angelina, sister Maria and brother John, Prince George returned to Belgrade where he succeeded, in 1486, the son of his father's brother, Vuk (Grigurovich), as the Despot of the Serbs in Srem, north of the Sava River. These times were some of the worst in the fallen kingdom of Serbia, as Turkish occupation of the territories since 1389 left the Serbs almost in a state of economic, political and religious collapse. As a result, the northern despotic of the Serbian kingdom was moved from Belgrade—which surrendered in the Battle of Smederevo on June 20, 1459—to the city of Kupinovo located in Srem, Voyvodina, just on the other side of the Sava River. The relics of St. Stephen the Blind were placed in the Church of St. Luke in Kupinovo, which was one of the oldest churches not only in Srem, but also in all of Voyvodina. Kupinovo was protected by the military forces of the Hungarian King Matthew Corvinus until September 9, 1521, when the Turks, in the Battle of Mohacs, crossed the Sava and Danube Rivers and destroyed everything in their path.

Despot George was a most benevolent ruler and beloved of all Serbian people. Often he risked his life in order to travel throughout the southern territories of the fallen kingdom in order to comfort and strengthen his people in the face of the Turkish onslaught and oppression. His contacts with various western European powers when he was a young prince in Albania was a great benefit to the Serbs at this time. His relationships with Hungary and Italy brought the Serbs badly needed food and supplies to stave off total destruction at the hands of the Turks. Serbs throughout the territories eagerly awaited his visits and treated him with tremendous respect and veneration each time he spoke to them or delivered goods to their aid. In 1493, Despot George pacified a political struggle for power among the princes of Slavonia; and, as an adviser to the Royal Court of Hungary, he was able to resolve peacefully

Sts. Maxim, Angelina, John and Stephen. 16th-century icon,
in the Museum of the Serbian Orthodox Church in Belgrade.

Monastery Manasia, also known as Resava. 15th-century fortification.

Apostle Peter

Prophet Habakkuk

Frescoes from Resava Monastery

Christ the Savior   St. Nicetas, Great Martyr

Prophet Habakkuk   Prophet Ezekiel

Frescos from Resava (Manasia) Monastery of the 15th century.

the dispute over the rightful heir to the throne of King Matthew of Hungary, after the latter's death on April 6, 1490.

Despot George was also considered a fortifier and pillar of the faith by the suffering Serbs, as he constantly urged his people to remain faithful to the Orthodox faith in Jesus Christ as delivered through God's Enlightener, St. Sava. The odds against the Serbs keeping their Orthodox faith intact were incredible, as the most difficult time of Islamic religious persecution took place precisely at this time, during the first one hundred years of Turkish occupation of the Balkans. Also, Despot George was pressured to convert to the Roman Catholic faith in return for support he received from the Hungarian King Matthew. In 1487, King Matthew offered his daughter, Princess Isabela, in marriage to Despot George. The only requirement of Despot George was that he convert to Roman Catholicism. This marriage, the King proposed, would solidify Serbo-Hungarian ties. Holy Despot George refused this offer, being very pious and truly a monastic in spirit. He also felt obligated, as the oldest son, to care for his aging mother, Queen Angelina. George also explained to King Matthew of Hungary that he would never depart from the Orthodox faith in favor of the Latin heresy, that he would never abandon the faith of St. Sava, the same faith for which his loyal Serbian people were now suffering. And, as time passed, after many conversations with Princess Isabela, Holy Despot George was able to convince her to devote her life to Christ. In the end, she too became a monastic.

Holy Despot George ruled the Serbs from Kupinovo, Srem, for ten years (1486-1496). He was a peacemaker, a protector of the Orthodox faith, and truly a man of his time who had a clear vision of the future. This is why, after many years of service to his people in the capacity of despot, he decided to abdicate the throne in favor of the monastic life. He sensed that the most important treasure of the Serbian people was their church and faith, which was the cornerstone and foundation of their entire identity and civilization. To help save the soul of the Orthodox Serb became for Despot George a matter of life and death.

Also, George had constantly sought the Lord in the kingdom of his own heart, a kingdom which was *not of this world.* Therefore, to fulfill this end, George abdicated the throne in 1496, at age 34, in favor of his younger brother John (Despot, 1496-1502), and traveled southward down the Morava river to the famous Serbian Orthodox monastery Manasia, founded previously by Despot Stephen Lazarevich (1389-1427), the son of Holy Great Martyr Prince Lazar (†1389; see June 15th).

Located on a plateau which drops sharply downward to the little Resava river in the mountains some twenty miles east of the Morava river, near the town known today as Despotovac, Manasia Monastery (or Resava, as it was known throughout the fifteenth century), was built from 1407-1418 like a strong fortified castle. It was erected on a well-chosen spot easily defensible from the Turks on all sides, encircled by a massive wall, and also strengthened by the addition of high towers (two at the entrance and nine at other strategic places along the outer wall). Throughout the fifteenth century, Manasia was the cultural center of the entire territory. Constantine the Philosopher, the biographer of the Monastery's founder, Despot Stephen Lazarevich, wrote that Stephen searched diligently for "highly skilled artisans, particularly a group of the most experienced fresco painters ... as far away as the islands (Greece), in order to illumine and beautify the main Church of the Holy Trinity with the lives and events of our Lord Jesus Christ, His Mother, all the disciples, apostles, and saints. The Despot also invited to the Monastery the most learned people of the time: writers, translators, copyists and illuminators." The popularity of the Manasia school was such that its influence was long felt outside the Despot's frontiers—in Macedonia and even in western Bulgaria.

The most attractive features of Manasia Monastery, besides its impressive physical structure and beauty, were its rich liturgical tradition, strong ascetic practice, and inspiring theological activity. Knowing this, one must stand in awe of the great Despot George, who became lowly monk Maxim after entrance into the monastic ranks, for within a short period of time he proved himself to be a wonderful example of this glowing spiritual tradition, surpassing all in ascetic labors, native intelligence and humanitarian service in Christ. Unfortunately, although he was considered a lowly monk by the brotherhood of Manasia, nevertheless Maxim did not go unnoticed by the ever watchful eye of the Turkish authorities. They knew of his past political skill and vehement defense of the Orthodox faith. Several times during his early monastic career at Manasia Monastery, holy father Maxim was sent death threats by the Turkish authorities. As a result of this disrupting activity, Maxim decided to flee to the mountains of northern Romania. Thus, after spending five years at Manasia, learning the obedient life of monasticism, holy father Maxim went into exile again, something to which he was quite accustomed since his early childhood in Albania.

Venerable Maxim built a monastic cell in a wooded area in the Diocese of Wallachia, central Romania, where he began to fight the demons night and day by trimming his body and sharpening his mind and spirit through rigorous fasting, long uninterrupted prayers, and hours of reading the Psalms. He did not go unnoticed in Romania either, for after a few years he opened up his cell and received many guests and visitors who sought a blessing or spiritual counsel from this genuine pillar of truth. Venerable Maxim was granted, by God's grace and love, the gift of spiritual discernment and unceasing prayer. He was especially loved by the pious populace of Wallachia, both Serbs of the diaspora and non-Slavs alike, who saw in Maxim a genuine compassion and care for their worries, fears, and daily problems. His popularity grew so great that the people went to the ecclesiastical authorities of the diocese, begging them to ordain Maxim a priest, and then hopefully a bishop. Thus, in 1502, at age 40, Maxim was ordained priest in the Diocese of Wallachia; and only five years later, when the then Archbishop of Wallachia suddenly fell asleep in the Lord, Holy Father Maxim was unanimously elected and consecrated as the new Archbishop of Wallachia.

Archbishop Maxim served the people of Wallachia for five years (1507-1512). His personal holiness was a source of unity to the various Orthodox in Wallachia—Romanians, Serbs, Greeks and Bulgars—as he was able to reveal to them that the spiritual bond of Orthodoxy can only be won in mutual cooperation, constant striving in the Lord, and seriously committed service and love for one another. His skill at discerning the truth amidst the numerous heretical visions of God and human life was truly a divine blessing for those there, as St. Maxim was considered a great "Defender and Protector of Orthodoxy" in Romania. Also, since St. Maxim was adept in the political arena as well, he was able, in the capacity of Archbishop of Wallachia, to reconcile, through prayer, fasting, and the spirit of mutual Christian cooperation, the opposing military commanders of the area, Radu and Bogdan, averting war between them. His memory in Wallachia is living proof that even in exile the Lord can work miracles through the believer who is open to His miracle-working grace and love!

Although he was beloved among the Christians in Wallachia, Maxim knew that he would someday return to his homeland, Srem. In 1512, at age 50, after many years of giving all his energies in spiritual warfare for the cause of peace in Christ the Lord, Maxim abdicated his archiepiscopal throne in Wallachia and retired to Srem, to Krushedol Monastery which is ten miles east of Irig, just south of Novi Sad. Maxim was in poor health when he returned home, as his many exiles as well as duties as both Despot and Archbishop took their toll on this suffering servant of Christ the Lord. Yet to his last breath he carried out the commandment of the Lord, which says, *He that endureth to the end shall be saved* (Matt. 10:22); as well as the words of St. Macarius of Egypt: "In afflictions and sufferings, and in endurance and faith, are concealed the promised glory of celestial beings."

Our Venerable Holy Father Maxim, Despot of Srem and Archbishop of Wallachia, fell asleep in the Lord on January 18, 1516, in Krushedol Monastery. He was 54 years of age. He was one of the very first saints of the Serbian Orthodox Church to be born under the

Turkish yoke. Venerable Maxim was given an honorable Christian burial in Krushedol Monastery; and shortly thereafter his body and relics were found to be incorrupt and miracle-working, granting to this very hour grace, healing and wholeness to those who venerate him in faith, hope and love

"O Holy Father Maxim, O Exiled One, thou didst prove that true worship of God can be carried out in any place, at any time, under any conditions; thou didst also demonstrate by thy pious actions that *God resisteth the proud, and giveth grace to the humble* (I Peter 5:5). Pray, therefore, O Pious One, that we too, exiles in this world of lust, godless power, and heretical vision, may receive, through prayer, fasting and thy intercessions, the eternal vision of the Celestial Heavens, so that we may glorify God here and now by our every word, deed and thought. For only our Lord Jesus Christ, Whose Kingdom has no end, deserves glory, honor and worship, together with His Unoriginate Father, and Life-giving Spirit, now and ever and unto ages of ages. Amen."

KONTAKION,
Tone 2

Taking up thy Cross thou didst endure many afflictions and exiles,* O holy hierarch Maxim;* deprived of thy homeland and the flock entrusted to thee by God,* thou didst endure all things cou-rageously* for the sake of the sanc-tification of thy soul.

Apostle Peter receives Communion from Christ's Hand.

142

Holy Apostle James preparing to receive Holy Communion from the Hands of Christ. A 15th-century fresco from Resava Monastery.

St. Pinnas

St. Nirras

St. Innas

TROPARION, Tone 4
O Lord, Thy Holy Martyrs Innas, Nirras and Pinnas,*
by their struggles have received from Thee, our God,* their
imperishable crowns of victory;* because, acquiring Thy
strength, they have demolished usurpers and crushed the
powerless might of satan;* therefore, through their
intercessions, O Christ God, save our souls.

January 20th

OUR HOLY MARTYRS

INNAS, PINNAS AND RIMMAS (NIRRAS)

OF SCYTHIA

(†2nd century)

A small suffering endured for God is better
than a great deed performed without suffering.
That which is done without labor is the righteousness
of worldly people, who bestow charity with the outer
person, but gain nothing within themselves. But you
must strive within yourself and suffer with Christ,
to be worthy to partake of the glory of Christ.
The mind will not be glorified with Jesus,
if the body does not suffer for Christ.
St. Peter Damascene

LIVING in the second century, these saints are regarded as the first group of Slavic martyrs recorded in Church history. Believed to be Serbs, Holy Great Martyrs Innas, Nirras and Pinnas were disciples of Holy Apostle Andrew and preached the Gospel to the pagans who lived in Scythia (west of the Black Sea and north of the Balkan mountains). The polytheistic pagans of Scythia, controlling the government, would not receive the Gospel of the Son of God and thus, after arresting these three divine preachers, they brought them to trial. Upon being ordered to reject the Christian faith and burn incense to idols, the Three Holy Martyrs stood up and exclaimed: "We worship neither wood nor marble nor stone, for our Lord and God, the Savior Jesus Christ, is He through Whom all things were made." After listening to this, the judge sentenced the Holy Three to death: they were to be frozen in the ice off the east bank of the Danube River, near Varna, Bulgaria.

The Three Holy Martyrs, bound hand and foot, were placed in a large net and then slowly lowered into the freezing waters of the Danube River. They suffered beyond comprehension, as they were literally frozen in the river like human icicles; yet, during the whole terrible ordeal, their souls were calm and at peace, being firmly protected by the warmth of the grace of the Holy Spirit. Each received a martyr's crown in the second half of the second century.

Oh, what a mystery! How is it that the saints of the Lord endure calmly such torture and suffering? How can mere mortals have such courage? The answer, of course, is found in their steadfast faith in the Savior, and especially in His saving Passion and Resurrection. "For if Christ did not rise from the dead, then our faith is in vain," says Great Martyr Apostle Paul. Yet, what spared the Holy Martyrs Innas, Nirras and Pinnas the pain of their torture? Truly their suffering was a real one. The answer is that they were filled with the Spirit of God, and were warmed and even enraptured by the grace and love of the Holy Spirit.

Listen to this teaching from St. Isaac the Syrian (honored Jan. 28th):

Love for God is by nature hot, and when it grips a person beyond measure, it throws the soul into ecstasy. A person who feels this love exhibits a remarkable change: his face becomes fiery and joyful, and his body is warmed; fear and shame leave him; a terrible death he counts as joy; the contemplation of his mind allows no kind of interruption in his thought of the celestial; he is aware of no impulse excited by objects, for, even if he does something, he is quite insensible to it—so ravished is his mind in contemplation, and his thought is always as it were conversing with someone.

This spiritual rapture filled the Apostles and Martyrs of old. Some travelled the world over, working and suffering persecutions, while others never lost heart in the most terrible tortures, but endured with courage. Yet others wandered in deserts, mountains, and caves, and amidst disorder were the most well ordered; they were thought to be out of their minds, but were the wisest of the wise.

"O Holy Great Martyrs Innas, Nirras and Pinnas, you three burning flames who have received your incorruptible crowns, pray to Christ our God for us miserable sinners, that His warmth, love, and grace may ravish and enrapture us, making us insensible to all trials, tortures, and tribulations, so that we may be witnesses to His Hallowed Passion and Life-giving Resurrection, to Whom belongs glory, honor and worship, together with His Unoriginate Father, and Life-giving Spirit, now and ever and unto ages of ages. Amen."

KONTAKION
Tone 8

To Thee, O Lord and Author of all creation,* the universe offers as the first-fruits of nature* the God-bearing Martyrs Innas, Nirras and Pinnas;* therefore, by their imploring,* preserve Thy Church in perfect safety,* for the sake of the Theotokos, O Most Merciful One.

Holy
Martyr
Theodore
Sladić

TROPARION, Tone 8

Thou didst refuse to fall to the passing fancies of a dying age,* confessing Christ and the knowledge of the Church* to be the true educator of soul and body;* with the fiery coals of thy godly words,* thou didst scorch the errors of the pagans, O Holy Martyr Theodore,* and thy trial by fire proved thee far more precious than gold;* therefore, pray to Christ God to strengthen our souls.

First Saturday of Great Lent

OUR HOLY NEW MARTYR
THEODORE SLADICH
(✝1788)

> *We should greatly honor the Church,*
> *venerate her holiness, her antiquity,*
> *her unshaken firmness, her divinely*
> *enlightened wisdom and spiritual experience,*
> *her soul-saving commandments and ordinances,*
> *her divine services, sacraments and rites.*
> St. John of Kronstadt

OUR HOLY NEW MARTYR THEODORE SLADICH was born in the mid-eighteenth century in the village of Kukuruzara, near the town of Komogovina, located in the foothills of Kozara, Banija (sixty miles northwest of Banja Luka, Bosnia). About his early life we know very little, which allows us to focus on the gift of his legacy, namely, his martyrdom for being unshakeably faithful to our Lord Jesus Christ and His Holy Church.

Martyrdom under any condition has traditionally been held in high regard by true followers of the Orthodox faith. Yet there are certain martyred saints who, due to extreme circumstances, especially stand out in the minds and hearts of faithful Orthodox as being prime examples

149

of courage and faith in the Risen Lord Jesus Christ and His Church. One such case is that of Theodore Sladich.

In order to understand the greatness of St. Theodore's martyrdom, we must delve into the era in which he lived. Throughout the eighteenth century, the Serbian Orthodox people were under tremendous pressure from the Uniate movement of the Roman Catholic Church in many parts of the Balkans—Voyvodina, Bosnia and Herzegovina, Slavonia, Lika, Banija and Kordun, Dalmatia, the Bay of Kotor—creating the impression that the Serbs might succumb to Roman Catholicism. To make matters worse, in 1766, by the decree of the Turkish sultan Mustapha III (1757-1773), the Patriarchate of Pech was officially abolished, subordinating the Serbian Church to the Patriarchate of Constantinople. These two problems resulted in many Serbs turning away from the Church and from everything else which it represented: culture, literacy, order, and leadership, making them resort to many pre-Christian customs and practices, and allowing them to be an easy prey to perhaps the most evil development of the eighteenth century— the modern "spirit of renovationism" of the Western European Enlightenment.

In the late eighteenth century, many confused Serbs who had grown weary under the Turkish yoke and who wanted nothing of the Roman heresy, decided to turn to the "new" ideas of the Enlightenment which came first to Voyvodina from Western Europe via Vienna, Bratislava, Budapest, and other European university centers. One of these ideas was the reduction of the number of holy days celebrated, in order to facilitate new economic plans and conditions. Some one hundred holy days were to be erased from the liturgical calendar. Also, under the Turkish system, Serbian clerical education was rather limited. Emperor Joseph II (1780-1790), "the enlightened despot" in Vienna, with the blessing of Metropolitan Moses Putnik (1781-1790) in Sremski Karlovci (Lower Karlovac), advocated the closing of a number of monasteries in order to generate revenue to build various educational institutions. One supporter of this idea was the famous Serbian man of the Age of Reason, Dositheus Obradovich (1739-1811). Beginning as a monk in the Monastery of New Hopovo, he then left for Western Europe, returning to Vojvodina and later to Serbia as a humanist philosopher, a fierce critic of Church practices, and as Serbia's first Minister of Education! In the end, this opting for the rationalism of the so-called Western European Enlightenment created within the pious Serbian peasantry a tremendous distrust of Church leadership, an abiding disdain for Church life and practices, and a many-faceted regression which was to last well into the nineteenth century.

With all this in mind, it can now be easily ascertained why pious Serbs everywhere especially venerate St. Theodore Sladich. Quite often in his lifetime he was approached by both propagandists of the Latin Unia and by Serbian converts to Western rationalism who wanted him to leave the Church and embrace "modernistic" ways of thought and living. Venerable Theodore was an ardent Orthodox and, due to his love for liturgical ritual and the vision of the doctrines of the Church, he became an outspoken proponent against the Latin Unia and the rationalistic innovations of Western Europe. He felt that the Unia would never "add" to the true Orthodox faith, and that attachment to the papacy was nothing more than an economic ploy on the part of Rome. Gaining new ecclesiastical territory only meant more wealth to the papacy. In regard to rationalism and so-called "modern" education, Theodore responded by explaining that the source of every true knowledge flowed from the Church—that all worldly education can never replace that which a true Christian receives in church, where God Himself educates the believer wholly: by acting upon his sight, hearing, smelling, feeling, taste, imagination, mind, and will, by the splendor of the images and of the building in general, by the fragrance of the incense, by the veneration of the Gospels, Cross and icons, by the singing and by the reading of the Scriptures. And most importantly, as Theodore once said: "In no way can secular education bring about the greatest mystery offered by the Church: the cleansing

151

from sins." It was prophetic thoughts and words such as these which eventually brought Holy New Martyr Theodore Sladich into conflict with his greatest adversary—the Turkish authorities.

Theodore's evangelical activities were quite inspiring to the common *seljacki* (villagers) in the area around Kukuruzara. His blameless way of life bolstered the practical teachings he offered to his pious followers. He taught his fellow Serbians that both communal prayer in church and personal prayer at home were necessary for believers to lead a Christ-like life; that too much food prior to going to Divine Services deadens the heart before prayer and obstructs the access of holy thoughts and feelings to it; that if one reads worldly magazines and newspapers and derives some benefit from them, then one ought to still more often read the Gospel and the writings of the Fathers and Ascetics of the Church in order to establish within the soul not only a concern for earthly matters, but, more importantly, a concern for divinely inspired ones, for *the world passeth away, and the lust thereof, but he that doeth the will of God abideth forever* (1 John 2:17).

Theodore also disagreed with some current Church practices, which he believed were induced by the Turks. For example, due to the exorbitant amount of taxes the Turkish *sipahi* (lords) imposed upon the monasteries and bishops, priests had to pay a tax to their local bishop. In turn, each household incurred a tax owed to the bishop, whether paid in money or goods, while priests also charged for their services: baptisms, marriages, funerals, and others. Many priests also began travelling to rich Serbian villages and towns in Wallachia (Romania) and Russia, where they collected large voluntary donations. The great attraction here was that the donors' names were read out after church services, and plaques and signs were posted in the church in their honor for future memory. St. Theodore felt this mocked the holiness of the Church and led many to view the Church in a very "human" way, something which was also taking root in the West. Thus Theodore and his followers began to speak out. And they paid a great price for their love of the purity of the Church—martyrdom.

During the first week of Great Lent in 1788, Theodore and 150 followers of true Orthodoxy were arrested by the Turkish authorities on the charge of political and religious treason: preaching salvation through Jesus Christ alone and refusing to degrade the holiness of Orthodoxy by participating in the evil tax system imposed on the Church by the Turks. After questioning, at which Theodore and his followers confessed openly their belief in the unconditional divine love of Jesus Christ and His saints—which cannot be measured, sold, or taxed by humans—these divine confessors of the Lord were led to the nearby Moshtanica Monastery (in northwest Kozara), where they were burned to death by the Turkish militia men. This took place on the First Saturday of great Lent, 1788. Throughout the fiery ordeal, St. Theodore comforted his true-believing followers with the Words of the Lord: *Verily, verily, I say unto you, that ye shall weep and lament, but the world shall rejoice; and ye shall be sorrowful, but your sorrow shall be turned into joy.... These things have I spoken unto you, that ye should not be offended ... yea, the time cometh that whosoever killeth you will think that he doeth God service. And these things will they do unto you, because they have not known the Father, nor me.... These things have I spoken unto you, that in me ye might have peace. In the world ye shall have tribulation; but be of good cheer; I have overcome the world* (John 16:20, 1-3, 33).

After their martyrdom, Theodore and the 150 followers were given an honorable Christian burial, attended by many pious Serbs of the surrounding territories. Unfortunately, only the right arm of Martyr Theodore survived the burning. This holy arm was placed in Moshtanica Monastery and venerated as an "arm of strength" by which the Lord Himself works miracles and directs His true followers on the right path to salvation. Several times since then has the holy arm of St. Theodore been transferred to different monasteries. In 1876 it was taken to Komogovina Monastery (northwest of Kostanica), and in 1940, just prior to World War II, it was placed in the Church of the Holy Archangels in Kostanica. In 1957, the righteous arm of our Holy Father Theodore was taken to the "Saborna Crkva" (Catholicon) in Upper

Karlovac[1] and then returned to Komogovina Monastery, where it remains to this present hour, granting holiness, courage and correct faith to all those who piously venerate it in faith, hope and love.

One of the most beautiful icons of Holy Martyr Theodore is the one in the Church of Holy Apostles Peter and Paul in Marindola (northwest of Karlovac) which depicts St. Theodore dressed in the *norodna noshnja* (peasant dress) of his birthplace in Banija. This icon has granted courage to many poor persons in the Church, for it has granted them strength not only to cope with the difficulties and trials of this world, but also helped to prepare them for the eternal world, won by leading a life well-pleasing to God, which means to be ready to sacrifice all for the love of Christ. Finally, St. Theodore is remembered and celebrated on Saturday of the First Week of Great Lent, called "Teodorva Subota" (the Saturday of St. Theodore the Tyro), a date which changes yearly due to the "moving" date of the yearly celebration of the Feast of Feasts, Pascha. Truly, Holy New Martyr Theodore

---

1. The town of Upper Karlovac (Gornji Karlovac) should not be confused with the town of Lower Karlovac (Sremski Karlovci). Upper Karlovac is located in Croatia and is the episcopal seat of the Diocese of Upper Karlovac (Gornjokarlovachka Eparhija) which includes most of the regions of Banija, Kordun and Lika. On the other hand, Lower Karlovac, located just south of Novi Sad on the north side of the Sava River, became an important ecclesiastical center as a result of the Austro-Turkish War (1716-1718), whereby it replaced Krushedola Monastery as the seat of the Metropolitinate of Lower Karlovac (Karlovachka Mitropolia). The Treaty of Passarowitz (Pozharevac) in 1718, ending the war, created a new and unusual situation: Serbia as far south as the western Morava region became part of the Austrian Empire, which included the Metropolitinate of Belgrade. Belgrade in this way became part of Orthodox Voyvodina. And the Serbian Orthodox residing in the restructured lands of the Austrian Hapsburg Empire ended up with two ecclesiastical leaders: the Metropolitan of Karlovci (Srem) and the Metropolitan of Belgrade. Thus the present official title of the Serbian Patriarch reads: Archbishop of Pech, Metropolitan of Belgrade-Karlovci and Serbian Patriarch. Finally, to note, the terms Upper and Lower are based upon the flow of the Sava River, whose source is in the northern territory of Slovenia (closer to Upper Karlovac), and whose flow is "downwards" toward the plains of Voyvodina, hence granting the term "Lower" for Sremski Karlovci.

Three ancient soldier-martyrs. 14th-century Ravanitsa fresco.

Sladich travels with us all to that Great Day which has no end, the Eternal Pascha of the Victorious Lord and Savior Jesus Christ.

KONTAKION

Tone 8

By thy words and deeds* thou didst teach thy fellow villagers to honor the Orthodox Church,* her sanctity and salvation open to all;* by thy martyrdom thou didst inherit the delightful abodes on High,* for thou didst greatly burn with the love of Christ, O Holy Theodore;* therefore, as thy name[2] reveals,* thou art a sweet gift from God* to all who call upon thee in faith.

---

2. The name Theodore Sladich is a most wonderful name. Theodore is a Greek word meaning "gift from God," while Sladich is a Serbian word meaning "sweet one," "sweet as in licorice," or just simply "sweetness." Combining the two meanings, Theodore Sladich means "a sweet gift from God."

St. Jacob
Archbishop
of Serbia

TROPARION, Tone 1

Truly thou hast been esteemed as a great hierarch of
the Church,* for thou didst fight the good fight and lovingly
pastor thy people;* yet thine eyes were always set on High,*
granting thee zeal and commitment to perform heroic deeds;*
therefore, with songs we cry out to thee;* Glory to the Father
who has revealed mysteries to thee;* Glory to the Son who
has given thee strength;* Glory to the Spirit who has
enlivened us to keep thy memory in
faith, hope and love.

February 3rd

OUR HOLY FATHER

JAMES (JACOB)

ARCHBISHOP OF SERBIA

(†1292)

The best moments on earth are those in which
we meditate upon heavenly things, or when we
recognize and defend the truth, which is of,
and from, the Heavens. Only then do we truly live.
It is therefore vital to the soul that we should more often
rise above the earth, and mount to Heaven, where alone is
our true life, our true country which shall have no end.
St. John of Kronstadt

V ERY LITTLE is known of the early life of our Holy Father James, Archbishop of Serbia (1286-1292). We do not know when he was born or from which area of the kingdom of Serbia he came, or even where he received his monastic training prior to becoming Archbishop of the Serbian Orthodox Church. This, of course, is of Divine Providence, for it allows us to concentrate on the aspects and deeds of his archpastoral life when he was chosen and consecrated in 1286 as the seventh Archbishop of Serbia, on the throne of St. Sava, following Archbishop Eustathius I's death on January 4th of that same year (see January 4th).

In order to understand and spiritually appreciate Archbishop James' contribution to the Serbian people for their own salvation, one must turn to the most valuable book of the early medieval period of Serbian history, *The Lives of the Serbian Kings and Archbishops,* written by Archbishop Daniel II (1324-1337), the eleventh and final archbishop prior to the establishment of the Patriarchate in 1346. This book describes the personalities of the great leaders of the Serbian Church and nation of this era as well as the conditions under which they lived and performed their virtuous deeds.

From *The Lives of the Serbian Kings and Archbishops,* we learn that Venerable Jacob was installed as Archbishop of Serbia during the fourth year of the reign of King Milutin (1282-1321), and that the kingdom of Serbia at this time was becoming one of the strongest states in the Balkans. Economically, due to her rich mining reserves, Serbia was able to compete with all other Balkan states. King Milutin, with the help of his brother Dragutin, had succeeded in settling the military accounts with all of Serbia's traditional rivals—Byzantium, Hungary, Bulgaria, and the Republic of Dubrovnik. Milutin's military victories necessitated the creation of many new ecclesiastical dioceses. Some had formerly been under the jurisdiction of the Archbishop of Ochrid, while others were new: the Dioceses of Lipanj, Machva, Konchul, Branichevo, Belgrade, and Skoplje. This expansion spelled the end to any plans calling for the return of the Serbs to the ecclesiastical jurisdiction of either Rome or Constantinople! It is this scenario which enables us to better appreciate the spiritual activities and greatness of Archbishop James.

St. James was one of the great protectors of Studenitsa Monastery, the foundational monastery of St. Simeon-Stephen Nemanja (see February 13th). Venerable James traveled throughout the Byzantine Commonwealth in order to provide Studenitsa with the proper liturgical and canonical texts for the upbuilding of monastic life as well as for the fortification of the Monastery's library and archives. Most importantly, the ascetic James was a shining spiritual example to the monks of Studenitsa (and various other monasteries), as he was an evangelical preacher of "the narrow and hard way" to salvation of the soul and body

Main Zhicha Monastery. Building begun in 1207.

through prayer, fasting, and the contemplative life of Orthodoxy. He truly loved the meditative life and was an advocate of the Christian life not only consisting of ascetical labors and community service, but also of personal meditation on the divine life of the Holy Trinity. His most powerful teachings and homilies from the New Testament centered on the prayer life of Jesus, Who so often was alone in personal prayer to His Loving Father. Archbishop Daniel II writes that James "was zealous in holiness in all things, as he daily placed all his talents in service to the Lord," ... "that he received his halo of sainthood because of his purity of faith and Christian commitment, as he ascetically worked toward every virtue and pressed on toward greater perfection, leading an honorable and righteous life, protecting the poor, guarding the welfare of the Church and working for the good hope of future generations." This saint lived solely for the glory of the Gospel of Christ, as his eyes were constantly fixed upon the Day without Evening, the coming Eternal Kingdom of Jesus which has no end.

Holy Father James did not escape suffering during his archiepiscopacy. In 1290 the marauding Bulgarians attacked Zhicha Monastery near Kraljevo, burning many of the Monastery's buildings and damaging much of the iconography and frescoes of the main church of Christ the Savior. This persecution on the part of the Bulgars provided the context for Archbishop James to be spiritually victorious against the works of the devil. During this vicious attack on Zhicha Monastery, Archbishop James, along with several ecclesiastical and military officials, secretly traveled to Kraljevo and freed many of the monastics there, and also exhumed and brought back the relics of his saintly predecessor, Archbishop Eustathius I (1279-1286). For this heroic deed, his spiritual disciple Dragoman wrote that "among the many divine and holy deeds performed by Holy Father James, this one—freeing the monastics and returning the relics of Eustathius I—demonstrates the Archbishop to be a great hierarch and servant of Christ and truly our Holy Father." Besides being an evangelical leader of the expanded territories of Serbia, a lover of peace, defender of the poor and jewel of the Orthodox

St. Peter, the Rock of the Apostles.
Fresco from Studenitsa Monastery depicting St. Peter as a rock
holding the Church.

161

meditative life, Archbishop James truly can be called a hero of the Faith of St. Sava and Christ's Holy Orthodox Church.

Our Holy Father James, Archbishop of Serbia (1286-1292), after six holy years of service to his Lord and the Orthodox Church of Serbia, peacefully fell asleep in the Lord on February 3, 1292. He was given an honorable burial and was laid to rest in Pech Monastery. In Orahovica Monastery there is an icon of Blessed Archbishop James, in a fresco depicting him as a loving and committed archpastor of the flock of Christ the Lord.

"O Holy Father James, thou didst fight the good fight, surrendering thy entire will to the Lord for the edification of the Church and her holy faithful; please, O Most Contemplative One, pray to Christ our true God for us miserable sinners, that we may receive that very same zeal, fortitude, and love for Christ and His Holy Church, to Whom belongs glory, honor and worship, together with His unoriginate Father, and Life-giving Spirit, now and ever and unto ages of ages. Amen."

KONTAKION, Tone 1

Thou didst love the contemplative life,* As thou didst know that all things pass away;* yet thy love for thy people was unmatched,* as thou didst guide them in the commitment to excellence in virtue;* having therefore won the crown of holiness, * pray to Christ God to save our souls.

King Milutin of Urosh, builder of Studenitsa.
A fresco of 1321, in the Monastery of Grachanitsa.

St. Sava II

Archbishop of Serbia

TROPARION, Tone 4

As guide of the faith and example of humility,* and like a
plant in the midst of Paradise,* thou didst enlighten the
world with thy venerable deeds, O Holy Father Sava;* therefore, we lovingly venerate thy relics in thy tomb,* and sing
piously:* come to the aid of those who praise thy holy and
God-bearing memory,* O Blessed Holy Father Sava;* we beg
thee to pray* for the salvation of our souls.

February 8th

OUR HOLY FATHER

SAVA II,

ARCHBISHOP OF SERBIA

(†1271)

If you have been found worthy of the divine and
venerable priesthood, you have committed yourself
sacrificially to die to the passions and to sensual pleasure.
Only then dare you approach the awesome, living sacrifice;
otherwise you will be consumed by the divine fire
like dry tinder. If the Seraphim did not dare touch
the divine coal without tongs (cf. Isaiah 6:6),
how can you do so unless you have attained dispassion?
You must through dispassion have a consecrated tongue,
purified lips, and a chaste soul and body; and your
very hands, as ministers of the fiery, supraessential
sacrifice, must be more burnished than any gold.

St. Theognostos

OUR HOLY FATHER ARCHBISHOP SAVA II was born in 1200, the son of Holy King Stephen the First-crowned, and the nephew of St. Sava, the Enlightener and first Archbishop of the Serbs. Before becoming a monk, his full name was Predislav Stephanovich Nemanja. As a youngster, Predislav was surrounded by the great leaders and ascetics of the Serbian Orthodox Church, namely, his uncle Sava and the monks of Hilandar Monastery who often came to visit the Royal Court of Serbia. Unfortunately for Predislav, his grandfather, Stephen Nemanja-St. Simeon the Myrrh-gusher, died on February 13, 1200, just prior to his birth. Yet, as Predislav *grew in grace and in wisdom before God and men,* he seemed to carry within himself the spirit of his grandfather, St. Simeon, for he was, like Simeon, always loyal to his royal family, his Serbian people, and his Serbian Church. Therefore, it came as no surprise to his father, King Stephen the First-crowned, when Predislav decided, at age 20, to leave the Royal Court in order to join the ranks of the pious ascetics and monastics on the Holy Mountain at the Serbian spiritual garden of Orthodoxy, Hilandar Monastery.

Being received with joy, honor and dignity—as he continued the Nemanjich monastic lineage—Predislav entered the monastic ranks of Hilandar on the twentieth anniversary of the feastday of his grandfather, St. Simeon—on February 13, 1220. Within a short period of time Predislav was tonsured a monk, and with humility and honor received the name Sava II, after his uncle Sava, the newly-consecrated first Archbishop of Serbia (see Jan. 14th). Hence, from the very beginning, Predislav-Sava II seemed destined for greatness in the ecclesiastical arena of the Church. At Hilandar, Monk Sava was transformed, by the grace of the Holy Spirit, into a spiritual man of God. Never once did he take advantage of his royal lineage and past, but instead, always preferred the most menial and mundane monastic tasks and labor. The lowly monk Sava learned quickly that "the person who has tasted the things of Heaven easily thinks nothing of what is below, but he who has had no taste of Heaven finds pleasure in possessions and worldly veneration";[1] and that *"to deny oneself* (cf. Matt. 6:24) is to be ready to give up everything for the brethren's sake and not to follow one's own will in anything, or to possess anything except one's own clothes. He who attains this state, and is thus freed from all things, joyfully does only what he is asked to do. He regards all the brethren, and especially the superiors and those appointed to bear the burdens of the monastery, as

---

1. John Climacus, *The Ladder of Divine Ascent,* Rung #17.

St. Sava II. Icon painted by Fr. Cyprian, a great contemporary
iconographer of Holy Trinity Monastery, Jordanville, New York, 1959.

lords and masters for Christ's sake. In this way he obeys Christ who said: 'If any man desire to be first, the same shall be last of all and servant of all' (cf. Mark 9:35), not inviting any glory, honor or praise from the brethren for his service and conduct" (St. Macarius of Egypt). By his ascetical exercises—especially his reading of the teachings of the early Fathers and Ascetics of the Church—and by his participation in the liturgical/sacramental life of the Monastery, Sava was able to place himself in the spiritual position necessary to acquire the Holy Spirit, Who transformed him into a flower of spiritual regeneration.

In 1250, at age 50, after spending over thirty years in monastic obedience, Sava was given the Abbot's blessing to leave Hilandar in order to travel to the Holy Land where our Lord and Savior Jesus Christ voluntarily shed His blood "for the life of the world." In Jerusalem, Sava venerated the Life-giving Tomb of Christ, and also visited the monastery of his uncle Sava's namesake, St. Sava the Sanctified (†532; honored Dec. 5th). Upon his return in 1253, the monks of Hilandar were spiritually edified to hear of the intense monastic life in the Middle East as well as of the experiences Sava acquired while venerating the Holy Places of the Lord. The Hilandar community also had a tribute and honor to bestow upon him: Sava was informed by them that he was unanimously elected by the ecclesiastical hierarchy in Serbia to become the new Bishop of Zahumlje, one of the very first dioceses (located in Hercegovina) previously established by his recently canonized uncle, St. Sava, the Enlightener of the Serbs. The newly consecrated Bishop Sava, although against his humble will, felt nonetheless honored to serve the Orthodox Church in his homeland which he truly loved and cherished. Thus, at age 53, after many years of ascetic struggle in the Lord, Sava was ready to serve his beloved people in the Diocese of Zahumlje.

Bishop Sava's pious life always preceded him, as he pastored and lead more by example than by words. He was a shining beacon of the divine grace of the Holy Spirit in the Diocese of Zahumlje. Bishop Sava was always filled with both divine wisdom and pastoral love, enabling him to enhance the spiritual life of his diocese in every way possible. He built new churches, preached and taught the Orthodox truth impeccably to his people, advised the civil leaders as to how to better care for the material needs of the people, and even developed one of the finest school systems for children in all of Serbia. Bishop Sava of Zahumlje was truly a bishop's bishop!

After thirteen years of service on the diocesan level in Zahumlje, Bishop Sava was given, in 1266, the greatest earthly honor and responsibility: he was selected by the entire episcopate of the Serbian Church to succeed the newly departed servant of God, Archbishop Arsenius (1237-1266), as the third Archbishop of Serbia. He ascended the archiepiscopal throne of St. Sava in the Monastery of the Holy Apostles in Pech, located at the entrance of the Rugovo Gorge and only twenty miles north of the beautiful Dechani Monastery (built later by King Stephen Urosh III (1321-1331), on the road to Prizren. Actually, the original ecclesiastical seat of the Archbishop of Serbia was located in Zhicha near Kraljevo; but, in 1253, when Serbia (and Zhicha Monastery) was besieged by the Bulgarian and Kumanovian[2] attacks, the archiepiscopal seat was transferred farther south to Pech.

Archbishop Sava II pastored the pious Serbian people for only five years (1266-1271), as he fell asleep in the Lord, at age 71, on February 8, 1271. Yet, following the example and spirit of our Lord Jesus Christ, Who preached the Eternal Kingdom of God for only three years, Archpastor Sava II was able "to heal the sick, free the spiritually captive, clothe the naked, feed the hungry, and preach salvation through repentance" to his Serbian flock. Perhaps the greatest tribute to our holy Father Sava II, Archbishop of Serbia, was given by his biographer, Archbishop Daniel II (1324-1337), who wrote: "As everyone must give account for his talents, Holy Father Sava II can be assured of eternal glory as he unfailingly served his flock of Christ with all the gifts and talents God imparted to him."

---

2. Kumanovo, located 40 miles northeast of Skoplje, was a city almost as powerful as Skoplje or Serres, Macedonia, in the mid-1200's.

Archbishop Sava II was given an honorable Christian burial in the Monastery of the Holy Apostles in Pech, on February 8, 1271—the day of his feastday—as the entire episcopate, clergy, monastics, and pious faithful of the Church were saddened at the loss of such a divine Archpastor. Yet they also were very joyful and praised the Lord, for from time immemorial all pious believers rejoice in the death of God's saints in their midst, since the saints have always been considered the salt of the earth and even to this very hour constantly guide and pastor us by their eternal prayers before the throne of the Archshepherd of all, the Eternal Word and Savior, our Lord Jesus Christ.

Oh, how difficult it is to be a leader and pastor for Christ! This certainly is the reason why Apostle Paul put such strict regulations and requirements on those being considered for ecclesiastical office. Listen to these words to his disciple Timothy:

> This is a true saying, If a man desire the office of a bishop, he desireth a good work. A bishop must then be blameless, the husband of one wife, vigilant, sober, of good behavior, given to hospitality, apt to teach; Not given to wine, no striker, not greedy of filthy lucre; but patient, not a brawler, not covetous; One that ruleth well his own house, having his children in subjection with all gravity; (For if a man know not how to rule his own house, how shall he take care of the church of God?) Not a novice, lest being lifted up with pride he fall into the condemnation of the devil. Moreover he must have a good report of them which are without; lest he fall into reproach and the snare of the devil.

This teaching on the qualifications for ecclesiastical office is true to human experience and most assuredly is the reason why, at the consecration or ordination of a bishop, priest or deacon, the candidate must receive the approval of not only the clergy present but also the entire faithful gathered together, signified by the shouting of the word:

Icon of the repose of Archbishop Sava II (✝1271),
a fresco from Pech Monastery painted in 1633-34 in the Church of the
Apostles. The fresco icon over the sepulchre with the relics of St. Sava II.

AXIOS! DOSTOJN! HE IS WORTHY!, as the respective candidate is clothed with each vestment symbolizing his leadership in Christ the Lord.

"Let not many of you become teachers, my brethren, for you know that we who teach shall be judged with greater strictness" (cf. James 3:1). To be a theologian is not simply to obtain an academic office or title, nor is it merely conceived as an intellectual exercise, but rather defined and measured by one's closeness to the Lord, by one's own intimacy with Him. It is something which can only be attained by years of prayer, fasting, vigil, and the conscious pursuit of virtue coupled with the contemplative life of placing the mind in the heart through unceasing prayer. This is the way of blessed leadership in the Church —and few have found it! This is why Apostle Paul gave the aforementioned warnings and requirements for ecclesiastical office, as we have all personally experienced, in the behavior and lifestyle of far too many ecclesiastical leaders, the inhuman and wretched qualities described by the following words of the Apostle Peter, in a letter he wrote almost two thousand years ago: *But there were false prophets also among the people, even as there shall be false teachers among you, who privily shall bring in damnable heresies, even denying the Lord that bought them, and bring upon themselves swift destruction. And many shall follow their pernicious ways; by reason of whom the way of truth shall be evil spoken of. And through covetousness shall they with feigned words make merchandise of you: whose judgment how of a long time lingereth not, and their damnation slumbereth not* (II Peter 2:1-3).

Therefore, let us continually pray to Christ our true God to grant us the gift of discernment in selecting our Church leaders. Let us pray that our Savior leads them not into temptation, but instead places within their hearts the fear of God, and the spirit of humility and contrition of heart, so that they may crucify the flesh within themselves, and lead us more by their example than by their words to a glorified life in Christ in the Church, the Temple of the Holy Spirit and Eternal Kingdom of our Heavenly Father.

And along the way, may the life of our Holy Father Archbishop Sava II of Serbia be discovered by all pious Christian leaders everywhere as a standard of excellence, a shining star and a pillar of truth in Christ Jesus.

"O Holy Father Sava, thou didst demonstrate that humility is the virtue which attracts all people to the Lord and Savior Jesus Christ; and thou didst also reveal that compassion is the crowning characteristic of righteous leadership in His Church. Pray, therefore, O Holy Archpastor, to Christ our true God, for us miserable and prideful sinners, that we may be imparted a measure of His love, His humility and His sacrificial spirit, so that our example may not tarnish any of the glory of His Eternal Kingdom, to Whom belongs glory, honor and worship, together with His Unoriginate Father and Life-giving Spirit, now and ever and unto ages of ages. Amen."

KONTAKION, Tone 8

Thou didst hold the throne of hierarch, O Holy Father Sava,* and as thou wast a stronghold of the saints,* thou didst protect thy homeland, habitation, city,* and the people who piously honored and venerated thy precious relics;* therefore, let us hymn thee in unison:* Rejoice, O Sava, endowed with divine wisdom!

Holy Martyr George of Kratovo

TROPARION, Tone 4

Fire and death thou didst bear* in the endurance of thy
many labors, O George,* and to thine own perfection,* in
the company of the martyrs* thou didst receive from Christ
the crown which does not fade away;* pray to Christ God*
that He grant our souls great mercy.

February 11th

OUR HOLY NEW MARTYR

GEORGE

OF KRATOVO

(†1515)

Let us strive after a good and God-loving life,
not for the sake of human praise,
but let us choose it for the sake of saving our soul.
For death is everyday before our eyes,
and all that is human is insecure.
St. Peter Damascene

OUR HOLY NEW MARTYR GEORGE was born in 1497 to pious Serbian parents, Demetrius and Sarah, in Kratovo, a small town some fifty miles east of Skoplje, Macedonia. At age 6, George began schooling in Kratovo and was quite successful in all subjects. However, his pious father Demetrius fell asleep in the Lord when George was barely 10 years old, leaving the household without a breadwinner. As a result, George decided sacrificially to give up schooling in order to support his mother Sarah and family; he opted for a trade and, within a short period of time, became an expert silversmith in one of the local craft shops. George was a handsome young lad, well-liked by all his peers and the townsfolk of Kratovo. Yet a black cloud seemed to hang over his head, for although he truly desired to stay in his hometown to care for his mother, the constant menace of the Turkish authorities, who accosted and indoctrinated young boys into their vicious customs and ways, forced George to leave his birthplace. Thus, at age 12, George was advised by his family to flee these attacks and to look for work elsewhere. His humble family arranged for George to travel north to Sophia, Bulgaria, where he stayed in the home of a kind priest, Father Peter.

Living with Father Peter, George was able to complete his education. Also, Father Peter made sure that George was "trained in the commandments of the Lord," developing within him a love for the liturgical life of the Church, the Lives of the Saints and the teachings of the Holy Fathers. Yet trouble and tribulation followed George even to Sophia, Bulgaria, as the Turkish authorities, fearing the spiritual power of Jesus Christ which sprouts from the hearts of His young followers, decided to send a shrewd lawyer to have a talk with George with the hope of converting him to the Muslim faith.

This cunning Turkish lawyer visited George, requesting him to make a hand-crafted silver box inlaid with jewels. George consented, and within a short period of time the box was completed. Seeing the beautiful and detailed work done by George, the lawyer praised him highly and paid him a huge sum of money. (George quickly sent the money home to help his mother Sarah and family.) The lawyer, in conversing with George, said, "If I were you, young man, I would accept our Muslim faith and marry one of our women, as you would most certainly receive the respect you deserve. You could even become a leading man of our city."

George thanked the lawyer for his compliments, but asked him, saying, "And is earthly glory permanent and eternal?"

"Of course, all things of the earth are not permanent, but believe me, George, Mohammed promised Paradise to all those who keep his commandments," answered the lawyer.

"And what do these commandments consist of?" asked George.

The lawyer answered, saying, "Of good faith and physical cleanliness; and cleanliness requires physical washing and prayer."

"Now if a person lives a promiscuous and insatiable life," asked George, "but still keeps the commandments concerning the body and stomach, can he enter Paradise?"

This confounded the follower of Mohammed, who was then compelled to admit the truth that a person without a clean heart and soul could not enter Paradise, but rather must necessarily receive eternal condemnation. "Moreover," George continued, "your rulers and the heads of the Court are expressing, by their unclean works and words, that they do not desire in the least to reject the unclean life. Are they not right now, by this very same uncleanliness, wallowing in eternal damnation?"

"God forgives sin through His mercy," retorted the unclean lawyer. "Look now, my friend, at how many mosques, bridges, waterworks, and hostels our Sultans and Pashas have built!"

To this George replied, saying, "Such magnificent buildings made by these unbelieving rulers! Such renowned works! Ha! You do not have the right to say that these unbelievers are in Paradise! Yet look at us Christians, how many rulers, priests, pious faithful, and loyal soldiers are counted among the saints, and have healed, by the redemptive sacrifice of Christ and the grace of the Holy Spirit, countless faithful who have venerated them in faith, hope and love! If you do not believe me, come, I will show you in your own city, where King Milutin [see Oct. 30th] lies at this very hour in his crypt as if asleep, and his relics right now exude a sweet-smelling fragrance and oil, healing many who come to him for spiritual regeneration. It is clear that these saints were pleasing to God, as their faith has been confirmed and recognized by God Who has endowed them with miraculous powers. Why, then, do you want me to reject the faith which leads to God and His Kingdom? I am certain that you comprehend everything I have said, but I know that it is a scandal to you and thus very far from the truth for you. Isn't that so?"

The defeated lawyer was dumbfounded and silent, and then left; but in his soul evil was lurking and stirring up against George, for he had fancied that this young man, not yet 18 years old, would have been easy prey for him to convert. Instead the man left insulted, and his pride as a well-known lawyer was destroyed. He had learned that this type of glorious defender of Christianity would not only denounce Mohammedism, but also had the ability to re-convert from Mohammed to Christ many who had accepted this faith for earthly reward and human glory. The lawyer then returned to his colleagues, and after relating his confrontation with George, said to them, "If we do not deal with him immediately, evil will come upon our faith."

The shameful lawyer then went to the Turkish Judge of the Court in Sophia and reported that George had blasphemed the Muslim faith, commenting that Sultan Selim I often said that they who do such things are condemned to eternal damnation. Then he added, "If George is allowed to remain a Christian, his faith will spread at our expense; he is a dangerous man!"

The Judge ordered George to appear before the Court, but not by force; he summoned him under the pretense that he wanted some silverwork done to decorate his chambers. However, George knew why he was summoned and did not refuse, hoping to witness to Jesus Christ. When he appeared before the Court, the Judge was impressed with George's physical stature and handsome appearance. After giving George his request, the Judge went on to say that the paradise of Mohammed was well worth a man's converting to the Muslim faith. George understood then that he was not called before the Court just to hear of the Judge's request; and secretly in his heart he had been praying to the Lord Jesus Christ to grant him wisdom and power. Then George boldly asked how the Moslems were able to prove that Mohammed and those who follow the Koran enjoy blessedness. The Judge answered, saying, "Has not our conquest led to an earthly kingdom? Do not your people pay us *danak* (tribute)? If God didn't love us, He would not have created a kingdom for us."

To this George replied, saying, "By the sword they have created a kingdom! Does this mean that since you are the victors you are doing the will of the Lord? Earthly happiness should not be confused with eternity; you have received your wealth in this life, but there your destiny will be different."

"Our law-giver Mohammed," said the Judge, "spoke with God and received the law from Him."

"Mohammed never proved," retorted George, "that he had a relationship with God: neither in miracles, nor in prophecy. Do you know that when Moses received the law from God, Mt. Sinai shook from earthquakes and lightning? The entire people saw and understood that Moses, the Messenger of God, was not simply expounding his own thoughts or opinions concerning the law. But what similar thing is found in the life of Mohammed? He spoke on different things about himself! Is it sufficient just to have faith in him? And what kind of law does he give? He taught an easy faith, very passive concerning human passions and sins. It does not uphold the striving for holiness, but allows all to be inclined as animals. Now, can we, in our right mind, believe that such repulsiveness came from Heaven?"

Listening to this courageous and truthful defense of the Christian faith, the Judge and the Muslims were beside themselves! The Judge then exclaimed, "Death to this unbeliever! He has shamed our faith!" The Judge then ordered Holy Confessor George to be bound and cast into prison.

Father Peter, upon hearing of George's arrest, came and pleaded with the jailer on behalf of George, hoping for some sort of clemency or posting of bail.

"If you love him," said the jailer, "urge him to accept the Muslim faith, and he will be set free."

Father Peter then went directly to the warden of the prison and with tears pleaded for George. The warden, out of respect for the venerable old priest, allowed George to be released and placed under temporary house arrest under the protection of Father Peter. When these two holy men of God returned to Father Peter's home, the blessed priest took George aside and spoke with him, saying, "George, you have now glorified the Lord, just as the Proto-Martyr Stephen. Martyrs are given glory throughout the world, and great glory awaits them at the Last Judgment."

"I am fearful that I will not be able to withstand the fire," George the Confessor said to the holy priest.

Then Father Peter strengthened him, saying, "But meditate, my dear one, on the eternal fire which is much more terrible. And what is our suffering in relation to the eternal crown of glory?! Our earthly life is but a moment compared to eternity."

Though listening to these truthful and inspiring words, George nonetheless asked Father Peter to offer a ransom for him, and then added, "I still desire to labor more for the Lord here on earth."

The next day the Turkish messengers came to the home of Father Peter to ask George again to reject Jesus Christ. The Confessor remained firm in his love for the Lord. As a result, they took him back to prison. In the meantime, Father Peter went to the Judge and promised him a great sum of money if he released George. A week later George was brought before the Judge. The Judge, telling George that he cared for him like a father cares for a son, then explained that he would make him a rich man and that George would even inherit some of his own (the Judge's) wealth if he would only renounce Jesus Christ and the Orthodox faith. To this George replied, saying, "If you love me so much, why don't you allow me to remain a Christian? I am not seeking, nor do I want any wealth or glory."

"I am ordering you," shouted the Judge, "to renounce Christ! I consider him to be a prophet who will judge people, but Mohammed is greater, since God gave him the keys to Heaven."

"Give thanks to God," exclaimed George, "since you acknowledge Christ to be the Messenger from God, for indeed He will judge the entire world! But Mohammed has never shown that he was a messenger of God. The Old Testament prophets did not speak of him. His sensual and physical paradise—is that Paradise? This is an insult and affront to the human mind! The Koran fell from Heaven to Mohammed? Where is proof of this?"

The Muslims, gnashing their teeth, could hardly restrain themselves from attacking George. They all began to cry out and chant, "Burn him alive! Burn him alive! He cursed Mohammed, the Sultan and our true faith!"

The Judge, turning toward Holy Confessor George, said, "Reconsider! Do you not hear what they wish to do to you?"

Then Holy Martyr George answered, saying, "I have not blasphemed God nor His creation, but rather have expressed the truth about what awaits those who are of similar unbelief; thus I am ready to die for 'the Way, the Truth, and the Life,' my Lord and God and Savior Jesus Christ!"

"Is this blasphemy?" the Judge asked the people present.

They answered, saying, "Earlier we heard his blasphemies. If you free him, we will appeal to the Sultan himself." The Judge then turned toward the people and said, "Let this be your doing; do as you wish."

All at once the Muslims lunged at George, hitting him and spitting in his face, and then bound his hands and feet. "Gather the wood," they bloodthirstily shouted. "Let's burn him alive, this blasphemer of our law!"

When the Holy Martyr passed in front of the Church of Holy Wisdom ("Sveta Mudrost") in Sophia, Father Peter came up to him and said, "You will not suffer long, my beloved George. Be courageous."

"Pray for me, Holy Father," said George, "that the Lord may strengthen my spirit."

Then the Turkish police pushed Father Peter aside. Standing by the church was another priest who, although he loved the Christian faith, nevertheless, for fear of his life, had never openly confessed his belief in the Lord Jesus Christ; moreover, he wore Turkish civilian clothes when he was out in public. Father Peter exhorted this priest to travel with the executioners so that he could watch all that was about to take place. Besides this, Father Peter told all the clergy and the people to come to

George's fiery ordeal in order to pray for him. The prayer which came from their lips was, "Lord, strengthen him."

On the square of Sophia was placed a large wooden stake. George was given one last chance to deny Christ. "I have already told you all," said George, "that I will not reject my Lord and my God, Christ, the Son of the Living God, Who was crucified for the salvation of the whole world." Then all his clothes except his trousers were removed as George was tied to the stake.

As the fire was lighted and the flames began to rise, the Muslims screamed at George, taunting him, "How's it going? Are you warm?"

The Great Martyr then replied, saying, "Believe me, I don't feel a thing; but as for you, an eternal fire is awaiting you on your judgment day." As the flames shot up to the sky, George managed to turn his body toward the East and, sealing himself with the Sign of the Cross, said with a loud voice, "Lord Jesus Christ, into Thy hands I commend my spirit."

One of the policemen heard him pray and, grabbing the large mallet used to pound the stake into the ground, hit Blessed George on the head. He was killed at once. Immediately the sun was darkened and a torrent of rain poured down. The Christians, glorifying God, asked for the body of the Martyr. "Don't even think of it," replied the Turks, "for his entire body will be burned and rot in hell." Then the martyred Saint's body was cast into a burning pit where animals were roasted, so that the Christians could not get to it. "We will continue to burn his remains until tomorrow," they said, "and if they are still undamaged, we will cast them into a dark crevice in the earth."

The Christians then decided it was better to leave and to go to the church to pray. In the night, however, one of the Christians came and took the body of the Martyr and brought it to his home. Then it was placed in the Cathedral Church of St. George the Great Martyr. The following morning, Father Peter went to the Court and spoke to the Judge, saying, "Early yesterday morning, I came into the church and found the body of George there. Do I have permission to bury him?"

The Judge answered, acknowledging, "George is a saint. Tell those who bury him to hand down as a part of his legacy the fact that even though much wood was used for the fire, his body did not burn." Then the Judge allowed George to be honorably buried.

Holy Great Martyr George of Kratovo suffered for the faith in Christ the Resurrected Son of the Living God, on Meatfare Sunday, February 11, 1515, during the reign of Sultan Selim I. He was 18 years old.

The Divine Service in honor of Holy New Martyr George is found in the Menaion[1] under May 26th. This is the day his life-giving relics were transferred to the Cathedral in Sophia, Bulgaria. Thus he is honored twice yearly, on February 11th, the day of his martyrdom, and on May 26th, the day of the transfer of his relics. May his eternal glory shine in our hearts every day of the year!

"O Holy Martyr George, thou didst demonstrate that all things of this world pass away, and thus cannot compare to what God has in store for those who love Him and witness to His Heavenly Kingdom. Therefore, pray to Christ our true God, O courageous one, that we humble sinners may desire more and more each day that which is above and beyond our senses, intellect, and total being, so as not to put our hope in earthly things, but rather to be illumined and fortified by the heavenly vision of the Resurrected and Ascended Christ, to Whom belongs glory, honor and worship, together with His Unoriginate Father, and Life-giving Spirit, now and ever and unto ages of ages. Amen."

---

1. The Menaion contains the texts and order for the Divine Services of the fixed feasts, fasts, and commemorations of the saints of the Orthodox Church. The material is found in twelve books, one per month, and is divided according to dates, beginning with September 1st. The word "Menaion" is of Greek origin, meaning "month" or "monthly."

ANOTHER TROPARION
Tone 4

By the grace of the Holy Spirit,* thou didst proclaim the Creator's dispensation,* and struggle as an athlete for Christ, O Holy Martyr George;* having endured the burning fire,* thou dost refresh us with divine grace;* O Holy Martyr, entreat Christ God that we may be granted great mercy.

KONTAKION
Tone 2

Desiring heavenly glory, O Most Blessed and Much Suffering One,* thou didst therefore cut to pieces the Persian falsehoods,* and received the victorious crown, Warrior George, follower of thy wonderworking namesake;* thou dost rejoice gloriously with Angels,* and with them thou dost unceasingly pray for us all.

ANOTHER KONTAKION
Tone 2

By the grace of Christ, O Glorious One,* thy godly tongue was like a trumpet blown by God,* sounding the great deeds of godliness* and dispelling the mythologies of the lawless;* therefore, as a mighty athlete, O Martyr George,* thou wast made a whole burnt offering unto God.

Early Christian martyr, a fresco from Sopochani Monastery,
built in 1260's by King Urosh I as a royal endowment
destined to be his burial place.

St. Simeon
The Myrrh-bearer

TROPARION, Tone 3

Illumined by divine grace,* even after death thou dost manifest the radiance of thy life,* for thou dost pour forth fragrant myrrh* for those who come to the tomb of thy relics;* thou dost also guide thy people to the light of the knowledge of God;* O our Father Simeon,* pray to Christ God* to grant us great mercy.

February 13th

LIFE OF OUR HOLY FATHER

SIMEON

THE MYRRH-GUSHER

(†1200)

The highest adornment of the head is the crown;
the highest adornment of the heart
is the knowledge of God.
St. Peter Damascene

OUR VENERABLE FATHER SIMEON the Myrrh-gusher was born in the year of our Lord 1114 in the town of Ribnica (near Podgorica today), in the territory of Zeta, one of the original regions of Serbia. He was the youngest of four sons born to Zhupan[1] David Nemanja (Serbian for "Nehemiah"), the ruler of Rashka, the other original region of Serbia which was located more inland around the town of Ras.[2] Actually, Zhupan David, St. Simeon's father, had to flee

---

1. "Zhupan" or Patriarchal Leader.
2. Ras, the ancient capital of Rashka, about 10 miles from Novi Pazar today, is first mentioned in history around 850, as the fortress on the border between Byzantium and Rashka. In the twelfth century Ras became the capital of the Serbian State, established by the Nemanja dynasty. In the fourteenth century, King Milutin (1282-1321), widening the borders of the state, moved his throne to Skoplje. At the end of the fourteenth century, the name Ras is no longer mentioned, but is called Trgovishte, or Pazarishte. Today there exist only parts of the fortress, its buildings and

187

his princedom of Rashka, being exiled by his brothers; and, since in coastal Zeta there were Latin priests, the divine child of God Simeon was first baptized in the Latin rite. When his father, Zhupan David, returned to his throne in Rashka a few months later, Simeon then was received properly into the Orthodox faith, in the oldest Serbian Orthodox church in history, the Church of the Holy Apostles Peter and Paul (built in 850) just north of Novi Pazar. At this baptism he was given the name Stephen, after the Proto-Martyr Stephen of the New Testament. Simeon, his monastic name, was received later in life.

Although the youngest of four brothers, Stephen Davidovich Nemanja was nonetheless "by the grace of God the wisest and the greatest." He was raised Orthodox in the pious royal family, and was provided with the finest education of the time. He excelled in all subjects, especially the study of Scripture and the teachings of the Fathers of the faith. When he was 15, Prince Stephen Nemanja was given part of his patrimony, the regions of Toplica, Ibar and Rasina, to rule as his own. For over twenty years (1129-1149), Prince Stephen ruled these areas astutely and also piously, as even foreign rulers were amazed at his Godly-wise statesmanship at such an early age. For example, Byzantine Emperor Manuel I Comnenos (1143-1180), in 1146, in his visit to the city of Nish, was so impressed with Prince Stephen that he honored him with the rank of "Sebastator" (Autocrat) and even gave him, in a gesture of peace and political friendship, part of his own domain, Glubochica (Metohija), saying, "This is for you and your descendants forever; this domain is to be shared neither with me, nor with my relatives."

In 1149, Prince Stephen's father, Zhupan David Nemanja, died. Even though he was the youngest son, Prince Stephen was named by his father in his will to be the ruler of all of Rashka (the eastern territories

---

monuments. In ancient documents, the title "Srpske zemlje" (Serbian lands) was interchangeable with "Rashka zemlje" (Rashkian lands), and the Serbian state was often called "Rascia," the Serbs being known as "Rasciani."

St. Simeon in schema, from a Pech Monastery
fresco of 1345, "The Synaxis of Simeon Nemanja"
in the Church of St. Demetrius.

from present day Novi Pazar to Nish). His three older brothers, Tihomir, Miroslav and Strazimir, were given lesser territories. This of course infuriated his brothers, who, like the brothers of Joseph in the Book of Genesis, were jealous, since *when his brothers saw that their father loved him more that all his brethren, they hated him, and could not speak peaceably unto him* (Gen. 37:4). This was a very trying experience for Prince Stephen, as he truly desired and believed the words of the Psalmist: *Behold now, what is so good or so joyous as for brethren to dwell together in unity?* (Ps. 132:1). Yet the Lord did not forget His faithful servant Stephen, as He granted him a great consolation and spiritual reward. In 1150, at age 36, Stephen was married to the beautiful Princess Anna, the 25-year-old daughter of the Greek Byzantine Emperor Romanos IV Diogenes.

This marriage was made in Heaven. Besides growing into a holy and divine union of love, peace and joy and producing two saints of the Orthodox Church—Sts. Sava and Stephen the First-crowned, their pious and glorious sons (along with Vukan)—this marriage also solidified Serbia's future ties to Byzantium and the way of Orthodoxy, something which to this very day has helped transform the Serbian race into a people of God. To show their love and gratitude to the Eternal Bridegroom, the Lord Jesus Christ, for their marital union, Stephen and Anna built the Monastery of the Holy Virgin in Kurshumlija at the mouth of the Kosanica River near Toplica. This monastery was proclaimed as the principal monastery of Princess Anna. This proclamation was a gesture of love on the part of Stephen, as he realized that his Greek wife was far away from her home in Constantinople. It was here that she later received the monastic tonsure with the name Anastasia at age 70, on the Feast of the Annunciation, March 25, 1196, spending the last five years of her blessed earthly life in peace, solitude, and humble service to her Eternal Bridegroom, the Savior Christ the Lord (see June 21st).

In the first years of their marriage, the Lord granted Stephen and Anna two beautiful sons: Vukan and Stephen. Once again, to show his

ST. SIMEON
Fresco from the Monastery of Lesnovo, 1342.

gratitude to Almighty God for granting these blessed children to him and his wife, Stephen built a monastery at the mouth of the Banja River to the glory and honor of his *Krsna Slava* (Family Patron), St. Nicholas the Wonderworker of Myra in Lycia (honored Dec. 6th). In 1165, when Stephen was 51 years of age, he became by popular decree the "Grand Zhupan of All Serbian Lands." He established his throne "in the center of the Serbian lands," the town of Ras (near Novi Pazar today). Both regions of Serbia—the coastal region of Zeta and the more inland region of Rashka—were placed under his dominion and officially recognized by the Emperor of the Byzantine Commonwealth in Constantinople. However, Zhupan Stephen's success was not attained without much tribulation, for his jealous older brothers were a constant threat to both his civil rule and religious endeavors. They constantly complained that he was building too many churches. When hearing this attack upon his person and work, Stephan wrote the following words to his brothers: "My dear brothers, we are the sons of the same mother and father; please do not find fault in my work and leadership, which I am accomplishing only by the grace of our Lord Jesus Christ. Whatever you desire in your heart to do in your appointed regions, please feel free to do so. But whatever I do, be it good or evil, let it stand as my responsibility before the Lord. And may the Lord God forgive us all by His grace and great mercy."

Unfortunately, this plea on the part of Stephen was to no avail. His three brothers, Tihomir, Miroslav and Strazmir, decided to go to war against Stephen. In 1167, they captured Stephen and threw him into prison. After giving thanks to Almighty God for having the opportunity of witness to the sufferings of Christ and His holy disciples and saints, Stephen prayed fervently to the great warrior and sufferer for Christ, St. George the Great Martyr: "O Holy George, thou didst suffer all sorts of terrible persecutions and tribulations for the love of God in Christ by the Holy Spirit. Please, O courageous one, pray to Christ God for me, an unworthy sinner and servant, so that He may send His Most Holy Spirit to comfort and deliver me from my enemies and all my

The pillars of St. George Church. 12th-century, in the town of Rash.

The church of Sts. Peter and Paul at Novi Pazar.

foes." Immediately after this prayer, the prison gates were miraculously opened by an angel of the Lord, freeing Stephen and allowing him to flee to safe territory. Hearing this news, his brothers quickly organized their troops—made up of Greek, Bulgarian, Venetian and Hungarian soldiers—and began the war once again. However, the Serbian people totally supported their benevolent Zhupan Stephen and, with the help of St. George, were able to defeat the renegade brother Princes Nemanja at the Battle of Pantine in 1168, thus enabling Stephen to ascend his throne in Ras once again. And as was his custom, Stephen gave thanks to Almighty God for being delivered from his enemies by building a most beautiful monastery dedicated to St. George the Great Martyr. Known as "Djurdjevi Stubovi" (The Pillars of St. George), this Monastery was thus named due to its two impressive bell towers which stood in front of the entrance to the main church. Located only four miles northwest of the Church of Sts. Peter and Paul in Ras (Novi Pazar), Djurdjevi Stubovi was built from 1168-1176. Only ruins and parts of the main church exist today, the most miraculous of which is the fresco above the entrance of the church which depicts St. George riding on horseback—for truly the love of "the riding St. George" still present among all pious Serbs originated and was fostered during the life of the most divine and blessed founder and unifier of the Serbian nation, Zhupan Stephen Nemanja.

Blessed Stephen and Anna had two sons, Vukan and Stephen; yet they desired in their later years, like Abraham and Sarah, (the parents of Isaac in their old age) of the Old Testament, and like Zechariah and Elizabeth (the aged parents of John the Baptist) of the New Testament, to have another child. Their pious prayers ascended before Almighty God, Who heard their petition and blessed them with their last child, a son born in the year of our Lord 1175. Stephen was 61 and Anna was 50 at the time; they had been married for over 25 years prior to the birth of this their last child. At baptism the child was given the name Rastko, a name derived from the Old Slavonic verb "rasti" which means "to grow." And grow divinely he did. There were many special things about

ST. JOHN THE MERCIFUL

Fresco-icon in the church at Novi Pazar of 1250. The beauty of the artwork
speaks of the great spiritual height of this period, the architecture of the
church is strikingly reminiscent of Celtic roots.

Rastko: he was a lovely child, with pronounced features and smooth skin, and possessed, already in his childhood, an unusually alert and pious demeanor.

After the conception of this holy child in their later years, blessed Stephen and Anna did not come together; but as they had promised God, they remained in chastity the rest of their lives. Moreover, after the birth of Rastko, the rulership of Zhupan Stephen became holier, more devout, and, like the great Byzantine Emperor of old, Constantine the Great (†337; honored May 21st), he was determined to create an Orthodox kingdom.

One of his first acts of transforming the Serbian nation into an Orthodox nation was to call, in 1186, a "Sobor" (National Assembly) in the Monastery of St. Nicholas located at the mouth of the Banja River (near Toplica today). Holy Zhupan Stephen summoned the Bishop of Ras, Euthymius, the various abbots with their monks, the honorable Priests, the "Starshine" (Elder Statesmen), the "Knezovi" (Princes) and the "Vojvode" (Military Generals) to the Sobor with the following words: "Come and see, fathers and brothers! Even though I am the least among my brothers, yet the Lord God and His Most Holy Mother the Theotokos did not look upon the outer man, but rather made me worthy, I who believe in the One-in-Essence and Undivided Trinity, to protect that which has been entrusted to me in behalf of my flock from the vicious snares of the devil. Even though I thought it impossible in my country, I now hear that there are evil-doers and blasphemers against the Holy Spirit, who like the heretic Arius of old, divide the Undivided Trinity. This must be stopped, and their teachings must be banished, or else the basis of our nation will be undermined and we will fall into hell along with these evil-doers." The Sobor's resolution and plan for the purification of the Orthodox soul of the Serbian people was quite successful under Nemanja, for within five years, due to the dedicated and sincere work of the bishops, clergy, monastics and civil and military leaders, the Serbian nation was once again restored to correct belief in the only true God: the Father, and the Son, and the Holy Spirit, the Trinity One in Essence and Undivided.

The humble Zhupan heeded the words of the Lord: *A fool is he that layeth up treasure for himself, and is not rich toward God* (Lk. 12:19-21). Thus he preferred to "empty his pockets" to the benefit of his own nation and the entire Christian world. He built many local churches and established schools even in remote villages of his kingdom, and also built two beautiful cathedrals in major cities outside it: the Church of Archangel Michael in Skoplje and the Church of St. Panteleimon near Nish. He also gave huge amounts of gold and silver (and religious gifts) to various churches throughout Christendom: the Churches of the Savior and of St. John the Baptist in Jerusalem, the Cathedral of Sts. Peter and Paul in Rome, the Church of St. Nicholas in Bari, Italy, the Church of the Theotokos the Grace-giver in Constantinople, and the Church of St. Demetrius in Thessalonica. Finally, in 1186, the Grand Zhupan built an everlasting monument to his own humble glory, his foundational Studenitsa Monastery, located to the glory of God on Mt. Radochelo, in the hilly region of the Ibar Valley on the right bank of the little Studenitsa River, only twenty miles from the present-day town of Ushche.

Yet the total religious "conversion" of the Serbs to Orthodoxy could not take place simply along these political lines, or be led solely by the convictions and spiritual hard work on the part of the Grand Zhupan himself. Something else was needed. That something else was a real true religious fervor which would thrust the territories of Serbia into the dominion of the Lord's Kingdom—committed Christian life—allowing the people to be transformed into an Orthodox people of God. The first great step in this total "conversion" took place in 1193, when Zhupan Stephen's youngest son, Rastko, decided to flee the Royal Palace in Ras in favor of the monastic life on the Holy Mountain of Athos.

This flight to the Holy Mountain on the part of Sava made a most profound impact upon Zhupan Stephen's life. Being a great believer in

Jesus Christ, he was led to see God working in all people and events associated with his own life. Sava's choice of the monastic life was therefore a sign and message for the Zhupan: a calling for him to become fully immersed in Orthodoxy, to lead his people to the ultimate Kingdom, that of God, and like Moses of old, to bring his Serbian people to the horizon and gates of the Promised Land, the Holy Orthodox Church and faith. Thus, only three years later, in 1196, due both to the many prayers to Almighty God in his behalf and to the numerous pleading letters sent to the Zhupan himself by his beloved son, Sava, Zhupan Stephen Nemanja decided to abdicate the throne of Serbia in favor of the monastic life in his foundational Studenitsa Monastery. This took place when he was 82 years old. He was tonsured a monk by Bishop Kalinik of Ras in the Church of Sts. Peter and Paul, on the Feast of the Annunciation, March 25, 1196. He received the name Simeon. On that same day, Princess Anna, his wife, also received the monastic tonsure (being 70 years old); having been separated from her husband, she retired to the Monastery of the Most Holy Virgin Mary in Kurshumlija. She received the name Anastasia (see June 21st). This royal abdication and opting for the monastic life was a first for Serbian royalty: it signified their total acceptance of Orthodoxy as the basis for the kingdom's religious life and practice, and also emphasized benevolent Christian rule as the criterion and requirement for all future royal leadership in the kingdom of Serbia. Thus, after thirty-one years of civil rule (1165-1196) of the earthly kingdom of Serbia as Grand Zhupan, Stephen Nemanja now entered the Eternal Kingdom of the Lord Jesus Christ as lowly monk Simeon.

Prior to his abdication, the Grand Zhupan appointed his second youngest son Stephen to the Royal Court in the position of Grand Zhupan, saying to all, "Have this one instead of me. He is a noble branch of my body. I am placing him on the throne which Christ bestowed upon me." To his oldest son Vukan he allotted the seacoast province of South Dalmatia, to rule with the title of Prince. Then he exhorted both his sons, saying, "My sons, put your hope in God and do not boast of

Monastery Studenitsa. The Catholicon is dedicated to the Theotokos, and the chapel to the right was built by King Milutin in the 14th century.

At right: detail of the west door.

HOLY PROPHET ELIAS
Fresco in the King's Chapel at Studenitsa. 14th-century masterpiece.

HOLY PROPHET HABAKKUK
Fresco in the King's Chapel at Studenitsa. 14th-century Serbian art.

your wisdom and power. I give you this commandment which is from above: Think no evil against each other, but have true love among you. *For he that loveth not knoweth not God; for God is love* (I John 4:8)." This was his last act prior to entering his beloved Studenitsa Monastery.

In Studenitsa, Simeon lived as a simple monk for about eighteen months, following strictly all the prescribed rules for prayer, fasting, learning, and work. He advanced incredibly in service to the Lord and his Monastery, as he was able, by the grace of God, to establish economic order in the Monastery, increase the number of monks, build his own crypt in the main church, and appoint a hieromonk, Dionysius, as abbot over all. After receiving an invitingly heartfelt letter from his youngest son, Monk Sava on the Holy Mountain, Simeon decided to leave Studenitsa to be reunited with him there. He left for the Holy Mountain on October 7, 1197, being escorted to the Greek frontier by his son, the newly appointed Grand Zhupan Stephen, and other Serbian dignitaries, and arrived to the loving arms of his soft-hearted son Sava on November 2, 1197, in the Greek Monastery of Vatopedi on the Holy Mountain. There for the first time in three years Simeon met his favorite child Sava, who by this time was an experienced monk. The biographer Theodosius writes: "They were both speechless, and had someone not supported his father (Simeon), he would have fallen. After he regained his composure, he poured many tears over the much longed-for and saintly head of his beloved son, embracing and kissing it and pressing it to his chest." And as Nikolai of Zhicha (see March 18th) writes: "Simeon was 84 and Sava 27, like snowy winter and blossoming spring, yet two hearts equally afire with the love of God. Parents and children can only know how much they love each other after a long separation. They discover, when they meet again, how immeasurable is that love."

The most wonderful element in the legacy of Monks Sava and Simeon—son and father—was their joint effort to bring to the Serbian nation a spiritual center in which Orthodox prayer and committed Christian life would be the eternal flame and vigil lamp guiding the Serbian people to the Kingdom of God. This eternal torch and divine light was the Hilandar Monastery. Hilandar Monastery was once a small monastic settlement which fell into ruin for many years. The property was owned by Vatopedi Monastery. Due to Sava's virtuous life and his representation of the Vatopedi brotherhood at the Imperial Court in Constantinople, and also because of Simeon's generous material support of Vatopedi, the ruins of Hilandar, by Imperial Decree, were given to the Serbs as an independent and self-governing property to be used as a monastery. This was made official by two foundational charters: The chrysobul of Byzantine Emperor Alexis III Angelos of Constantinople in June of 1198, and the charter of Hilandar Monastery's co-founder, Zhupan Stephen Nemanja–Monk Simeon in late 1198. Hence, the idea of a Serbian monastery on the Holy Mountain became a reality when father became obedient to son, when both of these spiritual pillars became totally dedicated to our Lord and Savior Jesus Christ and Holy Orthodoxy.

Within a year and a half—November 1197 to May 1199—Simeon was able, just like he had done so often before, to build the main church, dedicated to the Feast of the Presentation of the Theotokos into the Temple (Nov. 21st), as well as to complete the necessary accommodations for many monastics—cells, library, refectory, and guest houses. What he saw develop before his very own eyes was even a greater miracle: the arrival of many young Serbian ascetics, eager like his son Sava to take up the totally committed life of coenobitic monasticism. Venerable Simeon's pious example was shown at all times; he spent many hours in personal prayer and served the monks as a God-loving mother serves her children. He literally "wore himself out for the Lord" in service to his brethren. As a result of his ascetic labor for the Lord, Venerable Simeon's body became weak, yet his spirit became strong .

On the 7th of February, 1200, Blessed Simeon became ill. He summoned his beloved son Sava and quietly began to speak with pure and sweet words: "My sweet child and the solace of my old age, please listen to my words. The time has come for us to part. Now the Lord is letting me depart in peace according to His word: *for dust thou art, and unto dust shalt thou return* (Gen. 3:19). Do not grieve, my child, over my parting, for from this cup everyone must partake. If we part here, we shall unite there where there is no more parting." Having raised his hands, Simeon placed them upon Sava's head, saying, "I bless you; may the Lord grant you salvation, and may you have at all times my indivisible but nevertheless sinful prayer as an aid and solace for you."

Sava then became saddened and fell before the Saint's feet and spoke with tears: "I enjoy many great gifts from you, my Blessed Master Simeon. I have become dead before my own passing, as I fall before your venerable feet for the mercy of your honorable prayers which will bring about alleviation for my soul in the day of the fearful coming of our Lord Jesus Christ."

Then Simeon sent Sava for the abbot and the Elders of the Holy Mountain in order to prepare for his passing. As many of the monastics arrived, Simeon said, "Stay with me until you all sing over my body and bury me with your holy and honorable songs." Blessed Simeon, from the 7th day of February until the day of his passing, the 13th, did not taste bread or water; he partook only of Communion of the Precious Body and Blood of our Lord and God and Savior Jesus Christ.

On February 12th, Simeon requested that Sava bring the Icon of the Theotokos, saying, "My child, bring me the Icon of the Holy Theotokos; it is my solemn vow to expire in front of Her." He then, in an act of extreme humility, asked Sava for a favor: "Put the burial covering on me and prepare me in a holy manner, for I will be entering the grave. Spread a rug on the earth and place me on it, and put a stone under my head; let me lie here until God visits me and takes me from here." The great founder and Father of the Serbian nation was now lying on the earth, wrapped in a black mantle, bowing to everyone, arousing pity, and asking for forgiveness, prayers, and blessings.

That night the monks took leave, and having blessed him, went to their cells to rest awhile. Only Sava and a hieromonk (priest-monk) stayed with Blessed Simeon all night. A little after midnight, on February 13th, Simeon became silent, not speaking to Sava any more. When

Hilandar: The Serbian Monastery on Mt. Athos. Aerial view of the monastery today, very similar to the way it looked in the time of its early flowering.

morning came, Simeon's face became illuminated, and raising his hands toward Heaven, he said, *Praise ye God in His saints, praise Him in the firmament of His power* (Ps. 150:1).

Then Sava asked him, saying, "Father, who do you see?"

Simeon then replied, saying, *Praise Him for His mighty acts; praise Him according to the multitude of His greatness* (Ps.150:2). After Holy Simeon said this, his spirit left his body and he fell asleep in the Lord. Sava then fell on his face and wept profusely for a long time; then standing up, he thanked God that he was granted to see the last days of his beloved father. He was 86 years of age at the time of his passing.

Then hundreds of monastics—Greeks, Russians, Bulgarians, and Serbs—along with many civil leaders, gathered for nine days at Hilandar Monastery, and day and night kept vigil over Simeon's body, chanting the burial hymns and serving the Divine Liturgy. St. Simeon's body, placed in a crypt along the south wall of Hilandar's main church, immediately showed signs of incorruptibility—pure soft skin totally aglow, along with myrrh exuding from his hands and face. And as eternal love creates a bond unbreakable, only four months later—on June 21, 1200—the Blessed Princess Anna-St. Anastasia, Simeon's beloved wife, fell asleep in the Lord in order to join her husband in singing praises to the Divine Trinity in Heaven.

Simeon's body and relics remained at Hilandar for four years after his death (1200-1204). In 1204, due to the pleading of Sava's brother Stephen in Serbia to heal the fratricidal struggle for political rule of the kingdom, Sava was forced to return to Studenitsa Monastery with the life-giving relics of St. Simeon. Upon the hearing of this terrible report from Serbia, the body of St. Simeon stopped pouring forth the miraculous myrrh. Also, Sava was visited by his father Simeon in a dream, who told him to return to Serbia to save his people, his royal family, and his Serbian Church. Finally, this return by Sava to Serbia was prompted by an ecclesiastical atrocity which took place on the Holy Mountain: due to the Fourth Crusade by the Latin Church, in which Constantinople was sacked, the entire Holy Mountain was placed under

St. Simeon, fresco from Lejeviska Church of the Theotokos.

KONTAKION, Tone 6

Loving the angelic life while on earth,* thou didst abandon worldly rulership and the world,* and followed Christ through fasting, O Simeon;* in an apostolic manner thou dost guide unto Christ those who love thee,* proclaiming: Love God as He loves us.

the authority of a Roman Catholic Bishop! Thus Sava departed in great sorrow; yet St. Simeon did not abandon Hilandar and the Holy Mountain. In the stone foundation of his crypt there miraculously grew a huge grapevine whose grapes and branches have granted miracles to this day, especially to married couples "with difficulties in child-bearing."[3]

When he returned, Sava brought with him the "medicine" to heal his people: the body and relics of his father. St. Sava invited his two brothers, Stephen and Vukan, to Studenitsa Monastery for a rightful *Pomen* (Memorial Service) for their father. As the casket was opened, before their eyes the body of their father was found to once again exude the fragrant oil and myrrh, and he looked very much alive, warm and aglow, as if he was only restfully sleeping. Sava exhorted his brothers to commence peace talks, which they did, having as their aim the last words of their beloved peace-loving father: "Think no evil against one another." Civil war was thus averted by the lovingkindness of Simeon. And to this very hour Simeon's body and relics, along with those of his wife Anastasia and son Stephen, lie in eternal repose in Studenitsa

---

3. The true story of the gigantic miracle-working grapevine of St. Simeon at Hilandar is as follows. When Sava prepared to take the body and relics of St. Simeon to Serbia, the entire brotherhood of Hilandar mourned the loss. Then Simeon appeared in a dream to Abbot Methodius, explaining to him the importance of the return of his relics, all the while comforting him with the message that from his tomb would grow a grapevine which would be miracle-working. Thus, incredibly, a huge vine grew from the stone upon which rested the tomb of St. Simeon. From that time on the grapes and branches have granted healing to many, as witnessed in the miracle scrolls of Hilandar Monastery. In particular, the consumption of the grapes (and grape-water), with appropriate prayers and fasting, has granted to believing married couples "with difficulties in having children" the miracle of childbirth. As the author of these volumes, I attest firsthand to this miraculous power. My wife suffered an early miscarriage while living in Vrshac, Banat (Yugoslavia) in 1985. I then visited Hilandar Monastery and brought back the life-giving grapes and a branch from the vineyard of St. Simeon. Following the prescribed practices, my wife gave birth to a wonderful daughter—named Anastasia which means "Resurrection"—witnessing to the amazing life-giving power of God manifested in His saints.

Studenitsa Monastery: Church of the Virgin Mary.

Monastery, granting healing and unity to all who venerate them in faith, hope and love.

"O Holy Father Simeon, thy righteousness and thy love for God and His people inspires us to imitate thy greatness of humility. Pray, O Venerable Warrior of the Lord, to Christ the Righteous King, for us sinners who lack the courage to imitate thy greatness, to be granted love for Christ, His Church, thy country and countrymen, thy own royal families and the Orthodox faith, the faith which propels us all to the true knowledge and experience of the humble Lord Jesus Christ, to Whom belongs glory, honor and worship, together with His Unoriginate Father, and Life-giving Spirit, now and ever and unto ages of ages. Amen."

St. Arsenius

Bishop of Iver

TROPARION, Tone 8

Teacher of mercy and treasury of compassion which
thou didst open to all;* upholder of the true faith,* thou
wast a divine adornment of hierarchs and defender of the
poor,* O our Father and Hierarch Arsenius;* therefore, pray
to Christ God to enlighten our souls,* that we may never
sleep unto death.

March 2nd

LIFE OF OUR HOLY FATHER

ARSENIUS

BISHOP OF TVER

(✝1409)

> *If thou wilt be perfect, go and sell*
> *that thou hast, and give to the poor;*
> *and thou shalt have treasure in heaven;*
> *and come and follow me*
> St. Matthew 19:21

OUR HOLY FATHER Arsenius was born in 1350 to pious and humble Serbian parents in the town of Tver, about 150 miles northwest of Moscow, Russia. (His grandparents had migrated to this territory in Russia some seventy-five years before his birth.) He was a very serious and intelligent boy, excelling in school while also delighting in serving the Lord as an acolyte in his local Orthodox Church. When Arsenius was still a young boy, both his parents became grievously ill; and just prior to his thirteenth birthday, they both fell asleep in the Lord. On their deathbed they asked Arsenius to fulfill one last wish: to live a holy and devout life, remembering the Lord God all his days, and to remember the poor and needy. At this time, because Arsenius was their only child, they willed all their possessions to him.

After the repose of his pious and God-loving parents, Arsenius spent many hours in prayer, seeking guidance from the Lord as to how to carry out his parents' last request. During this time, two particular passages of the New Testament continually spoke to his heart: *For what is a man profited, if he shall gain the whole world, and lose his own soul? or what shall a man give in exchange for his soul?* (Matt. 16:26). This passage made Arsenius realize the serious nature of Christian commitment, as well as the priority that must be given to the spiritual over the material. The following second passage made it clear to him exactly what he should do in order to fulfill this commitment: *Go and sell that thou hast, and give to the poor, and thou shalt have treasure in heaven: and come and follow me* (Matt. 19:21). Motivated by these sayings of the Lord, the young Arsenius, not yet fifteen years old, decided to sell all his family's possessions—and they were great indeed—and give the resulting money to the poor of Tver. He then announced to all his relatives that he desired to become a monk, so that he could remember the Lord God continually in the depths of his heart and truly identify with the poor and needy by becoming one of them in the fullest sense. His relatives, shocked at such a thought, tried hard to dissuade him and even arranged for him to marry a young Russian maiden of Tver. However, the teenage ascetic for Christ would have no part of this, and he secretly fled his birthplace and traveled to Kiev-Caves Monastery, where the famous Russian Orthodox ascetics, Anthony and Theodosius, had previously persevered in the virtuous life of monasticism in Jesus Christ the Lord.

Arriving at the Kiev-Caves Monastery, the Christ-loving 15-year-old fell on his knees before the abbot of the Monastery and begged him, saying, "Have mercy, holy Father, on me, a sinner! Please do not deny me entrance into this holy place; please remember that Christ did not cast away the repentant sinner."

The abbot, taken aback by such extreme humility, asked the youth, "Why do you, my son, feel so powerfully the grip of sin? You are still a young boy!"

"I am also a great sinner," answered the youth, "for there is no one who lives and does not sin, even if he only lives one day on this earth. We are all born into this mortal and passing age. Please, holy Father, do

The city of Tver, dominated by the Cathedral, 1907.

Zheltikov Monastery, photograph, 1907.

not turn me away. I truly believe in and understand the awesome judgment seat of Christ. What kind of account will I possibly give to Christ?!"

This reply of the youth astonished the abbot. He truly felt the grace of God pouring forth from this young lover of Christ. Yet, still fearing that the boy was too young for the monastic vocation, the abbot replied, saying, "The monastic life is difficult, and its trials and temptations are many. It would be fearfully difficult for a young man such as yourself to carry out the ascetic practices of the monastic life. Pray to God, my son, that He Who reveals many ways to His Kingdom will show you an easier path for the time being."

"I am not afraid of monastic labor and ascesis," said the holy youth. "For me they are pleasant, sweet and life-giving. I ask, then, only one thing: let me be considered the least of the entire brotherhood, and I will do, by the grace of God, all that is required. God will be my Protector, and your prayers, holy Father, will strengthen me. I am constantly motivated by these zealous and sober words of the Lord: *No man, having put his hand to the plough, and looking back, is fit for the kingdom of God* (Luke 9:62)."

The abbot, by this reply, was finally convinced of the ardent desire and willingness on the part of Arsenius to enter the monastery. Thus Arsenius was received into the brotherhood, being clothed with the cassock, as he began his journey on *the narrow path* (cf. Matt. 7:14).

The Kiev-Caves Monastery was a strictly regulated coenobitic community. Each monk served his obedience and progressed from degree to degree in the ascetic life. Arsenius, as the rule required, began with the easier tasks, such as collecting wood for heating and cooking, and only then went on to the more difficult ones: working in the chapel and serving the elder monks who were ill. All of these tasks he fulfilled with zeal, and never once did anyone hear a grumbling word from his mouth. The entire brotherhood was amazed at such zeal, endurance and desire to acquire virtue through ascetic labor.

As time passed, the young man became one of the great ascetics of the Kiev-Caves Monastery. His humility and virtue surpassed all; the light and love of Christ were so visible in him that many elder monks came to him to seek spiritual advice and counsel. He was an accomplished ascetic by the age of twenty, and when he reached the canonical age of twenty-five, was ordained deacon in Kiev by the Metropolitan of Kiev, Cyprian.[1] Although Arsenius accepted ordination reluctantly, feeling totally unworthy of the vocation, he nevertheless consented with the plea that Cyprian would not elevate him to the priesthood. However, in Tver, Arsenius' birthplace, there was an ecclesiastical disruption. The spiritual situation of the diocese deteriorated to such a degree that the Prince of Tver, Michael Alexandrovich, petitioned Cyprian in Moscow to investigate matters. Archbishop Cyprian traveled to Tver, taking with him two Greek Metropolitans, Michael and Nikandros, St. Stephen of Perm, Bishop Michael of Smolensk, venerable Archdeacon Arsenius, and several other archimandrites[2] and abbots. After Divine Liturgy in the Transfiguration Cathedral in Tver, a synod was held. Arsenius was to be elevated to the rank of priest and then bishop, and assume the episcopal duties of the Diocese of Tver.

Ascending the archpastoral throne in Tver, Blessed Arsenius began immediately, by sincere prayers, fasting, evangelical words and virtuous deeds, to restore the faithful of the diocese to spiritual health and vitality. He was inspired at this time by the words of Prophet Ezekiel: *So thou, O son of man, I have set thee a watchman unto the house of Israel; therefore thou shalt hear the word at my mouth, and warn them from me* (Ez. 33:7). Arsenius' greatest gift to his flock was his pure and devout life. He continued to lead a strict ascetic life, constantly keeping vigil over his entire person by fasting. News about this holy man of God quickly spread, prompting many to come to receive his blessing, forgiveness of

---

1. St. Cyprian, a Bulgarian by birth, was consecrated Metropolitan of Kiev on December 2, 1375; and in May 1381, he assumed the archiepiscopal throne in Moscow. He is commemorated on Sept. 16.

2. An archimandrite oversees two or more monasteries. In recent centuries he is an ordained igumen (abbot) of a brotherhood or monastery.

sins and spiritual healing. Also at this time St. Arsenius was granted, by the grace of God, the gift of healing. He healed many of their physical woes, as pious believers after being blessed by water or anointed with oil by the Saint were made physically whole as well as confirmed spiritually in faith in the Lord.

Coming to Tver, St. Arsenius did not forget the monastic community of the Kiev-Caves, where he had first entered as a novice some twenty-five years before. The examples and teachings of the founders of the Caves Monastery, Anthony and Theodosius, were permanently etched in Arsenius' mind and heart, as their lives and works inspired him to build his own monastery where he would someday be buried. Prince Michael of Tver was pleased with this desire of Arsenius and vowed to aid him materially to fulfill his God-inspired plan. The saint then chose for his monastery a place called Zheltikov, some seven miles from Tver, near a quiet spot on the Tmaka River. Invoking the Holy Spirit of God, venerable Arsenius built a chapel in Zheltikov in honor of Sts. Anthony and Theodosius. Arsenius' chapel was completed in 1394, and the brotherhood who gathered around him chose him as their abbot. Ten years later, on August 30, 1004, the main church of Zheltikovo Monastery, dedicated to the Dormition of the Theotokos —following the pattern of the Caves Monastery—was completed and consecrated. The Church was truly beautiful, as Prince Alexandrovich, fulfilling his promise, provided all the materials necessary to decorate and beautify the Church. And it was next to this main Church that Blessed Arsenius, with his own hands, dug his own grave and constructed his crypt out of white stone.

As Bishop of Tver, venerable Arsenius often visited his Monastery, encouraging the monks to continue spiritual warfare in the Lord. Under his direction the *Kiev Caves Patericon* was published. Arsenius at this time was inspired by the words of Scripture: *And the servant of the Lord must not strive; but be gentle unto all men, apt to teach, patient, in meekness instructing those that oppose themselves...* (II Tim. 2:24-25). Truly Arsenius was a blessed archpastor! His personality and character were so

Apparition of St. Arsenius to Monk Sabbatius. An illustration by
N. Adamovich, in *Russky Palomnik*, 1906.

much like that of our Lord and Savior Jesus Christ that all who came
in contact with him were touched by God's grace and divine life of love.
This great lover of peace was even able to resolve political difficulties
and differences among the various governors and princes throughout
Russia; several times Archbishop Cyprian called him to Moscow to solve
and pacify these political struggles. And as a result of his spiritual
guidance and example, Blessed Prince Michael, in his later years,
abdicated the throne and chose the totally devoted monastic life, being
tonsured Monk Matthew and spending his remaining years in Zheltikov
Monastery. This virtuous saint of Serbian descent was truly one of the
great Church leaders from all walks of life in the Russian Church in the
second half of the fourteenth century.

The blessed repose of St. Arsenius took place during Great Lent,
1409. On the Sunday of Orthodoxy Arsenius gave his last sermon in
the Cathedral of the Transfiguration in Tver, calling upon all to remain

217

firm in the Faith and *to guard the inheritance* which our Lord and Savior Jesus Christ had entrusted to them. On Thursday of the Second Week of Great Lent, he became grievously ill; and the following night, March 2, 1409, at age 55 the blessed archpastor fell asleep in the Lord, ascending the heavenly ladder to the mansions of the righteous. The following day, his holy body and relics were taken from the Cathedral in Tver to his Monastery in Zheltikov where the burial service was held. He was honorably laid to rest in the tomb he had dug himself next to the main Church of the Dormition of the Theotokos.

As many pious faithful came from near and far to venerate his body and relics, a sweet fragrance and myrrh exuded from his crypt, a true sign expressing his incorruptibility in the grace and divine life of the Holy Trinity. Many miracles were reported after his repose. Here is the report of the official canonization found in the "Miracle Scrolls" of Zheltikov Monastery: "In 1483, seventy-four years after his death, Bishop Basil of Tver, by the decree of Tsar John Vasilievich, had the crypt of St. Arsenius transferred from Zheltikov Monastery to the Cathedral in Tver where many pious faithful could venerate him and receive healings and blessings. Upon opening the crypt, the body was found completely intact, sweet-smelling and aglow. At this time the Divine Services and hymns were composed, and his feastday—March 2nd— was officially established by the Church of Russia, as well as by the entire Orthodox Church.

St. Arsenius was known for his miracles. On a silver reliquary there are seven depictions of his miracles. First, the resurrection of a fisherman, Tirentius. The second is a depiction of the deliverance of the son of John Kartash; third is the healing of Archpriest Alexis, who suffered from bad legs. The fourth is the healing of virgin Justina Golovenka. Fifth, the saving of a strangled man; sixth, a miracle from the shroud of the Saint. And the seventh, the delivery from madness of Gregory and his wife.

In the manuscript collection of miracles, one is no less wondrous than the next. In 1637, when the Cathedral was renovated, the relics of the Saint were temporarily brought out and place in the Church of Anthony and Theodosius. At that time a certain monk, Sabbatius once entered that church in an unsober state, and fell asleep near the reliquary of the Saint, thus performing an act of sinful disrespect to it. Suddenly he felt someone waking him up. Opening his eyes he saw a bright light in church that came from the sepulchre and on top of it the Saint was sitting. Sabbatius, in horror, attempted to flee. But suddenly he heard from the sepulchre a voice saying, "O unworthy monk, how dare you enter church in a drunken state?" In the morning, they found the monk barely alive. He was sick for a long time and then, confessing to the abbot his sin, told everyone, adding how he was healed and that people should have piety.

"O Holy Father Arsenius, thou didst demonstrate that the only purpose and reason for existence is to love the Lord God and to humbly serve our neighbor with our whole heart. Pray to Christ our true God that we, miserable and helpless sinners, may receive His life, comfort and love, so as to manifest His humility in our lives, to Whom belongs glory, honor and worship, together with His unoriginate Father, and the Life-giving Spirit, now and ever and unto ages of ages. Amen."

KONTAKION

Tone 2

Nourishing thy spiritual children with the food of thy words, O God-bearing Arsenius,* and praising with thy tongue,* making songs with thy lips and preaching,* thou didst cry: O Christ, Thou art the Light inexpressible.

St. Nikolai of Žiča

TROPARION, Tone 4

Thy righteous acts have revealed thee to thy flock* as a model of faith, a reflection of humility* and a teacher of abstinence, O Holy Father Nikolai;* therefore, through humility thou hast obtained exaltation and through poverty, riches;* pray to Christ God to save our souls.

LIFE OF OUR HOLY FATHER

NIKOLAI
"THE NEW CHRYSOSTOM"
BISHOP OF OCHRID AND ZHICHA
(†1956)

Beloved, even if we should attain the very pinnacle
of virtue, let us consider ourselves least of all,
as we have learned that pride is able to cast down
even from the heavens the person who does not take heed,
and humility of mind is able to bring up on High
from the very abyss of sin the person who knows how
to be sober. For this is what placed the Publican before
the Pharisee. By pride I mean an overwhelming
boastful spirit, surpassing even incorporeal powers,
that of the devil himself; while humility of mind
and acknowledgment of sins by the robber is
what brought him into Paradise before the Apostles.
St. John Chrysostom

OUR HOLY AND GOD-BEARING FATHER, Bishop Nikolai, was born at dawn on December 23, 1880, on the feast of St. Naum of Ochrid, to pious Orthodox parents, Dragomir and Katarina Velimirovich, in the small village of Lelich, only five miles southwest of Valjevo, a city located in the valley of the Povlen Mountains of western

Serbia. Because he was born physically weak, this divine child of God was baptized soon after his birth. He was given the name Nikolai, after his family's *Krsna Slav* (family patron saint), "Sveti Nikola" (St. Nicholas of Myra, Lycia). Nikola was the first-born of Dragomir and Katarina, who had eight other children, all of whom unfortunately perished later during World War II. The baptism of young Nikola took place in Chelije Monastery, and was performed by beloved "Pop Andrija" (Fr. Andrew), the parish priest in Lelich.

Nikola's parents were pious farmers who always interrupted their work schedule for daily prayer, which included keeping the yearly fasting routine as well as the liturgical cycle of the Church. His mother Katarina, quite pious and truly a holy woman, provided Nikola with his first lessons about God, Jesus Christ, the lives of the saints, and the holy days of the Church year. Often Nikola was seen being led by the hand of his mother to Chelije Monastery—a walk of three miles—for prayer and Holy Communion. Later Nikola (as Bishop Nikolai) recalled these lessons on God and "walks with my mother" as being some of the most influential experiences in his life. He wrote of them in an autobiographical poem entitled "Prayers of a Captive in Prison" (1952).

Nikola's formal education began in Chelije Monastery, dedicated to the Holy Archangels Michael and Gabriel, where his father Dragomir had hoped he "would learn to read the call to service from the government," in order to be a leading man and protector of his village Lelich. "Pop Andrija" taught "mali Nikola" (Little Nicky), as he was known in Lelich, his first lessons in reading, writing and mathematics. Besides these lessons, Fr. Andrew, being Nikola's spiritual father, taught him about the Scriptures and the teachings of the early Fathers of the Church, as well as his heritage. This latter education was inspiring to little Nicky from the very beginning. He demonstrated, even as a youngster, a tremendously penetrating mind and a zeal for learning. Quite often during summer breaks Nikola would climb the bell tower of the catholicon (main church) of Chelije Monastery and hide there all day long, occupying himself with prayer and the reading of books.

Above: Bishop Nikolai with
his mother Katarina in front
of his hometown church,
Lelich, 1932

At right: Nikola as a student
in Berne, Switzerland,
1907-8.

Thus, due to the influence of his mother Katarina and the lessons of beloved Pop Andrija, Nikola seemed headed for far more than just being a leading citizen of his small village of Lelich.

After finishing sixth grade in grammar school in Valjevo, Nikola petitioned for entrance into the Military Academy. However, he could not pass the physical exam, as he was, in the words of the physical fitness commission, "too small, not having large enough shoulders and a frame strong enough for such activities." This was certainly the divine will of our Heavenly Father, Who desired that Nikola travel on another path—to be a soldier of the Heavenly Kingdom and not of the earthly one. Immediately thereafter, Nikola applied for entrance into the Seminary of St. Sava in Belgrade, where he was accepted to begin studies as a seminarian. Besides studying the usual subjects, Nikola began reading the significant texts of the most famous writers of western and eastern European culture: Shakespeare, Voltaire, Nietzsche, Marx, Pushkin, Tolstoy, Dostoevsky, and others. His favorite author was without a doubt the Montenegrin Peter Njegosh, whose writings he had been reading since his early school days in Valjevo. His final examination for seminary studies was a discourse on the poetry and thought of Njegosh. This discussion, held in 1902 in Rakovitsa Monastery, located just ten miles south of Belgrade, amazed not only his fellow students, but even his professors and instructors as well.

Life was difficult for Nikola during his years as a seminarian in Belgrade. Due to his poor eating habits and the terrible living conditions of the seminary's housing facilities, Nikola contracted scrofulosis, a disease affecting the body's glands. After his seminary days, Nikola taught for a short while in the villages of Drachich and Leskovac, as well as in Valjevo. In Valjevo, he befriended Fr. Sava Popovich, whom he helped in parish activities and from whom he "learned the ropes" of being involved with the faithful on an everyday basis. During summer breaks, at the advice of his doctor, Nikola spent time on the sea coast. It was during these "resting times" that he wrote the life of Bokel the Montenegrin and Dalmatian. Also at this time, Nikola founded a newspaper, "Chrischanski Vesnik" (Christian News), in which appeared his first writings and articles.

In 1905, due to his astute knowledge and evangelical activities, Nikola was chosen, along with several other students, to continue studies in Russia or Western Europe. Nikola chose to study in Europe, in the Old Roman Catholic Theological Faculty at the University of Berne, Switzerland. Besides studies in Berne, Nikola studied in Germany, England, and later in Russia. He was exposed to the finest education Western Europe had to offer. He even became knowledgeable in the spiritual and philosophical books of ancient India. This learning made Nikola into a "Renaissance man," whose erudition and profundity of thought were considered by everyone as both a wellspring of knowledge and a unique treasury of wisdom and spirituality. In 1908, Nikola received his Doctorate in Theology in Berne, with the dissertation entitled "Faith in the Resurrection of Christ as the Foundation of the Dogmas of the Apostolic Church." This original work was written in German, published in Switzerland, and later translated into Serbian. In the following year, 1909, this veritable genius, at age twenty-nine, prepared his Doctorate in Philosophy at Oxford, England; and during the summer of that same year, in Geneva, Switzerland, Nikola wrote his second doctoral dissertation entitled "The Philosophy of Berkeley," in French.

In the fall of 1909, Nikola returned home from Europe and became grievously ill with dysentery. This illness changed his life. Like the great theologian of the early Church, St. Gregory of Nazianzus (†390), whose life was also dramatically changed due to a personal difficulty,[1] Nikola decided to apply all his gifts and talents in service to God and His holy Church. Lying in the hospital for over two months, Nikola prayed in his heart, saying, "If my service to the Lord is needed, He will save me."

---

1. St. Gregory of Nazianzus' life was dramatically changed after the boat in which he was traveling from Athens to Cappadocia (Asia Minor) was wrecked in the Aegean Sea. He then vowed, if God desired him to be saved, to place all his talents in service of the Lord Jesus Christ and His Church.

He then vowed that if he returned to health he would become a monk and serve God's people in His Church. Thus as a Doctor in Theology and Philosophy, Nikola became the lowly monk Nikolai. After his tonsure into the monastic ranks, Monk Nikolai was ordained to the priesthood on the same day, December 20, 1909, in Rakovitsa Monastery. Hieromonk Nikolai now placed his entire being—his knowledge and all his talents—in the service of God and His Serbian Orthodox people; and within a short period of time, pious Fr. Nikolai was elevated to the rank of Archimandrite.

After his tonsure and ordination, Archimandrite Nikolai was chosen to be a teacher in the Seminary of St. Sava in Belgrade. However, it was discovered that he had not completed the final two years of gymnasium (grammar school), the seventh and eighth grades; he had to take a test in order to fulfill these requirements which would in turn validate his status as a teacher. The commission before whom Fr. Nikolai spoke was amazed with his wealth of insight. According to the words of one of its members, "Listening to his discourse on Christ, we were astonished, as no one could ask him one question or even say one word in reply." Yet it was decided that before Fr. Nikolai could become a teacher in the Seminary, he would be sent, with the blessing of Metropolitan Demetrius of Serbia, to Russia. Spending over a year in Russia, Archimandrite Nikolai learned of the passionate Russian spirit and of the rich Orthodox soul of the peasantry. It was during this time that Blessed Nikolai wrote his first great work—*The Religion of Njegosh*. One of the contemporary critics said of this work that "from a religious-philosophical point of view, or a religiously critical point of view, the young seminary professor [Fr. Nikolai] is no less interesting than the Bishop of Cetinje [Njegosh]."

Returning to Belgrade as a seminary professor, Nikolai published, in 1912, an anthology of homilies entitled *Besede Pod Gorom (Sermons at the Foot of the Mount)*. Explaining the title, the humble Nikolai wrote, "Christ spoke on the Mount; I dare to speak only at the foot of the Mount." In 1914 Fr. Nikolai wrote the book *Iznad Greha i Smrti*

Monastery on Ochrid Lake.

Bitol Seminary students with instructors: Archbishop John Maximovitch and Fr. Justin Popovich in center, 1933.

(Beyond Sin and Death), a writing of immense profundity yet with the ability to reach the soul of the common person. Nikolai was most inspiring to his students. Under his spiritual influence and guidance, many went on to become monks, clergy and theologians. One of them, Justin Popovich, a spiritual disciple of Fr. Nikolai, became one of the greatest theologians in the history of the Serbian Church (see March 25th). Thus, besides teaching philosophy, logic, history, and foreign languages in Belgrade, Rev. Dr. Nikolai Velimirovich was fast becoming a great Serbian literary figure as well as a beloved spiritual pastor; soon he would become a well-respected international figure as well.

With the outbreak of World War I in the summer of 1914, the entire Balkan peninsula was thrown into turmoil. The imperiled Serbian nation badly needed a leader to help them survive this international crisis. To this end, Archimandrite Nikolai was called to embark upon an official diplomatic mission to England in order to obtain support from the British government for the suffering Serbian people. Having received a doctorate from Oxford, Nikolai was received with honor and dignity by the British authorities. His political astuteness was revealed in several lectures and homilies delivered in England, which not only invoked a profound concern for the suppressed Serbs, but also addressed the issue of world peace and the methods to attain such a political ideal. Besides receiving British support for the Serbs, Nikolai was also personally awarded a Doctorate of Divinity—*honoris causa*—from Cambridge University. His short tracts, "The Lord's Commandments" and "Meditations on the Lord's Prayer," electrified the Church of England, and also shattered many false conceptions of what the Orthodox faith entailed.

In the late summer of 1915, Archimandrite Nikolai continued his "war mission" by traveling across the Atlantic Ocean to New York City, America. His mission was to rally the emigrant Serbs, Croats, and Slovenes against the Austrian government, for the majority of them had fled to America. His mission was quite successful, as America sent over 20,000 freedom-loving Slavic volunteers—called "the Third Army of

Bishop Nikolai," most of whom fought on the Salonican Front—and hundreds of thousands of dollars worth of aid to their suffering brothers and sisters in the homeland. This trip was also quite revelatory for Nikolai: in a dream he received a message from an Angel of the Lord, who revealed to him that he would someday return to America and help organize the fledgling Serbian Orthodox communities .

In early 1916 Nikolai returned to his beloved England, where he decided to sojourn until the end of the war. He continued his literary activities by writing several articles and books: *The Religious Spirit of the Slavs* (1916, sent to the soldiers in the homeland); *Serbia in Light and Darkness* (1916); *The Serbian Soul, The Agony of the Church, The Serbian Orthodox Church,* and *The Spiritual Rebirth of Europe* (all in 1917). Oriented towards a British audience, these essays and books appealed to their sense of justice for suffering Serbia. In particular, *The Spiritual Rebirth of Europe* was of great interest to the Anglicans, for it promoted the possibility of a return of the Anglican Church to her rightful mother, the Orthodox Church. As a result of his academic excellence, Nikolai received another Honorary Doctorate of Divinity, in 1919, from the University of Glasglow in Scotland.

Feeling tremendously homesick, the patriotic Nikolai returned to Belgrade toward the end of the war. He then became involved in the formation of the new Yugoslav state as the interpreter for the then President of the government, Nikola Pashich. Yet Nikolai felt that there was something missing in his life. He wanted to be involved with his suffering people on a more daily basis. The fulfillment of this yearning came quickly: on March 12, 1919, the Holy Synod of the Serbian Orthodox Church selected Fr. Nikolai, at age 39, as the new Bishop of Zhicha, the historical seat of the First Archbishopric of Serbia. During his episcopal consecration, Blessed Nikolai wept as a newborn babe in the Lord. Thus after four years of seeking support from England and America in behalf of Serbia, Bishop Nikolai was now ready to personally help in healing the war-torn hearts and souls of his beloved people.

For two years (1919-1921), Bishop Nikolai spiritually soothed pious Serbs not only in the Diocese of Zhicha, but also throughout newly formed Yugoslavia. Like the Lord and Savior Jesus Christ, Archpastor Nikolai "healed the sick, set free the spiritually captive and preached salvation" to these humble souls. In 1921, Bishop Nikolai was transferred to the Diocese of Ochrid and Bitola. This was done to facilitate the union of the Serbian and Macedonian Churches which occurred as a result of the formation of the kingdom of Yugoslavia. Blessed Father Nikolai, always a man of unity, peacefully engaged in the union of the Serbs and Macedonians of these regions. Besides sowing seeds of unity in his diocese, Nikolai also visited Athens, Constantinople, and the Holy Mountain, where he was received as a unifier of all Orthodox in the bond of love for Christ and His Church. During this time Nikolai wrote two books: *Rechi O Svechoveku (Orations on the Universal Man*, 1920) and *Molitve Na Jezeru (Prayers at the Lake*, 1921). This latter work, written during his resting periods at Lake Ochrid, was in poetic-prose style, so deep and profound, similar in spirituality to the great Psalms of David. Yet Bishop Nikolai was not destined to stay in his homeland. Like a "beacon set upon a hill," his divine radiance was seen from afar, as he was invited to deliver lectures at various universities and Anglican Churches in America. At first, the Royal Government of the kingdom of Yugoslavia as well as the Holy Synod of Bishops refused these requests for Bishop Nikolai; but the invitations kept coming, so that in the end they both resolved to send beloved Nikolai to America for a second time.

On June 24, 1921, Blessed Bishop Nikolai arrived in New York City. He had three immediate goals while in America: 1) to deliver lectures and homilies in universities and churches with the purpose of presenting World War I from the Eastern European viewpoint; 2) to collect funds for the setting up of orphanages in Serbia for those poor children who lost parents and relatives during World War I; and 3) to visit many Serbian Orthodox communities in order to thank them for their patriotic war efforts, along with making a report on the possibility of creating an American Serbian Church.

The brilliant Bishop Nikolai was successful in all three phases of his mission. He delivered approximately 150 lectures and homilies in the following three months. He spoke at a variety of places including Columbia University in New York City, various Serbian communities, and even the African American Congregation of St. Philip in Harlem, New York, to over 1,500 parishioners. Wherever he spoke concerning the past World War, his message was clear. Do not blame the (Eastern) European peasant for the war, he proposed, but rather, look to the artificially created intellectual class of the European university system. He wrote, "The European peasant is a noble spirit, but it is the intellectuals in charge of the peasants who are on the wrong track." Nikolai said that if these conditions in Western Europe continued, a second world war was likely to happen. And how right he was. One of his most enlightening sermons was delivered on the Sunday after Ascension, 1921, in the Episcopalian Cathedral of St. John the Divine in New York City, entitled "The Stone which the Builders Rejected" (Matt. 21:42), in which he called for a return on the part of Western Europe to the true source and rock of their entire culture and civilization, to the Lord and Savior Jesus Christ, *the way, the truth, and the life.*

Nikolai also proposed that America, such a rich multi-national country, could possibly hold high the torch of hope for all of humanity. "The world has become small, but it waits to be proclaimed a united being. Europe has discovered the world. Can America organize it?" proclaimed Nikolai time and time again, with the hope that America would lead the way to a peaceful and just world for all. As a result of these speeches, Nikolai was called a "second Isaiah" and a "New Chrysostom" of our times; furthermore, his activities helped in obtaining acceptance of Yugoslavia into the League of Nations.

Concerning the development of orphanages for suffering Serbians both in the United States and Yugoslavia, Nikolai was motivated by the commandments of the Lord Jesus Christ: *Let the children come unto Me, and do not hinder them; for of such is the Kingdom of Heaven.... Take heed that ye despise not one of these little ones; for I say unto you, That in heaven their angels do always behold the face of my Father which is in heaven* (Matt. 18:10). *Come unto me, all ye that labor and are heavy laden, and I will give you rest...For my yoke is easy, and my burden is light* (Matt. 11:28, 30). *For I was an hungered, and ye gave me meat: I was thirsty, and ye gave me drink: I was a stranger and ye took me in: Naked, and ye clothed me. I was sick, and ye visited me: I was in prison, and ye came unto me.... Verily...inasmuch as ye have done it unto one of the least of these my brethren, ye have done it unto me* (Matt. 25:35-36, 40). Nikolai felt the pain of the loss of beloved ones so acutely that he often broke into tears upon visiting orphans and the poor in his homeland. Prior to coming to America he set up an orphanage in Bitola, placing at its head the exiled Abbess Anna—previously known as the social worker Nada Adjich—in Vrachevshina Monastery. To the poor children in Yugoslavia, Bishop Nikolai became known as "Deda Vladika" (Grandfather Bishop), as one who really cared and "practiced what he preached" to alleviate their plight and difficulties. As head of the Council of Serbian Child Welfare in Belgrade, Nikolai, while in America, secured thousands of dollars for the cause of taking care of "these little ones." With this money he personally organized and supervised orphanages in Kraljevo, Chachak, Gornji Milanovac and Kragujevac, where over 600 poor children were granted the love of Christ in action.

Finally, concerning the creation of an American Diocese of the Serbian Orthodox Church, Bishop Nikolai wrote a Paschal Epistle in 1921 to all the Serbian parishes in America. Nikolai, being the first Serbian hierarch ever to travel in America, was greeted with utmost respect upon visiting the Serbian communities. The problems of the Serbs in America were many: they were often pastored by Russian priests who did not understand their language; there were no monasteries to lead the people in the spiritual life; there was no seminary for education of clergy and the faithful; mixed marriages created confusion among the faithful; schisms in leadership among all Orthodox in America; hetero-

Bishop Nikolai Velimirovich in 1930

dox church practices, as well as secularism, were creeping into the life of the churches.

Bishop Nikolai returned to Belgrade on June 16, 1921, after six months of missionary activities in America. When he left, the American Serbians mourned the loss; but they all hoped that he would return as their new Bishop of the American Serbs. Yet this was not the will of the Lord. Ten days later, on June 26th, he gave his report on the American situation in a session of the Synod of Bishops held in Sremski Karlovac; and on September 21st, Metropolitan Varnava nominated Bishop Nikolai to assume the duties of Bishop of America, with Archimandrite Mardarius Uskokovich of Rakovitsa Monastery (south of Belgrade) as his administrative assistant. This decision upset many pious people in the homeland, as none of them were ready to relinquish their beloved "New Chrysostom". Somewhat frustrated over this situation, in January 1922, Bishop Nikolai went on a pilgrimage to the Holy Land, then traveled to the Holy Mountain, to Hilandar Monastery, to spend Pascha with the monks there. This sojourn was a spiritual necessity for Bishop Nikolai, as he retreated from the pressing problems and sought counsel from his Heavenly Father.

Upon his return for the gathering of the Synod of Bishops, Nikolai was convinced that the American situation needed a full-time bishop to carry out the ecclesiastical plans which the Angel of the Lord had previously revealed to him in his dream. Thus, he himself nominated Archimandrite Mardarije Uskokovich to be the future first permanent Serbian Bishop in America. This nomination was confirmed by the entire Synod of Bishops, and on October 18, 1923, Archimandrite Mardarius was appointed the sole administrator of the Serbian Church in America. This decision relieved Bishop Nikolai from some of his many duties. He was now able to devote himself fully to writing inspiring works as well as pastoring his faithful to be more fully immersed in the love of Jesus Christ and His Church. In 1923, Nikolai wrote *Nove Besede Pod Gorm (New Sermons at the Foot of the Mount)*, *Misli o Dobru i Zlu (Thoughts on Good and Evil)*, and a lengthy work

St. Sava Serbian Orthodox Monastery, Libertyville, Illinois.

Holy Trinity Monastery
near Jordanville, New York.

Bishop Mardarius Uskokovich

entitled, *Omilije na Nedeljna i Praznichna Evandjelja (Homilies on the Sunday and Festal Gospels)*.

Besides writing, Nikolai began a popular religious movement, later affectionately called *Bogomoljacki Pokret* (Movement of God-Prayers). The venerable Bishop's disciples loved to gather at his episcopal residence to sing the very moving and edifying songs he had written. Praising the Lord in their own tongue was a joy and delight to these zealous Serbs. The once-maligned Serbian Christians experienced in Nikolai an evangelical freshness which renewed their spirits after the war and which allowed them to once again be fully immersed in the love of Jesus Christ. By praying to the Lord in the vernacular Serbian, these Serbs desirous of a fuller Christian life were able to be built up into a people of God with the God-praising Nikolai leading the way. There were many priests who were jealous of Nikolai's "Bogomoljacki Pokret," but as they began to experience the spiritual growth among their parishioners, they slowly supported this prayer movement. These zealots—by their constant reading of the Scriptures, singing of spiritual songs, quickness of prayer, travels from monastery to monastery, regular confession of their sins, keeping of the fasts, and frequent communing of the Precious Body and Blood of Jesus Christ—began to slowly transform the clergy. Bishop Nikolai, a master at pastoring his people, allowed his passionate God-seekers to lead the way in renewing the Serbian Church. Through this prayer movement, monasticism was revitalized as well as the study of theology, as was clearly evidenced, for example, in the life of the great theologian and ascetic, St. Justin Popovich (see March 25th).

In 1927, at the invitation of the American Yugoslav Society, the Institute of Politics in Williamstown, Massachusetts, and the Carnegie Endowment for International Peace, Bishop Nikolai once again traveled to America for his third visit. He spent only three months in America, speaking at various universities and churches as well as inquiring into the progress of the St. Sava Serbian Orthodox Monastery in Libertyville, Illinois, under the direction of newly consecrated Bishop Mardarius.

On his way home, Nikolai stopped in London where he stayed for two weeks, prophesying that an impending catastrophe was threatening Europe. The prophet Nikolai, a man rooted in the present with a clear vision of the future, was a "voice crying in the wilderness" to a people in search of hope for a peaceful future. His message was clear: *Repent, for the Kingdom of God is at hand!*

Returning to Ochrid, the venerable bishop began writing once again. It seemed as though his sojourns in foreign lands filled his mind and heart—his total being—with restless divine thoughts of the promised Eternal Paradise; and the only way to relieve himself of these majestic longings was to write of them. In 1928 he wrote *Vera Obrazovanih Ljudi (The Faith of Educated People), Rat i Biblija (War and the Bible)* and *Ochridski Prolog (The Prologue of Ochrid)*. This latter book, over 1,000 pages, was patterned after ancient hagiographical literature which included both brief Lives and edifying incidents from the lives of holy men and women, as well as ordinary sinners. Also entitled *Zhitije Svetih (The Lives of the Saints)*, this text was based upon the daily calendar of Orthodox saints. Translated into English in 1985, *The Prologue of Ochrid* has become a spiritual classic to all Christians living in the West. The Bishop of Montenegro, Amphilocius Radovich, a disciple of Nikolai, once said that "the only two books one needs to digest and put into practice to obtain salvation are the Bible and *The Prologue of Ochrid.*"

In the town of Bitola in Bishop Nikolai's diocese was the Serbian Seminary of St. John the Theologian. From 1929 to 1934, one of the theology instructors there was the young Hieromonk John Maximovitch, the future Archbishop John. Bishop Nikolai valued and loved Fr. John, and exerted a beneficial influence upon him. More than once he was heard to say, "If you wish to see a living saint, go to Bitola to Fr. John." The lives of Bishop Nikolai and Fr. John would one day parallel each other: both of them would spend the last years of their lives in America and die there, and both would be canonized as saints.

In early 1930, Bishop Nikolai participated in the Pan-Orthodox Conference held at Vatopedi Monastery on the Holy Mountain. It can be said that Bishop Nikolai was "the Voice of Orthodoxy" during this time, as he was not only able to lead pious Orthodox Greeks, Serbs, Russians, and Bulgarians to transcend any nationalistic tendencies which might threaten the bond of love and unity of spirit among them; but also, perhaps more importantly, the venerable bishop, by his ability to abstract the true Tradition from all local traditions, was able to present to Western Christians in a precise and comprehensive manner the true and eternal faith of the One, Holy, Catholic and Apostolic Church.

Prior to World War II, Nikolai wrote *Simvoli i Signali (Symbols and Signs,* 1932) and *Nomologija (Nomology,* i.e., *The Science of Law,* 1940); and in 1937 until the outbreak of war in 1941, Nikolai began a compilation of his letters entitled, *Misionarska Pisma (Missionary Letters).* This anthology of hundreds of letters witnessed to the amazing evangelical activity of Bishop Nikolai, as he was uniquely attuned to the spiritual crises of these perilous times.

In 1941, with the German occupation of Yugoslavia, Bishop Nikolai, together with Patriarch Gabriel Dozhich, was arrested and sentenced to imprisonment in the infamous Dachau Prison Camp in Germany. He spent two years in Dachau, witnessing and suffering some of the cruelest torture of human beings the world has ever known. Nikolai attributed his survival of this terrible ordeal to the Theotokos. While in prison, he wrote *Molbeni Kanon i Molitva Presvetoj Bogorodici (Petitionary Canon and Prayers to the Most Holy Mother of God),* along with *Tri Molitve u Senci Nemachkih Bajoneta (Three Prayers in the Shadow of the German Bayonets)* which reads as a spiritual diary of his captive years. On May 8, 1945, as a result of the freedom secured by the 36th American Division of the Allied Forces, holy confessors Nikolai and Gabriel were released from prison. They both then sought sanctuary in England. Afterwards, the confessor Gabriel returned to Belgrade as Patriarch, while the confessor Nikolai moved on to America for the

Bishop Nikolai arrested by the Germans, Zhicha Monastery, 1941.

fourth and final time. After recuperating from back and leg problems, the exiled Bishop began lecturing, as usual, in various educational institutions. In June 1946, he was awarded for his academic excellence his final Doctorate of Sacred Theology from Columbia University. In all, Bishop Nikolai obtained five doctorates.

From 1946-1949, Venerable Nikolai taught at the St. Sava Seminary in Libertyville, Illinois. Realizing the need for American-born Serbians to have an Orthodox catechism in English, he published *The Faith of the Saints* (1949). In 1950, he wrote an essay on Orthodox mysticism in English, *The Universe as Signs and Symbols,* and a book in Serbian entitled, *Zemlja Nedodjia (The Unattainable Land)*. In 1951, his last book written while teaching at St. Sava's was, fittingly, *The Life of St. Sava*. According to the words of the distinguished professor Dr. Veselin Kesich, "this book reveals something about [Bishop Nikolai] himself in his meditation on the end of St. Sava's Life: 'Sava withdrew to his House of Silence in Studenitsa and offered a prayer to God to let him die in a foreign country.' Why did he pray for this? Bishop Nikolai considers several reasons: Sava's protest against political disorder at home, his appeal to the conscience of his people, and his conviction that he would work for their salvation from the outside. These three reasons probably influenced the Bishop's decision to come to America and not to return to Yugoslavia after the war."

In 1951, beloved Bishop Nikolai moved to St. Tikhon's Russian Orthodox Monastery in South Canaan, Pennsylvania. Here he spent the last five years of his earthly life as a professor, dean, and eventually rector of the Seminary, as well as an elder to the monastics at St. Tikhon's Monastery. To the students of the Seminary, the old Bishop was a loving father figure whom they would never forget. To the laity and faithful of the monastery parish, as well as all who came in contact with the Bishop, he was a hierarch in whom they saw manifest the grace of God. Being all things to all people, Nikolai published articles in Russian for the God-seekers at St. Tikhon's, but taught solely in the English language, at a time when very few courses were taught in that language.

Bishop Nikolai at St. Tikhon's Seminary.

Below: With the Rector, professors and students.

For him, "class" could be any time. Anything said to him could be turned around and assigned a deeper meaning. For example, one day, in class a student mentioned the fact that it was such a terribly dismal day because of the rain. Bishop Nikolai walked over to the window, looked out, and expounded on the further dimensions of rain, from Noah to the present time: "What is rain? It is like Christ Who was also sent by the Father from Heaven to water a thirsty earth."

His ease and facility with languages was amazing to all. Nikolai could read, write, and speak fluently seven different languages. Besides his activities at St. Tikhon's, he lectured at St. Vladimir's Seminary in Crestwood, New York, as well as at the Russian Orthodox Seminary and Monastery of the Holy Trinity in Jordanville, New York. Yet he did not forget his Serbian flock, as he published, in 1952, *Zhetve Gospodnje (The Harvests of the Lord)* and *Kasijana (Cassiana)*, a story of a penitent. In 1953, he wrote *Divan (Conversations)*, a book on the *Bogomoljci* and their miracles. His final book, *Jedini Chovekoljubac (The Only Love of Mankind)* was published posthumously in 1958. Bishop Nikolai's final undertaking was the Serbian Bible Institute, which published a series of seven short tracts on various theological topics: "Christ Died for Us," "Meditations on Seven Days," "Angels Our Elder Brethren," "Seven Petitions," "Bible and Power," "Missionary Letters," and "The Mystery of Touch."

Our holy and God-bearing Father Bishop Nikolai fell asleep in the Lord on Sunday, March 18th, 1956, in his humble cell at St. Tikhon's Russian Orthodox Seminary. As related by the late Abbot Afanasy, "The Bishop served the Holy Liturgy on Saturday, March 17. Everything was unusually beautiful. Following the service, he went to the monks' dining room. After a short talk, with a low bow, three times he humbly muttered, 'Forgive me, brothers,' as he was leaving. This was something special, for he never did that before...."[2] That Sunday morning, the late Fr. Vasily went down to Bishop Nikolai's room at the Seminary, and upon knocking at the door, received no answer. Opening it, he found

---

2. From *The Tikhonaire* for 1986 and 1988.

ST. NIKOLAI VELIMIROVICH

the Bishop dead, stretched out on the floor in a kneeling position. In all probability, he had died between seven and eight that morning. He was 76 years old. He was given an honorable Orthodox Christian burial service in St. Sava Serbian Orthodox Cathedral in New York City, as pious Christians from all parts of the world came to hear eulogies in honor of one of the greatest hierarchs of the entire Orthodox Church in the twentieth century. From New York City his life-giving body was transferred to Libertyville, Illinois, just north of Chicago, to St. Sava Serbian Orthodox Monastery, where more *Pomeni* (memorial services) were held. He was laid to rest on the south side of the Monastery church, on March 27, 1956.

Like St. Sava, the Enlightener of Serbia, holy Bishop Nikolai died in a foreign land. Behind the main church of Chelije Monastery in his home village of Lelich, next to the grave of Archimandrite Justin Popovich (†1979), was marked a place for his return to the homeland and the people he so very much loved. Thus, on April 27, 1991, after twenty-five years of repose in the Lord in America, holy Bishop Nikolai's body was returned to his homeland in western Serbia. Pious American Orthodox, particularly many Russian Orthodox, did not forget the blessed Nikolai, as at St. Tikhon's Monastery his room was made into a shrine for prayer and meditation. His beloved disciple, Justin Popovich, wrote these words in 1961, at the fifth anniversary of Blessed Nikolai's repose in the Lord: "Thank you, Lord—in him we have a new Apostle! Thank you, Lord—in him we have a new Evangelist! Thank you, Lord—in him we have a new Confessor! Thank you, Lord—in him we have a new Martyr! Thank you, Lord—in him we have a new saint!"

"O Holy Father Nikolai, the magnificence of thy glory shines forth for all to see, as thy divine brilliance illumines us all with the superabundant love of Christ the Prince of Peace and Humble Shepherd. Pray to Christ the only Lover of Mankind, O most loving Archshepherd, for us weak and decrepit sinners, that His mind, His brilliance, His care, His energy, His divinity, His strength, His sacrifice, His humility and His

St. Tikhon's Seminary, South Canaan, Pennsylvania, at the time
St. Nikolai was Rector there.

resurrected glory may shine within our hearts so that we may in some
small way spread His love to the ends of the earth, to Whom belongs
glory, honor and worship, together with His Unoriginate Father and
Life-giving Spirit, now and ever and unto ages of ages. Amen."

ANOTHER TROPARION, Tone 8

Loving thy homeland thou didst sojourn as a patriot to secure aid
for God's suffering children,* and as a new Chrysostom thou didst
preach to those in darkness* the rediscovery of the Foundational Rock,
Christ the Lord,* in the eternal homeland of God's Kingdom;* thy
pastoral love for all, O Confessor Nikolai, was purified in captivity by
the godless,* demonstrating thy commitment to the truth and thy
people;* therefore, O venerable hierarch, thou hast attained the crown
of eternal life.

Venerable Justin

of Ćelije

TROPARION, Tone 4

As Orthodox sweetness and divine nectar, Venerable
Father* thou dost flow into the hearts of believers as a
wealth;* by thy life and teachings thou didst reveal thyself to
be a living book of the Spirit, most wise Justin;* therefore
pray to Christ God the Word* that the Word may
dwell in those who honor thee.
*(Composed in Greek by Fr. Athanasius of Simonos Petras
Monastery on the Holy Mountain, May 31, 1979.)*

March 25th

LIFE OF OUR FATHER

JUSTIN

ARCHIMANDRITE OF CHELIJE

(†1979)

> *Holy love has a way of consuming some. This is what is
> meant by one who said,* Thou hast ravished our hearts,
> ravished them *(Song of Songs 4:9). And it makes others
> bright and overjoyed. In this regard it has been said:*
> My heart hath hoped in Him, and I am helped and
> my flesh hath flourished again *(Ps. 27:7). For when the
> heart is cheerful, the face beams (cf. Prov. 15:13), and a
> person flooded with the love of God reveals in his body, as
> if in a mirror, the splendor of his soul, a glory like that of
> Moses when he came face to face with God (cf. Ex. 34:29-35).*
> St. John Climacus

OUR HOLY FATHER JUSTIN, Abbot of Chelije Monastery in
Valjevo, western Serbia, was born to pious and God-fearing parents,
Proto Spyridon and Prontonica Anastasia Popovich, in Vranje, South
Serbia, on the Feast of the Annunciation, March 25, 1894. He was born
into a priestly family, as seven previous generations of the Popoviches
(Popovich in Serbian actually means "family or son of a priest") were
headed by priests. At baptism, he was given the name Blagoje, after the
Feast of the Annunciation *(Blagovest* means Annunciation or Good

News). Being raised in a pious Christian atmosphere, young Blagoje learned quite early of the virtuous life in Christ as dedicated in service to God's holy Church. As a child, he often visited with his parents the Prohor Pchinjski Monastery, dedicated to St. Prohor the Miracle-worker (see Oct. 19th). He witnessed firsthand the miraculous power of the Lord manifested through St. Prohor, as his mother Anastasia was healed of a deadly disease by the Saint's intercessions when Blagoje was still a young boy.

Blagoje was an excellent student in elementary school. His greatest love was for the Bible, and the four Gospels in particular. He began serious reading of the Bible at age fourteen, and throughout the rest of his life he carried the New Testament on his person, reading faithfully three chapters a day. In 1905 after finishing the fourth grade in Vranje, following the tradition of the Popovich family, young Blagoje entered the nine-year program of secular and religious study at the Seminary and Faculty of St. Sava in Belgrade. In the early twentieth century the School of St. Sava in Belgrade was renowned throughout the Orthodox world as a holy place of extreme asceticism as well as of a high quality of scholarship. Some of the well-known professors were the rector, Fr. Domentian; Professors Fr. Dositheus, later a bishop, and Athanasius Popovich, and the great ecclesiastical composer, Stevan Mokranjac. Yet one professor stood head and shoulders above the rest: the then Hieromonk Nikolai Velimirovich, Ph.D (see March 18th). Fr. Nikolai was Blagoje's Father Confessor during his years as a seminarian and became, without a doubt, the single most influential person in his life. From the venerable Nikolai, Blagoje learned of the virtuous ascetic life in Christ the Lord, of the doctrinal genius of the great Fathers of the Church, and of the spiritual and intellectual effort needed to probe the important philosophical and theological questions of the day. In the end, both of these two spiritual geniuses possessed a commonality: tremendously penetrating minds which, being regenerated constantly by their total commitment to Christ the Lord, provided them with a truly Orthodox vision of life, which in turn made them the two greatest voices of the Serbian Orthodox Church in modern times. Both Nikolai and Blagoje, later Monk Justin, sought to "speak the truth in love" to a passing world. They sought the answers to the world's most pressing problems in the teachings of the Scriptures and the Fathers of the Church, and especially in the experiences found in the Lives of the Saints. The saints were for them "living Bibles," "incarnate dogmas," and the true source of Orthodox theology, experiential knowledge of God and existential pedagogical truth valid for all times.

In 1914, at age twenty, Blagoje finished the nine-year program of St. Sava's in Belgrade. At this time he had only one desire in mind: *that I may dwell in the house of the Lord all the days of my life, that I may behold the delight of the Lord, and that I may visit His holy temple* (Ps. 26:4). With this hunger and thirst for righteousness driving him, Blagoje wanted to radically devote his life to Christ in the monastic vocation. However, due to the beginning of World War I in 1914, and the declining health of his parents, Blagoje decided to postpone his entrance into the monastic ranks.

During the early part of World War I, autumn of 1914, Blagoje served as a student nurse primarily in South Serbia—Skadar, Nish, Kosovo, etc. Unfortunately, while in this capacity, he contracted typhus during the winter of 1914 and had to spend over a month in a hospital in Nish. On January 8, 1915, he resumed his duties. It suffices to say that Blagoje and the rest of the aids and nurses, as well as all of the freedom-loving Serbian Christians in South Serbia, suffered bitterly from the effects of war.

On the eve of the Feast of St. Nicholas, his *Krsna Slava* (family patron saint), 1915, Blagoje returned to Skadar in order to visit Metropolitan Demetrius, who later became the first Patriarch after the patriarchal throne was renewed in 1920.[1] Blagoje came in order to petition the Metropolitan to become a monk. Then, on January 1, 1916, Blagoje

---

1. By the decree of Sultan Mustapha II in 1765, the Patriarchate of Serbia was abolished and subordinated to the Patriarch of Constantinople. This throne was re-established in 1920 and moved to Belgrade.

received the monastic tonsure in the church in Skadar, taking the name Justin, after the great Christian philosopher and martyr for Christ, St. Justin the Philosopher (†166). This name was truly a gift and sign from Heaven, for it was as a philosopher and seeker of Christian truth that the humble Monk Justin would later receive glory from God.

Shortly after becoming a monk, Justin, along with several other students who received the Metropolitan's blessing, traveled to Petrograd, Russia, to begin a year's study in the Orthodox Seminary there. It was here that young Monk Justin first dedicated himself more fully to Orthodoxy and the monastic way. He learned of the great ascetics of Russia: Anthony and Theodosius of the Caves in Kiev, Seraphim of Sarov, Sergius of Radonezh, John of Kronstadt, and others. Justin fell in love with Russian spirituality and piety, especially that exhibited by the common folk of the countryside.

After his year's study and sojourn in Russia, Justin entered, by the prompting of his spiritual father Nikolai, the Theological School in Oxford, England. He spent seven semesters at Oxford—November 1916 to May 1919—yet he did not receive a diploma since his doctoral dissertation entitled, "The Philosophy and Religion of Dostoevsky," was not accepted.[2] As a result, Justin returned to Belgrade after the war and became a teacher in the seminary at Karlovac, Srem. At Sremski Karlovac, Justin renewed the ancient study of the Lives of the Saints as being a proper theological focus and most important course of study. It was at this time that he received the calling and vision from God to translate into modern Serbian the entire Lives of the Saints of the Orthodox Church, a feat which to this day is truly astounding. In September of 1919, Justin entered the Greek Orthodox School of Theology in Athens, Greece. He spent two years there to finish his doctoral course work. Just as in Russia, Monk Justin traveled through-

---

2. With all due respect to the venerable theological institution at Oxford, it seems as though at that time after World War I, western theologians were not ready, as they now seem to be, to accept a healthy and correct critique on western thought, theology, and civilization, such as Justin proposed.

Above: Spiyridon and Anastasia Popovich (1930), parents
of Fr. Justin.

At right: Fr. Justin as a young
monastic in Athens Theological School, 1919.

251

out the countryside of Greece, especially benefitting spiritually from the Greek Orthodox heritage commonly known as the Byzantine legacy. In 1920, venerable Justin was ordained deacon and began to experience another side of the Church's liturgical life: leadership of the worship services. As his liturgical and ascetical life increased, Justin matured spiritually and became known throughout all of Greece as a most pious ascetic. At this time, due to his unceasing prayer to the Most Sweet Jesus, Justin was granted by the grace of the Holy Spirit the gift of *umilenije* coupled with tears.[3]

In May 1921, Deacon Justin returned to Sremski Karlovac and resumed his teaching duties at the Seminary. He lectured on the New Testament, Dogmatics, Patristics, and the Lives of the Saints. Prior to each lesson on the Scriptures he opened with this short prayer: "O Most Sweet Lord, by the power of Thy Holy Gospel and through Thy Apostles, teach me and announce through me what I am to say."

One year later, on the Feast of the Beheading of John the Baptist, 1922, Venerable Justin was ordained priest by His Holiness Patriarch Dimitrije. Throughout the ordination service, Justin was in tears, crying as a newborn babe in the Lord. His humility attracted many, as his disciples grew rapidly in number. Not only students, but also many lay people came to him for confession, counsel, and spiritual healing. His most beloved disciples were those pious men and women of the *Bogomoljack Pokret* (Serbian Prayer Movement) originally formed and led by the newly consecrated Bishop Nikolai. The great Bishop Nikolai and the blossoming Fr. Justin were as "living water" to all Christians desirous of a deeper experience of the Church's faith, liturgy, mission, and vision. And Justin, as always, considered Nikolai as the Great Apostle of the twentieth century, as the "New Chrysostom" of his times. These two were as Anthony and Athanasius, and Basil and Gregory of old—"two bodies, yet one mind"—as their love for our Lord Jesus Christ produced much spiritual fruit in the lives of many zealots. Everyone especially enjoyed singing the spiritual songs written by

---

3. For the definition of *umilenije* see note two, p. 122.

Bishop Nikolai. These songs, written in the vernacular language of the people, were not only quite spiritual and edifying, but also were very didactic and doctrinal in nature. And it was this "praising the Lord in the people's language" which inspired Justin to translate into modern Serbian, from the original Greek text, the Divine Liturgy of St. John Chrysostom. Following the scriptural and liturgical tradition of the Church given to the Slavs by the great evangelical missionaries, Cyril and Methodius and their disciples, that is, the tradition of hearing the Word of God and praying in the mother tongue of the people (I Cor. 14:19), both Justin and Nikolai were able by the energy of the Holy Spirit to edify, enlighten, and confirm in Orthodoxy the pious faithful in their own tongue.

The zealous Fr. Justin was also in close contact at this time with two great Russian Orthodox pastors: Metropolitan Anthony Khrapovitsky, who taught at the Seminary in Sremski Karlova, and the exiled Russian Bishop John Maximovitch. Holy Father John, a man of extreme asceticism, was truly a miracle-worker, and his coming later to America—where he reposed in the Lord in San Francisco—became a blessing and visitation from the Lord for those God-seekers there.

In 1923, Fr. Justin became the editor of the Orthodox journal *Christian Life;* and in this journal appeared his first doctoral dissertation, "The Philosophy and Religion of Dostoevsky," for which he was persecuted at Oxford. Three years later, in 1926, his second doctoral dissertation, "The Problem of Person and Knowledge in St. Macarius of Egypt," was published in Greek in Athens. Fr. Justin was now on his way to establishing himself as a modern Father of the Church. For his course on the Lives of the Saints, Justin began to translate into Serbian the Lives of the Saints from the Greek, Syriac and Slavonic sources, as well as numerous minor works of the Fathers—homilies of John Chrysostom, Macarius, and Isaac the Syrian. He also wrote an exquisite book, *The Theory of Knowledge According to St. Isaac.* Justin's blossoming literary genius amazed everyone.

In 1931, after a stint as Professor in the Theological Academy in Prizren, the brilliant Fr. Justin was requested by the Holy Synod in Belgrade to assist Bishop Joseph (Cvijovich) of Bitola in reorganizing the Church of the Carpatho-Russians in Czechoslovakia. This area had been besieged by those espousing Uniatism.[4] Justin, an established defender of the faith, was a great aid to the reorganization of the Orthodox Church of Czechoslovakia. This experience made him realize a tremendous need of the Serbs: to have in their mother tongue an exact and complete exposition of the Orthodox faith. As a result, he began writing, after his return to Bitola in 1932, his monumental work, *The Dogmas of the Orthodox Church,* in three volumes. Volume one, published in late 1932, dealt with the sources and method of theology, the nature of God and the teaching on the Holy Trinity, creation, and divine providence. This volume was so well received that Dr. Justin was chosen, in 1934, as Professor of Dogmatics at the Theological Faculty of St. Sava in Belgrade. One year later, this hard-working writer completed the second volume, entitled, *The God-Man and His Work: Christology and Soteriology.* There is so doubt that these two volumes— and the third and final volume, *Ecclesiology: Teaching on the Church,* published later in 1970—are the most complete and thorough treatment on Orthodox Christian truth available in the world today. Justin's knowledge of Hebrew, Syriac, Greek, Latin, Russian, Romanian, and all western languages, coupled with his most ascetical vision of life, produced for all Christians a magnificent analysis of the ancient faith of the Church.[5]

In 1938, Fr. Justin, along with a number of noted intellectuals of Belgrade, founded the Serbian Philosophical Society. Holy Father Justin

---

4. Uniatism, for most Serbian Orthodox, represents a serious affront and grave violation of Christian love on the part of the Latin Church. Begun officially at the Union of Brest-Litovsk in 1595, it was an attempt of the papacy to absorb into the Latin Church the Eastern Orthodox Churches outside her fold.

5. Unfortunately, these volumes have not yet been translated into a western language; but when they are translated, they will no doubt be considered as "sources of living water" and theological classics.

A portrait of St. Justin as he was most remembered.

began at this time to probe the philosophical and world issues of his day. His penetrating mind was fully displayed in two books: *The Foundations of Theology* (1939) and *Dostoevsky on Europe and Slavism* (1940). Both of these works dealt with the nature and method of theology, and the spirit and vision of western civilization. Fr. Justin was never fearful of telling the truth concerning the fallen state of human-kind and, particularly, the follies of Western European religious and secular life.

Fr. Justin remained in the capacity of Professor of Dogmatics in Belgrade until the end of World War II. Within the perspective of the newly established communist and atheistic regime, the likes of a zealous Christian such as Fr. Justin, who was now beginning to convert the intellectuals to faith in Jesus Christ, had no place. He, along with several other teachers, was ousted from the university system in Belgrade and told never to return. Thus ended the university teaching career in Belgrade of the great Rev. Dr. Justin Popovich.

For two years after his exile from Belgrade, the ascetic Justin lived in several monasteries in Serbia—Kalenich, Ovchar, Sukovo, and Ravanitsa—and on May 14, 1948, he entered Chelije Monastery near the village of Lelich,[6] only a few miles from the major town of Valjevo, Western Serbia. Fr. Justin remained in Chelije Monastery until his repose in the Lord on March 25, 1979. He became Archimandrite there and was the spiritual head of the Monastery. Under his guidance, Chelije Monastery became a convent. A school of iconography, renewing the Serbo-Byzantine style, was also begun there, and a new chapel dedicated to St. John Chrysostom as well as residential quarters were constructed in 1970. Many pious people from all parts of Yugoslavia, Greece, the Balkans, and literally all parts of the world came to hear him preach and teach the correct faith and life in Christ by the energy of the Holy Spirit. Without a doubt, from the end of World War I until his repose in the Lord, Archimandrite Justin was the pillar of Orthodoxy in his home-land.

---

6. The birthplace of Bishop Nikolai Velimirivich. See March 18th.

Fr. Justin overlooking the fields and dales of Chelije Monastery.

General view of Chelije Monastery in Fr. Justin's time.

During the time of confinement in Chelije Monastery, he accomplished an amazing literary feat: he translated and compiled from various sources twelve volumes (one per month) of the *Lives of the Saints*. St. Justin also wrote a thirteenth volume on the Triodion and the Pentecostarion. Published from 1972-1977, these texts amount to over 7,000 pages of writing. He also was a great ascetic, in constant prayer, as he served daily in either the chapel or catholicon all the services of the Orthodox liturgical cycle: Vespers, Matins, Vigil, Divine Liturgy, etc. Fr. Justin communed of the Holy Gifts daily, for the Eucharist, the Precious Body and Blood of our Lord Jesus Christ, was his "daily bread" and the true source of his entire life, work, teaching, and existence. His words, deed and thoughts exuded a lifestyle reminiscent of the ancient Fathers of the Church. Another Father of the Church walked this earth in the person of St. Justin.

In addition to the *Lives of the Saints*, the following is an incomplete list of the writings he produced in Chelije, some of which are still unpublished:

> Commentaries on all the Epistles of St. Paul and St. John
> Commentaries on the Gospels of Matthew and John
> The Theology of St. Sava as a Philosophy of Life (1953)
> Life of Sts. Sava and Simeon (1962); in Greek (1975)
> Man and the God-Man (1966 in Greek)
> The Orthodox Church and Ecumenism (1978)
> Three Divine Liturgies (1978)
> The Theandric Way (posthumously in 1980)
> Serbian Translations: "Trebnik" (Prayer Book of Needs);
> Akathist Services to the Lord, the Theotokos and various saints.

His literary genius, when summarized, is amazing. Not only did he write so many and such a wide variety of works, but each one of them is so thoroughly Orthodox and patterned after the ancient literary way of the Fathers of the Church. Each of his books is highly dogmatic, correct in vision and detailed; kerygmatic, proclaiming the truth in Christ; and pastoral—exhortive, directional, and inspiring. Each dis-

Sisters of Chelije Monastery.

Fr . Justin in his monastery court in 1978.

Chelije Monastery surrounded
by wilderness.

plays a highly analytical and perceptive mind and heart. He actually created a new theological and philosophical language necessary to reach the heart of the modern human being. And his writings and teachings reflect a genuine and total commitment to the Lord Jesus Christ, a commitment characterized by extreme asceticism, as well as by the contemplative vision of the Divine Light of God the Holy Trinity. He was a "living dogma" and a "flute of the Spirit" reflecting the divine love of God the Holy Trinity. Theology was life to St. Justin.

St. Justin fell asleep in the Lord on March 25, 1979, on his birthday, the Feast of the Annunciation. He was 85 years of age. After his most honorable burial which was attended by hundreds of pious believers who came from many parts of the world, he was laid to rest facing east behind the main church of Chelije Monastery. To this day eulogies praising his virtue and love of Christ continue to be heard from all parts of the Orthodox world. Also, miracles have occurred at his gravesite, such as healings, flashes of brilliant and divine light from his tomb, as well as many conversions of unbelievers who have either read his writings or have been personally visited by Almighty God through the prayers of St. Justin.

Truly St. Justin's legacy is a great one. Many disciples are now extolling his name and imitating his life by drinking from the inexhaustible riches of grace and truth which he revealed to us. Add another modern Orthodox Christian saint to the Church calendar!

"O Holy Father Justin, thy sweetness of life refreshes our souls. Thy love for truth and desire to live with all the saints is a reminder to us of our own calling from God to pursue virtue, that we, most unenlightened and miserable sinners, may open our hearts to the knowledge of Truth Incarnate, the Lord Jesus Christ, to Whom belongs glory, honor and worship, together with His Unoriginate Father, and Life-giving Spirit, now and ever and unto the ages of ages. Amen."

Righteous Elder Justin in his later years.

St. Irenaeus

Bishop of Srem

TROPARION, Tone 2
As a pure diamond of the faith,* and as a solid
rock unmovable from the truth,* thou didst confess Christ
openly as hierarch of thy flock of Srem,* O holy father,
Hieromartyr Irenaeus;* therefore, O invincible one,*
pray to Christ God to save our souls.

March 26th

OUR HOLY HIEROMARTYR

IRENAEUS

BISHOP OF SREM

(✝304)

*Blessed are those who are
persecuted for righteousness sake,
for theirs is the kingdom of Heaven.*
St.Matthew 5:10

DURING the godless persecution of Christians under the reign of pagan Roman Emperors Maximian and Diocletian (284-305), there lived in Srem[1] a devout and pious Serbian Orthodox Bishop, Irenaeus, who in the face of terrible torture and brutal persecution, courageously confessed the Lord Jesus Christ as the only true God and Savior of the world.

St. Irenaeus, the Bishop of Srem, was married[2] and had children. As Bishop of Srem, he was well known as a glorious defender of the Faith, a powerful preacher of the words of the Gospel, and a fierce spiritual warrior for Christ. In an effort to weaken the Christian cause, the

---

1. Sirmium, 100 miles west of Belgrade on the Sava River, or Srem.

2. In the early church, married bishops was the custom (I Tim. 3:2), and was only changed by the decrees of the Apostolic Constitutions (pre-318); but as late as the fifth century in the East there were still a few married bishops. In 692, the Council of Trullo put forth canons concerning this issue—the marriage of clergy—which are still followed by the Orthodox East, the "black" monastic and "white" lay clergy.

Governor of Srem, Probus, decided to arrest venerable Irenaeus and imprison him until he renounced his faith in the Lord.

"Comply with the government statute," ordered Probus, as he interrogated Irenaeus in trial. "Offer incense to the gods!"

"Whoever does such an act," replied the Saint, "is not worthy of the Kingdom of Christ which is not of this world. No, I will not sacrifice to your false gods."

"The most holy Emperor has ordered that you either sacrifice to the gods or be tortured," the Governor retorted, hoping to frighten the holy man of the Lord.

"For me, to suffer for Christ is an honor and a privilege, not a punishment. No human torture can compare to that eternal life which is given to those who truly take up their cross and follow the Lord," answered Blessed Irenaeus.

Then Governor Probus ordered the court soldiers to torture Irenaeus. As they beat his bare back with leather straps embedded with nails, the Governor taunted him: "What do you say now, my friend, do you still refuse to sacrifice to the gods?!"

The Saint answered, saying, "My sacrifice to the Lord is a true confession of faith in Him. Nothing in this world will prevent me from confessing Him as Lord and King."

Seeing the blessed archpastor remain obstinate in his belief in the Lord, Probus tried another avenue: he brought before Irenaeus his parents, wife, children, relatives and friends, telling them that they could save Irenaeus and their own lives if they persuaded him to renounce Christ. The venerable Father, discovering this cunning plot, forestalled his relatives, not allowing them to sin: "These are the words of our Lord Jesus Christ, *Whoever renounces me before men, I too will renounce before my Father Who is in Heaven* (Matt. 10:33). Believe and understand, then, my beloved relatives in Christ, the exhortation of the Holy Great Martyr Apostle Paul: *Who shall separate us from the love of Christ? shall tribulation, or distress, or persecution, or famine, or nakedness, or peril, or sword? As it is written, For thy sake we are killed all the day long; we are*

A saint-martyr of the 2nd century.
Ancient fresco in Studenitsa Monastery.

accounted as sheep for the slaughter. Nay, in all these things we are more than conquerors through him that loved us. For I am persuaded, that neither death, nor life, nor angels, nor principalities, nor powers, nor things present, nor things to come, nor height, nor depth, nor any other creature, shall be able to separate us from the love of God, which is in Christ Jesus our Lord (Romans 8:35-39). Therefore, let us pray to be worthy of such a high calling. Let us all run to this hope and joyful end."

After this futile attempt on the part of Probus, St. Irenaeus was imprisoned for several months. Afterwards, the Governor approached the blessed confessor once again. "Don't you understand that I have the power to punish your relatives and Christian followers?!" said the Governor angrily. "Come now, simply offer incense to the true gods, and I will set you free."

Then Bishop Irenaeus replied to this vicious tempter concerning his relatives and spiritual flock, saying, "These are the words of the Lord Jesus Christ, *He that loveth father or mother more than me is not worthy of me: and he that loveth son or daughter more than me is not worthy of me* (Matt. 10:37). Therefore, those who love the only true God, our Lord Jesus Christ, with their whole heart, soul, mind, and strength, will comprehend the passing nature of this world and will prefer eternal life to any so-called earthly salvation, possession, or glory."

Having realized his defeat, the Governor had in his own thinking only one recourse—to put the holy confessor Irenaeus to death. Probus ordered him to be beheaded in public and his remains cast into the Sava River. Upon hearing the sentence, Blessed Irenaeus prayed to the Lord: "I bless Thee, Lord Jesus, since Thou hast given me a victorious faith; make me worthy, also, of Thy eternal crown of glory." After completing this prayer, Venerable Irenaeus was taken to the Artemidian Bridge. His clothes were stripped off and a crown of thorns was placed on his head. He then raised his arms in prayer once more: "Lord Jesus Christ, Thou didst suffer for the life of the world; let Thy Heavens open now to receive the spirit of Thy faithful servant, Irenaeus, who for Thy name's sake was taken from the Orthodox Church in Srem and persecuted unto death.

I will not renounce Thee even at this hour, and ask only, dear Lord, that Thou, in Thy abundant mercy, protect from all danger and evil, both visible and invisible, the pious Orthodox Christians of Srem, and that Thou wilt strengthen them in Thy faith."

Having finished this prayer, Irenaeus, the pious Bishop of Srem, was martyred for the true faith in the Lord Jesus Christ on March 26, 304, when Probus was the Governor of Panonia, Srem. May the memory of St. Irenaeus be eternal!

"O Holy Father and Great Martyr Irenaeus, the champion and victor of true faith in our Lord Jesus Christ, pray to Christ, the only true God and Hope, that our faith may be strengthened to match thine, so that we, too, most sinful servants, may be found worthy of His eternal crown of glory, to Whom belongs glory, honor and worship, together with His Unorginate Father, and Life-giving Spirit, now and ever and unto ages of ages. Amen."

KONTAKION
Tone 2

O holy martyr, Hierarch Irenaeus,* thou hast received thy incorruptible crown of glory,* won by thy steadfastness of faith and holiness of life,* repelling the godless threats of the pagans;* therefore, by virtue of thy love for Christ's victory,* pray for thy spiritual children* who honor thy memory in faith, hope, and love.

Holy Martyr Nicetas

TROPARION, Tone 1
Thy faith was pure and zealous,* as thou didst face the
godless persecutors,* preferring the treasures of eternal life,*
to the follies of mankind.* Therefore, O Holy Martyr
Nicetas,* thy resurrected beauty shines for all ages;*
pray to Christ God to strengthen us in the truth*
of His glorious Passion and Resurrection.

April 4th

SUFFERING OF NEW MARTYR

NICETAS

OF ALBANIA AND SERRES

(†1808)

*Suffering for God and for His sake are more
precious to God than any prayer or offering;
and the smell of their sweat is better than incense.*
St. Peter Damascene

OUR VENERABLE NEW MARTYR NICETAS was a Serb born in Albania in the late eighteenth century. Very little is known of his childhood, his parents, or family background. This may very well be the will of God, for it allows us to concentrate on Nicetas' ultimate Christian contribution and claim to glory: when he became, as an adult, an undefiled witness to the Life-giving Cross and incorruptible Resurrection of our Lord Jesus Christ, by his voluntary act of martyrdom for the true Orthodox faith in God.

As a young man, Nicetas resolved upon the radically devoted Christian life in Christ—monasticism. He left Albania as a youth and traveled to the Holy Mountain, Athos, residing at first in the Russian Orthodox Monastery of Great Martyr Panteleimon. Being received into the monastic ranks there, Nicetas spent his entire time in strict ascetic labor, acquiring virtue upon virtue, while also receiving the grace of the Holy Spirit in the divine contemplation of the Holy Trinity. Within a short period of time, Blessed Nicetas was granted the abbot's blessing to live in the Skete of St. Anna. The grace of the Holy Spirit often welled up within Nicetas, filling him with an ecstatic love for God, man, and all of creation. This love of God granted him a peaceful and radiant countenance, and helped him ward off all the assaults of the foul-smelling demons. His thoughts were constantly centered upon the Cross of our Lord Jesus Christ, particularly on the kenotic love Jesus exhibited in His humble and reconciling death on the Cross. The fact that God Himself would become flesh and shed His own divine blood "for the life of the world" made Nicetas believe more and more, as time passed, that it would certainly be a privilege and honor to die for belief in Him, the only true God and Savior of the world.

With this experiential knowledge filling his life with tremendous Christian zeal, Blessed Nicetas was asked to leave the Holy Mountain and to travel to the town of Serres[1] in order to strengthen the monastic communities there who were suffering under Turkish persecution. Upon arrival, Nicetas, whose zealous reputation preceded him, was summoned by the Turkish court to appear for questioning. There he disputed with the musselmen concerning the faith in Christ, explaining to them, like the martyrs of old, that Jesus the Lord is the only true God, *the Way, the Truth, and the Life,* He Who was in the beginning with the Father and the Spirit before time began, Who also became a human being for *us and for our salvation,* being crucified by the ungodly unbelievers, and Who was raised from the dead, establishing a Kingdom without end. The Turkish authorities, overcome by his radical commitment to Christ Jesus, judged that Nicetas had blasphemed their faith in Mohammed. Thus, being fearful that Nicetas would convert and reconvert many to Christ, they decided to offer him a position at the Royal Court, hoping to perhaps silence him with gifts and royalties, and eventually persuade him to accept the Muslim faith.

These gifts were foolishness and vanity to holy Father Nicetas, and he stopped them at once, saying that he would never reject the Lord

---

1. Seventy-five miles southeast of Skoplje.

Jesus Christ. The Turks then decided to try their second-best method—torture. Taking Holy Confessor Nicetas to the public square for all to see, they encased his holy head with an iron cage and pulled off his finger- and toe-nails, all the while keeping a large flame of fire before his face. This took place at the beginning of the Great and Holy Week of the Lord's Passion and Resurrection, 1808. After this, Nicetas was thrown into a huge hole in the earth, only to be taken up for daily beatings and similar torture.

Having praised and blessed the Lord God for the privilege of suffering for His name's sake, Blessed Nicetas passed on to the eternal mansions of the righteous on Holy Saturday, April 4, 1808. Three days later the Orthodox Christians of Serres, with boldness and Godly courage, took the blessed body and relics of Holy Martyr Nicetas out of the hole and gave him an honorable Christian burial. The hole became bright as the sun as they raised his body; and as they proceeded to the Church of St. Nicholas the Miracle-worker in Serres, Nicetas' body exuded a fragrant myrrh. And ever since his burial, miracles have been granted to those pious followers who venerate Blessed New Martyr Nicetas in faith, hope, and love.

And the Turks of Serres and the surrounding territories were dealt a most vicious blow: the entire populace became followers of Nicetas, as many were converted and strengthened in the faith in the Risen and Victorious Lord Jesus Christ.

"O Holy Father Nicetas, thy wish was granted: to die for Christ truly is an honor and privilege only received by purity of faith and steadfastness of heart. Therefore, O pure and incorruptible one, pray to Christ the exalted King that we, too, most unworthy and corrupt sinners, may be granted that very same zeal, desire, love, commitment, and energetic grace to witness to His Cross and Resurrection before all ungodly persecutors, to Whom belongs glory, honor, and worship, together with His Unoriginate Father, and Life-giving Spirit, now and ever and unto ages of ages. Amen."

Venerable Joseph of Meteora

TROPARION, Tone 3

We honor you, holy fathers Athanasius and Ioasaph* and reverence your divine ladder and net* that has uplifted souls to heaven* who were attracted by the divine light* that shone from atop Meteora.

April 20th

LIFE OF OUR FATHER

IOASAPH

OF METEORA

(✝1422)

Human life extends cyclically through years, months,
weeks, days and nights, hours and minutes.
Through these periods we should extend our ascetic labors
—our watchfulness, our prayer, our sweetness of heart,
our diligent stillness—until our departure from this life.
St. Peter Damascene

OUR HOLY Father Ioasaph was born in 1350, being the son of
Serbian King Simeon Urosh (1355-1369) of the Nemanja dynasty, who
was the brother of the great Serbian Emperor Dushan the Powerful
(1331-1355). St. Ioasaph's mother, Queen Tomaida, was the daughter
of the Byzantine Empress Maria Paleologos and Emperor John II Orsine
Paleologos, Despot of Epirus (1323-1335). At baptism, St. Ioasaph was
given the name John.[1] He progressed in grace and wisdom before the
face of the Lord and all people, and received the finest education the
kingdom of Serbia had to offer.

---

1. Ioasaph was his monastic name received later in life.

During his youth, the royal throne of King Simeon, his father, was located in Trekala, Thessaly (northern Greece). King Simeon was a blessed benefactor of the Church of Serbia at this time, as he built in Trekala a church in honor of St. Simeon the God-receiver. Also, by the nearby town of Kalambaka, atop the forest of rock pinnacles called Meteora, was located the Greek Orthodox Monastery of the Transfiguration, founded by St. Athanasius (whose feastday is also celebrated on April 20th). During King Simeon's reign existing monasteries were rebuilt and new ones were founded at Meteora.

Meteora—these rocky pinnacles suddenly thrust heavenwards in the midst of the Thessalonian plains and reach vertiginous heights which will humble even the mind of a high-thinking man. One is reduced to a state of pure wonder upon seeing the monastic dwellings situated atop these rocks whose lofty summits surpass even the eagles' nests. One is also bewildered imagining how the first monks surmounted these summits whose sheer cliffs lack even the most basic footholds. Learned philosophers and scientists have proposed various schemes such as gigantic kites flying heavy rope across the peaks or other such implausible methods in order to explain how such an ascent could be possible. These same philosophers and scientists also fail to comprehend the virgin birth of Mary, the mother of God. If they cannot fathom Her, who is "the height transcending heaven above," we cannot expect that they will understand how men of God ascended these rocky pinnacles. In these cases we are reduced to reverent silence as we contemplate those who by the grace of God attained yet greater achievements than the scaling of sheer rock walls in mortifying their self-will and pride, conquering the passions, and acquiring virtues.

According to tradition the first hermits came as long ago as the ninth century, and imperial and patriarchal documents indicate for certain that they were there by the 11th or 12th century. The first hermits lived in hollows, clefts of rocks, overhangs, and caves. Warding off the privations of thirst, cold, and exposure to the elements in their love for God, they with their lives of unimaginable hardships inspired the souls

General view of Meteora monasteries.
A 19th-century engraving showing in one glance the Meteora panorama
of the rock forest with monastic communities perched on cliffs.
Beneath is the present day town of Kalambaka.

of men, and they attracted fellow servants of God who sought to mortify the flesh so as to live among the angels. Athanasios Kouros writes, "The Meteoric landscape and asceticism are two things very much alike. The total refusal of the world coupled with great devotion to the Christian faith; the redemption of the soul; prayer, deep whole-hearted prayer; and, the gathering of self, concentration and religious meditation, all need a place like Meteora. Something rough but imposing. Bare stone and sky. A lot of sky!" Living atop these rocky pinnacles far above the world, men lived closer to the stars in the heavens and their souls responded with fervent tears of longing for what is yet to come.

As the first hermits watered the ground with their blood, sweat, and tears, more souls desirous for the angelic life sprang up out of the earth, yearning for the heights of virtue, and eager to be raised to heaven by the elders' prayers. Sketes began to be formed in which several men shared a prayer rule and yet lived as hermits, only coming together for weekly celebrations of the day of Resurrection and for feasts. The first skete to be established was atop what is known as St. Stephen the Protomartyr's Rock. Access to this skete is easier than to other lofty dwellings because the nearby hill of Koukoulas reaches a peak that is only some twenty-five feet away from the top of St. Stephen's Rock. Only in the 20th century a movable bridge spans the abyss quite easily. As communities began to be established atop other lofty peaks, more secure—though by no means altogether safe—ways of ascent replaced the extremely arduous climb by hand. Scaffolding from the occasional cliff-side caves and hollows in which hermits and ascetics dwelt was erected, and rickety ladders were hung. Monks who made the long and arduous climb to the foot of the final heavenwards thrust of Great Meteoron (the widest and highest in this forest of immense stony pillars) were able to ascend the sheer rock wall by means of a net in which they were drawn up from the world below some eight-hundred feet to the angelic life above. Altogether there were 18 monasteries on rocks. Now only five are functioning as such with a few monastics.

General view of the rocks from the village of Kalambaka.

Monastery of St. Barlaam, neighbor to Sts. Athanasius and Ioasaph's
Great Meteora.

Great Meteoron, also known as the Monastery of the Transfiguration, was founded by St. Athanasius.[2] St. Athanasius was born in Ypati of Phthiotis in 1302 and baptized as Andronicus. His mother died after his birth and his father died within a short time from that. Left an orphan, Andronicus was raised by his father's brother. During his youth, Andronicus was captured by the Catalans but managed to escape with his uncle to Thessalonica where he set about learning Greek and cultivating his mind. Being too poor to afford tutelage, he often stood without the classroom listening for whatever might profit him. At seventeen years of age, Andronikos left to go to the holy Mount Athos. He was not able to stay as he could not yet grow a beard, so he returned to the world and sought to gather what he could from the spiritual lights in the area. His travels took him to Crete and finally he was able to return to the Skete of Magoula on Mt. Athos where he became the spiritual son of Elder Gregorius and the younger brother of Elder Moses, and received the monastic habit with the name of Antonios. Within a short time he was tonsured into the Schema and was named Athanasius. After a pirate raid in which Elder Moses was abducted, St. Athanasius and Fr. Gregorius were forced to flee and decided to go to Meteora (at the time known as the rocky district of Stagi). They lived for some time on a style, but due to the desire for greater solitude and the inconvenience of visitors (both well- and ill-intentioned ones), Antonios eventually settled atop Great Meteoron. There he established the coenobitic rule and began to provide for the spiritual upbringing of the young souls who came, thirsty for God.

Thus John from his youth was surrounded not only by blessed royalty in the Lord, but also by the Orthodox ascetic life at nearby Meteora monasteries. As he grew, Blessed John exhibited a tremendous zeal for the pious and ascetic life, being inspired by the monks of

---

2. St. Athanasius also created the name "Meteora" from the Greek *meta-* (after) and *aeipo* (raise) which literally means raised or suspended. The name originally applied only to what is now known as the Great Meteoron, but came to be applied to all the rocky pinnacles in that locale.

Aerial view of the top of Transfiguration Monastery Rock.

Side view of Great Meteora, showing the original dwelling and chapel of St. Athanasius (with columns).

Meteora. He was enthralled by the Divine Services, the chanting and reading of the Gospels and the Lives of the Saints. He read and spoke Greek, learning this from his Byzantine Greek mother, Queen Tomaida, and thus was able to read and comprehend the liturgical texts and the many ancient writings of the great ascetics and Fathers of the Church. Hence it came as no surprise to his father, King Simeon, when young John, upon completing gymnasium (high school) in 1369, petitioned the Royal Court for its blessing to travel to Hilandar Monastery on the Holy Mountain of Athos, in order to join the monastic ranks there.

When his father died in 1371, the lawful and only crown prince, John Ouressis Paleologos, was summoned to take over the command of the kingdom. When the God-seeking John returned from Mt. Athos to Trekala he first visited the Monastery of the Great Meteoron. Reaching the base of the Great Meteoron Monastery, a net was lowered for the royal prince the same as it was for any lowly man who wished to ascend the rocky crag to partake of true monastic life. Some eight hundred feet above, the monks began operating the winch and slowly drew John up the precipice. Arriving at the summit, he passed by the bakery and soon met the enlightened figure of St. Athanasios. The clear gaze of St. Athanasios, the poverty of his cell, and all the surroundings spoke deeply to the soul of the young king: Athanasios had found "the way that leads to life." Why could not the young king follow this way as well?

A tremendous dilemma appeared: whether or not to forsake his earthly kingdom in pursuit of a heavenly one. He thought of the words of the Gospel, *What does it profit a man if he gains the whole world and loses his own soul?* Then he made the strong, unbending decision to refuse! He considered "everything but dung" and asked to put on the monastic habit, preferring the coarse, hair shirt and ryassa of a monk to the imperial purple of a king. The consequent sorrow of his relatives, the disappointment of his fellow country-men, and his own realization that because of his monastic life he was to forever end the imperial

Sts. Athanasius and Ioasaph, the founders of Great Meteora Monastery.

Sts. Theophanes and Nectarius, founders of Varlaam Monastery
of All Saints.

blood-line of his family, all these made up for him the narrow gate and just the beginning of the painful path that he chose.

The writer of his hymns, Joustinos Dekadio, in his inspired verses has the whole universe celebrating for this high self-denial:

Angels agree with the intention,* the Heavens rejoice,* earth exults,* seeing through him God glorified.

He refused his crown for the love of the thorn-crowned King. He laid down his sceptre to take up the cross of Christ, and he trode the narrow path that leads to the eternal Kingdom.

John handed over the royal leadership to his first cousin, Alexis Angelos Philanthropinos, and with this the title of "King and Autocrat of the Greeks, Serbs and Albanians."[3] With this abdication, John was now able to pursue his true love: zealous service and discipleship to the Lord Jesus Christ in the monastic vocation. He entered the Great Meteoron, and under the spiritual tutorship of venerable Athanasius, was tonsured a monk and given the name Ioasaph. This name was not given to him by chance. It is the name of the saint, Ioasaph the king of India, who left his kingdom and went to live with his spiritual father, the hermit Varlaam, when he found the "precious pearl" of Christian truth.

The relationship in the names and lives of these two men is sung in hymns:

With what songs shall we honour*Athanasius and Ioasaph*the Meteoritic founders,*and builders of the holy church?*The one lived as the Athonite,*the other followed Ioasaph's *virtues and ways.*And all of them,*both the former and the latter,*Christ the merciful, crowns.

Unfortunately, no hagiographical literature concerning St. Ioasaph exists. The only information about his life as a monk comes from St.

---

3. King Alexis was the last Christian ruler in Thessaly, as the Turkish hordes conquered Thessaly in 1393.

Athanasios' biography and from a letter concerning Ioasaph written by the abbot of the Monastery of Vatopedi on Mt. Athos.

Perhaps St. Ioasaph's life did not reach the spiritual heights of his teacher. Maybe he had no gift of miracles or of prophesying future events. But Ioasaph was himself a miracle in the choice of his life when he decided to abandon everything for Jesus' sake. It is a miracle that he managed to remain a monk to his last day, living a monastic life which demands from everyone perfect lack of property, inuring to hardships, death to one's own will and personal opinions.

Although it is true that he still had some say in the governing of the country, nonetheless in the royal seals he is referred to as "Ioasaph, the Saint King, the most honoured among monks." He himself used to sign as "✝ John Ouressis Paleologos, the monk named Ioasaph by receiving the angelic habit." Even though he was not included in the strict fasts and the heavy work of his brother-monks because of his spiritual father's discretion, the student of St. Athanasios could not but live humbly, obediently, and in want. And when sometimes he was worn-out by the hardships and the even harder crushing of the ego, the devil must have tempted him with reminders of the neighbouring kingdom and of its comforts and honours. Then, he must have sent the devil away by remembering the terrible promises he had given when he was being dressed with the cassock, the Angelic Habit:

"Will you be patient in every sorrow and hardship of the monastic call that you may win the Heavenly Kingdom?

"Will you remain a monk up to your last hour?"

And he had answered, "Yes, holy Father, by God's help I shall!"

And by God's help he remained a monk up to his last hour. He put on the monastic habit in 1381 and died about 1422.

Although technically still considered the rightful heir to the royal throne, venerable Ioasaph was nonetheless humbly obedient in all things to both his spiritual father Athanasius and to the entire brotherhood of Meteora. He practiced the strict and well-regulated

coenobitic[4] life of the Monastery. Monk Ioasaph progressed in virtue
and in the contemplative life in Christ to such a degree that venerable
Abbot Athanasius decreed that after his repose Ioasaph was to succeed
him as abbot of the Meteora Monastery. From 1369 until the repose
of his spiritual father in 1382, Sts. Ioasaph and Athanasius lived in
oneness of soul—"having two bodies, yet one mind"—and built three
churches on the Monastery's grounds; one is dedicated to Christ the
Savior, another to the Most Holy and Ever-Virgin Mary, and the last
to the Transfiguration of Christ. St. Ioasaph endowed them with
much gold and silver, and by royal decree provided for the renewal of
iconostases, frescoes, bell towers, etc., of many other monasteries
throughout Thessaly. Also, the inheritance of his sister, Marian Angelina, the Princess of Epirus, Ioasaph used for the construction of
several monastery hospitals, water and irrigations systems, and for
other civic needs. Even up to the present day within the eso-narthex
of the Great Meteoron Monastery candelabras—dating from the 12th
and 13th centuries and having been in all likelihood given to the
Monastery by Angelina, St. Ioasaph's sister—may be seen in front of
the two east columns. As a result, from 1369-1382 the monasteries of
Thessaly were considered materially some of the finest in the entire
Byzantine Commonwealth and Empire.

Yet this is not to suggest that Ioasaph was solely interested in the
material prosperity of the monasteries. On the contrary, his virtuous
character and reputation were always much in evidence, as many
considered him to be equal in stature to the ancient ascetics and teachers
on the spiritual life in Christ Jesus. His cell was constantly flooded by
visitors seeking spiritual counsel. Humble Ioasaph has forever since been
considered first and foremost in the spiritual history and tradition of
Thessaly as a "divine flower of regeneration" and "spiritual genius of

---

4. Coenobitic monasticism is the form of monastic life which stresses communal
worship, shared living and housing, and regulated personal prayer. The other two
major forms of monastic life are the semi-eremitic (skete) life and the eremitic.

Fresco icons of St. Ioasaph from main Monastery of Meteora,
dating from the 15th-century.

Orthodoxy," and only after this as a great and benevolent benefactor of Meteora Monastery.

Before his repose in the Lord in the year 1382, St. Athanasius disclosed his final wishes, saying, "My brothers and fathers, to all of you I leave a small and last command. First of all, I entrust you to the protection of the Most Blessed Theotokos and Ever-Virgin Mary, as our Monastery is under her patronage. I have my hopes and faith in her to this day. She has not deprived us of anything we needed. Moreover, I hope with her mediation and grace to be saved, though I have not done one good thing all my life. However, since by the grace of God I ascended this place and not another, and I was the first to inhabit this rock, building and embellishing our ascetical habitation, and all at Meteora have come with me, I give the command that you have as first brother and spiritual father the Priest-monk Macarios. This is because, from the outset, before I became ill, I entrusted him with the supervision of the daily and practical needs of the monastery. Now, however, it is beneficial for him to guide and regulate your spiritual conduct.

"Moreover, as you know, by reason of our sins, Lord Ioasaph left our monastery.[5] He no longer abides with us, as he first agreed. However, when he returns here and he accepts to live in concert with the regular Typicon of the Monastery—because I hope that he will return again—then have him as your head to govern the brotherhood and all that are found here. Render him all submissiveness and obedience."

After the Saint spoke these things, the disease lasted another forty days. St. Athanasius was about seventy-eight years old when he reposed on the 20th of April, 1382. Hence he was translated unto the Lord and counted with the choirs of the holy fathers.

Ioasaph did indeed return and he undertook leadership of the brotherhood, but he did not have the title of "abbot" which was at the

---

5. Turkish invasions in the year 1382 and perhaps difficulties within the monastery's community life forced St. Ioasaph to leave Meteora and go to Mt. Athos.

time reserved for the elder governing the Skete of Doupiani, who was called the "first of the skete."[6] For eleven years (1382-1393) St. Ioasaph wisely governed the Monastery until the cruel Turks conquered all of Thessaly in 1393. Then, St. Ioasaph was advised to flee for his life, since being of royal lineage he was a potential target of Turkish attacks. In 1394, at the age of 44, St. Ioasaph along with three monks withdrew from their beloved Meteoron temporarily to seek refuge at the Holy Mountain of Athos. Their stay, as St. Ioasaph had hoped, proved to be short. Before 1401, Ioasaph returned to Great Meteoron.

Evidently during these travels St. Ioasaph met Metropolitan Ioasaph of Larisa. In a letter (written in 1401 or 1402), the Metropolitan described St. Ioasaph as "one who warmed all. He was holy, sweet, meek, serene, and clever." After St. Ioasaph's return, he never went afar again. He remained at his beloved Meteoron occupying himself with prayer and unrelenting asceticism. Till the end of his days he remained a simple monk, never receiving the dignity of priesthood. Out of humility, even in official documents, he desired to be known only as Ioasaph the monk. Continuing in this conduct of life until the end, he was called by our Lord unto Himself on April 20, 1422, at seventy-two years of age. His precious relics, including his honorable skull, are stored in the Church of the Transfiguration of Christ of the Great Meteoron Monastery next to his spiritual father St. Athanasius. Thus, just as St. Ioasaph is united with his spiritual father in the heavenly mansions of the righteous where *there is neither Jew nor Greek, there is neither bond nor free, there is neither male nor female: for ye are all one in Christ Jesus* (Gal. 3:28), so too on earth are they united by the day of repose and the location of their relics. The life and deeds of St. Ioasaph continue to this very hour to inspire all pious Christians by the power of the uncreated grace and energy of God, the Holy and consubstantial Trinity, which illuminated him.

---

6. This skete was established upon St. Stephen's Rock and preceded all other sketes. In 1490, the title of "Abbot" was given instead to the elder governing the Monastery of the Transfiguration, also known as the Great Meteoron, which had for some time been of greater influence and importance.

"O Holy Father Ioasaph, life to thee was one of constant giving and sacrifice to the Lord God, Who wills all things with His life and love, so that every atom and molecule of created existence may be able, through the incarnate love of Christ, to be transfigured and offered by human beings as a continual sacrifice of praise to God the Holy Trinity. Pray, therefore, O honored one, that the Lord Jesus Christ, by the power of the uncreated grace of the Holy Spirit, may enliven us to that deep yearning within each of us to remain in constant union with and full participation in Christ, the Humble Giver, to Whom belongs glory, honor and worship, together with His Unoriginate Father, and Life-giving Spirit, now and ever and unto ages of ages. Amen."

ANOTHER TROPARION, Tone 4

Thou didst give up the earthly life but did not forget thy people,* as thy striving in the Lord edified both their souls and bodies.* Thy vigilance attracted all to the blessed ascetic life,* having as their image thy giving and love.* Pray, therefore, O God-illumined Ioasaph,* that Christ's giving may be made incarnate in us.

KONTAKION, Tone 4

Seeing thy most praiseworthy life and purity* and unworldly humble wisdom,* Venerable Athanasius named thee as his own successor.* Thou didst demonstrate thy worthiness, as it is written,* by serving the Tri-personal God.* Thou didst faithfully preserve the Meteora habitation,* therefore, pray, Father Ioasaph,* not only for thy homeland and the entire Serbian race,* but always for all of us.

ANOTHER KONTAKION, Tone 5

Thou wast left as a orphan* O our Father Athanasius* but thou, O Father Ioasaph* didst leave thy royal family voluntarily* and abandon the throne,* to be pulled up to angelic life* by thy Father in Christ, Athanasius.* And together you did ascend the lofty heights of virtue.

Other Sources: Meteora, the Rocky Forest of Greece by Sister Theoktekna, Meteora-Athens, 1977; *Meteora 600th Anniversary,* by Theocaris M. Provatakis, Athens, 1991; *Great Synaxaris,* 1979.

Iconostasis of the main Transfiguration Church of Sts. Athanasius and Ioasaph.

St. Sava

Metropolitan of Erdel

TROPARION, Tone 8

Being a Confessor of Orthodoxy, a good archpastor
of the Church of Christ,* and a leader of the people, most
blessed and victorious Holy Sava,* thou hast been found worthy of the crown of life;* therefore, pray to the Lord
for the salvation of our souls.

April 24th

LIFE OF OUR HOLY FATHER

SAVA

METROPOLITAN OF ARDEAL

(†1681)

*That good thing which was committed unto thee
keep by the Holy Spirit which dwelleth in us.*
II Timothy 1:14

Our HOLY FATHER SAVA (Brankovich), Metropolitan of
Ardeal, was born in 1615 in Podgorica, Montenegro. His descendants
were royal leaders of Serbia. His grandfather, George Brankovich, was
the last of the Serbian medieval rulers (1427-1458), and his father John,
together with his uncle, Despot George–St. Maxim (see Jan. 18th), held
at separate times the title of "Despot by the Grace of God" of all of
Voyvodina—Srem, Bachka and Banat. At baptism, the child of God
was given the name Simeon. Shortly thereafter, the Brankovich family,
like many other Montenegrin and Hercegovinian families during the
seventeenth century, emigrated north, settling north of Belgrade, in the
town of Pomorishe, Banat. Young Simeon received the best education
possible, as his uncle, Metropolitan Longin, was his personal tutor in
both secular and religious subjects. Yet it was the tumultuous era in
which young Simeon lived which was to provide the necessary educational and experiential context for his future greatness and glory.

The late sixteenth and early seventeenth centuries in the Balkans—

and in the entire Christian East for that matter—were some of the most turbulent and confusing times in Church history. In 1595, the relics of St. Sava were burned on Vrachar hill in Belgrade, a brutal Turkish answer to the "insurrection and cult of St. Sava" (see April 27th). The mutual hatred of the Latins and Byzantine Greeks was prevalent among the Serbs. We need only recall the reply of former Despot George Brankovich (1486-96) to the Hungarian King John Hunyadi's offer of military assistance to overthrow the Turks: "I would rather remain under the Ottoman yoke than acquiesce to the heretical Latin faith." Under Ottoman rule, religious life and theological education in particular virtually came to a standstill in practically all Orthodox countries. Many Orthodox leaders and theologians received their training in the West. As a result, heresy entered the Orthodox Church from high ecclesiastical positions. For example, Cyril Loukaris, the Ecumenical Patriarch of Constantinople,[1] in 1620 wrote a Confession of Faith which was totally Calvinistic both in spirit and content. Therefore, the encroachments of Uniatism, coupled with the Turkish and Hungarian problem, spelled for the Serbs most difficult, confusing and even frightening times. Yet it was this context which our Holy Father Sava "used" in order to show himself a pillar of Orthodoxy and divine flower of spiritual regeneration.

After receiving a theological education under Metropolitan Longin, Blessed Simeon was married at age thirty and then ordained to the priesthood. Unfortunately, shortly after his ordination his wife died. Simeon remained a priest for ten years, patiently enduring in the vineyard of the Lord, helping to convert and re-convert many from the Moslem religion unto eternal life in the belief in the only true and personal salvific God, our Lord Jesus Christ. In 1656, due to his tremendous evangelical Orthodox spirit, the entire episcopacy of the Serbian Church unanimously elected Father Simeon as the new Bishop of Ardeal.[2] Having been tonsured a monk, he was consecrated to the

---

1. Changed to Istanbul.
2. Transylvania, or western Romania.

St. Sava Brankovich (†1683) at right, and St. Iorest (†1657)
of Transylvania. Icon prepared for their canonization
by the Romanian Church in 1955.

episcopal office and given the name Sava, after St. Sava, the great Enlightener of the Serbs.

Metropolitan Sava served as an ecclesiastical diplomat in Transylvania. As an expert in international affairs, due to his experience at the Royal Court of Voyvodina, Sava traveled several times to Russia on behalf of the Transylvanian authorities in order to strengthen religious and political ties.

Venerable Sava also played the role of defender of the Faith in Transylvania. At this time Calvinism began making inroads into Transylvania and was increasingly gaining the upper hand, for certain princes—particularly, the Prince of Ardeal, Michael Apafi—and other political figures hoping to receive favors from the West, gave it support. Confessor Sava soon came into conflict with these leaders, and he carried out an arduous fight for the Orthodox Faith for over twenty years. He used every means to instruct the people so as to strengthen them in Orthodoxy. He created a print shop at his diocesan residence and published several books and articles: divine service books, teaching manuals for the clergy and faithful, and a most inspiring and eloquent confessional catechism, all the while preaching and pastoring his people using as a model the Lives of Saints and the teachings of the ancient ascetics of the Church.

As a true Confessor of the Faith, Sava suffered persecution for his preaching, teaching, and virtuous life: several times he was imprisoned and beaten for his evangelical Orthodox witness against the Calvinists.

After his final release from prison in 1681, due to the efforts of Prince Sherban of Wallachia, Sava became grievously ill; and exhausted from his many brutal sufferings, he fell asleep in the Lord on April 24, 1681. He was 66 years old. Immediately following his martyrdom in the Lord, the Orthodox Church in Transylvania began to venerate Sava as a saint, confessor and martyr for the cause of the faith in the one true Lord and Savior Jesus Christ. For the Serbs in the homeland, as well as for the "holy remnant" of true Orthodox in the entire Balkans, Blessed Confessor Metropolitan Sava Brankovich of Ardeal represented the supreme example of faith, that is, one who *guarded the precious jewel and deposit given him,* who did not hide the true faith under a bushel basket, but instead let his divine radiance shine forth in brilliance and splendor before all of humankind.

The Holy Synod of Bishops of the Romanian Orthodox Church, at its session on February 28, 1950, officially proclaimed Metropolitan Sava a saint, canonizing him; and in 1962 the Serbian Orthodox Synod of Bishops entered St. Sava, Metropolitan of Ardeal, in the list of saints of the Serbian Orthodox Church.

"O Holy Father Sava, thy zeal and virtuous efforts for Orthodoxy and thy people shine as a brilliant divine light before our eyes. O right-believing and right-living one, please pray to Christ our God to strengthen us in our belief in Him, in our pronouncement of Him, and in our witness of Him, in His Church, His body, the Orthodox Church of the Divine Trinity, for to Christ alone belongs glory, honor and worship, together with His Unoriginate Father, and Life-giving Spirit, now and ever and unto ages of ages. Amen."

KONTAKION
Tone 4

Most worthy archpastor and defender of the Church of Christ,* protect all true believers who always sing to thee:* Rejoice, Sava, holy Confessor of the Lord.

ANOTHER KONTAKION
Tone 4

Being an exile among heretics,* thou didst proclaim the truth of Christ Jesus to those darkened in their faith.* As a witness to Orthodoxy,* thou didst suffer for thy preaching and teaching of the God-Man Christ our Savior.* Therefore, O most Blessed Sava, pray that Christ may illumine our souls.

Venerable Janik

The Miracle-Worker of Devič

TROPARION, Tone 1

Through prayer and fasting thou wast enlightened
with divine grace,* being illumined by the blessed Light
which is not of this world.* Receiving from God the gift of
miracles* thou dost heal the infirm* and expel spiritual evils
from those who run with faith* to the might of thy holiness,
O our venerable Father Ioannikios:* Glory to Him Who has
granted thee grace,* Glory to Him Who has strengthened
thee,* Glory to Him Who heals all through thy chastity.

OUR GOD-BEARING FATHER

IOANNIKIOS

MIRACLE-WORKER OF DEVICH

(†1430)

*He who keeps in mind the way of the saints
by imitating them not only shakes off
the deadly paralysis of sin, but also
takes up the life of virtues.*
St. Peter Damascene

OUR VENERABLE and God-bearing Father Ioannikios (Janik) was born in Zeta, on the coast of Old Metohija, near the Adriatic Sea. He lived and persevered in the faith in Jesus Christ during the reign of the last Serbian Medieval ruler, Despot George Brankovich (1427-1458). All that is known of his parents is that they were God-fearing and pious Orthodox Serbs. From his youth, St. Ioannikios delighted in solitude and the quiet contemplative life; as a result, he forsook his parents as a teenager and journeyed to east Serbia, settling in the wooded area known as "Chrna Reka" (Black River), only a few miles from the Ibar River. The Black River area was already a famous site, since it was, according to the Serbian spiritual tradition, the place where St. Peter Korisha (see June 5th), the great Serbian ascetic of the mid-thirteenth century, spent many years in prayer and fighting the demons. Continuing this tradition, hermit Ioannikios built a cell and began his quest to subdue the flesh by calling upon the Lord Jesus Christ in incessant prayer.

As years passed, ascetic Ioannikios' spiritual prowess became well known throughout all the Serbian lands, as many zealous Serbs gathered around him with the hope of hearing his messages and receiving his blessings. After a sufficient and determined group of ascetics banded together, Blessed Ioannikios led them in building a church near his cell. However, as a result of his growing fame and reputation, venerable Ioannikios decided to flee the "follies of the flesh" by withdrawing to the town of Drenica, west of Kosova Mitrovica, to a wooded area called Devich. Years passed once again as Ioannikios persevered in hesychia and silence. He struggled with intensity against the demons, and was able, by the grace of the Holy Spirit and practicing the Jesus Prayer, to conquer the flesh and defeat the devil. Ioannikios was granted the gift of incessant prayer coupled with tears, being able to make the demons flee at the sound of his voice.

Being informed of his great asceticism and holiness, the Serbian Despot George Brankovich brought before Ioannikios his terminally ill daughter Maria. The Saint healed her at once. Despot George, amazed and astonished, asked Ioannikios how he could repay him. The Saint then persuaded George to build an Orthodox monastery in Devich, dedicating it to the Feastday of the Entrance into the Temple of the Most Holy and Ever-Virgin Mary the Theotokos (November 21st).

Father Ioannikios lived in God-pleasing asceticism to a venerable old age. He fell asleep in the Lord in Devich Monastery on December 2, 1430, being nearly 100 years old. His holy body and relics were buried in the cemetery within the monastery walls, and ever since then have been a source of numerous miracles and healings. Many of those healed did not forget their blessing from Almighty God through His Saint, as several hospitals and public works have been built in honor of St. Ioannikios. Also, an *Ispostnica* (House of Silence) was built in 1895 in honor of St. Ioannikios by the Nun Euphemia, known throughout

Devich Monastery chapel in which St. Ioannikios is buried.

St. Ioannikios' grave in the Devich Monastery church.

Kosovo as Blessed Stojna.[1] During World War I and II, when the enemies of the Serbs destroyed Devich Monastery, they could not destroy his gravesite—each time Blessed Ioannikios forbade them. After World War II, in 1947, Devich Monastery was renewed by two nuns, Paraskeva and Thecla, with Abbot Macarius Popovich. Also, the healing Saint did not forget his people, for the "Miracle Scrolls" of Devich Monastery provide us with evidence of his immortality and incorruptibility.[2]

"O Holy Father Ioannikios, O healing saint of the Lord, thou didst demonstrate the truth that the gift of healing comes from purity of heart, soul, mind, and body. Pray, therefore, to Christ our true Source of life and wholeness, that we, most miserable and needy sinners, may be delivered from all infirmities of both body and soul, so as to attain a measure of His holiness and deification in order to grant healing to others. To Him belongs glory, honor, and worship, together with His Unoriginate Father and Life-giving Spirit, now and ever and unto ages of ages. Amen."

---

1. The Life of Nun Euphemia was written by Bishop Nikolai Velimirovich, entitled *Blessed Stojna,* Belgrade (1924).

2. Here are but a few recorded healings by St. Ioannikios in these modern times: May 1947, Krsta Donish of the village of Binch, Metohija, healed of an incurable disease while praying at the gravesite of St. Ioannikios; May 1949, Radovan Krstich of the same village, healed of a deadly disease; July 1957, Nada Bebich from Pristina, healed of paralysis by St. Ioannikios; May 1959, Decimir Milanovich of the village of Mirnica near Prokuplje, completely healed of epilepsy while praying at the gravesite of St. Ioannikios; March 1963, Milorad Patkovich of Viche near Uroshevac, healed of a brain tumor while praying at the gravesite of St. Ioannikios; August 29, 1964, Slavica Brbich of Prishtina, healed also of epilepsy by the prayer of St. Ioannikios; October 10 and 18, 1964, Bozhana Niktarevich from Kragujevac and Dobrivoj Stevich from Negotin, healed at the gravesite of St. Ioannikios; June 1973, Mira Kovich of Trstenik, healed at the gravesite of St. Ioannikios. Many Albanians and Moslems have also been healed by St. Ioannikios: September 15, 1955, Ramik Aljimet from Muxhevina, healed by St. Ioannikios; May 30, 1956, Isinaj Chuf from Dragoljevac, healed by St. Ioannikios; and April 1972, Ramadan Kazitraj of Kosh near Klina, healed by St. Ioannikios.

Devich Monastery surrounded by wilderness as it looks today

KONTAKION TO ST. IOANNIKIOS

Tone 8

From thy youth, O God-wise one, thou didst love the angelic life,* as thou didst forsake all worldly pleasures;* shining as a star out of the world in Christ* thou didst radiate spiritual truth and righteous sunshine,* from Christ receiving the grace of healing thou dost heal of various diseases* those who run with love to thy holy grave.* Therefore, we also venerate thy most honorable memory,* and with love cry out to thee: Rejoice, Father Ioannikios.

Abbess Paraskeva, who renewed Devich Monastery.

Burning of the Relics of St. Sava on Vračar

TROPARION, Tone 4

Thy life and glory inspired thy people,* O Blessed Father
Sava,* as thou wast the spiritual heart from which pulsed the
life-blood of thy race.* Thy memory and veneration caused
the godless to lose control,* as they believed they could kill
the spirit along with the body.* Instead, thy memory inflames
us with eternal love for Christ God,* forever enshrined
in the temple of our hearts, souls, and minds.

April 27th

THE BURNING OF THE RELICS
OF OUR FATHER

SAVA I

ENLIGHTENER AND FIRST
ARCHBISHOP OF SERBIA

(Which took place in 1595 on Holy Saturday)

The Lord is my helper, and I will not fear
what man shall do unto me.
The Lord is my helper, and
I shall look down upon mine enemies.
Psalm 117: 6-7

OUR HOLY Father Sava, the Enlightener and First Archbishop of Serbia, died during the night between Saturday and Sunday, January 14, 1235, in Trnovo, Bulgaria. He had officiated at the Hierarchical Divine Liturgy on Epiphany, January 6, in the Imperial Cathedral of the Holy Forty Martyrs in Trnovo. After the service, as was the custom, Archbishop Sava participated in the Blessing of the Waters at the nearby Jantra River, where he caught a cold, which developed into pneumonia, eventually causing his death on January 14, 1235. He was sixty years of age.

St. Sava received a most honorable burial and was laid to rest in the Cathedral of the Holy Forty Martyrs in Trnovo. He remained in Trnovo for over two years until May 6, 1237, when a solemn procession journeyed from Trnovo to Mileshevo Monastery in Serbia, where the Saint was finally laid to rest in his homeland (see May 6th). Although renowned for its beautiful icons and frescoes, the Angel at the Tomb of Christ in particular, the Monastery could never have imagined the attention it would receive after the placing of the holy body of Sava in the main church. Upon opening his casket for the burial service, St. Sava's body was found completely intact and sweet-smelling. Thousands of pilgrims—Serbs, Roman Catholics, and even Jews—came to venerate the divine Sava. As a result, only eighteen years later, in 1253, the Orthodox Church of Serbia officially canonized their beloved St. Sava.

This love for St. Sava continued unabated even until the time of the Turkish occupation of the Serbian lands, beginning with the Battle of Kosovo on June 15, 1389. The Serbs firmly believed that St. Sava, the Spiritual Father of the Serbian Orthodox Church and nation, would not permit their total destruction or permanent enslavement under the Turks. The Serbs, especially during these oppressive times, often visited his tomb in order to receive the spiritual courage needed to endure the cruel suffering and treatment received from the hands of the Turks. St. Sava was for them hope, medicine, comfort, joy, faith, healing, spirit, strength, courage, and unity. The icon of Sava was often placed on flags. And as time passed many Turks came to venerate Sava—perhaps fearing the wrath of God—as numerous miracles of healing of Turks by St. Sava were recorded.

Yet it was this ever-present national unity based on *Svetosavlje,* the country's veneration of St. Sava, that became a constant "thorn in the flesh" to the Turkish authorities. In 1595 a Serbian revolution took place, called the Insurrection of St. Sava, led by Patriarch John Kantul of Pech, Metropolitan Visarion of Hercegovina, and Bishop Theodore of Banat. The Turkish military leader in Belgrade, Sinan Pasha, quickly sent troops to crush the rebellion. But this time the Serbs had gone too far. At the request of Sinan Pasha, Sultan Mohammed II ordered, to the horror of all Serbs, the burning of the body of St. Sava, the Serbian

ST. SAVA I
Fresco in Lesnovo Monastery, 1392.

religious inspirational leader. On Orthodox Holy Friday, 1595, Turkish troops descended upon Mileshevo Monastery and removed from the crypt the body of St. Sava. These troops returned to Belgrade; and on Holy Saturday, April 27, 1595, they ascended Savinac Hill in the district of Vrachar and before the eyes of the horrified Serbs burned the relics of St. Sava.

By this inhuman act, Sava was crowned with the highest expression of true faith in the Lord Jesus Christ—Great Martyrdom, even after death—and the faithful and pious Serbs, watching the Turks burning his body and then scatter his ashes in the winds, were touched beyond measure. The end result was not despondency, but rather a greater love and zeal for Jesus Christ, Holy Orthodoxy, and God's faithful servant, St. Sava. His martyrdom seemed to inflame the Serbs with even greater Christian passion and national unity. Although the relics of St. Sava were destroyed, his glory and influence nevertheless increased. The Turks, desiring to crush the religious and national spirit of the Serbs, failed once again, for the burning of the body of St. Sava made all Serbians realize once and for all that religious life—Orthodoxy—and national unity and independence had to complement and interpenetrate one another if ever a true Orthodox Serbia was to develop once again.

When total independence came in 1879, the Serbs did not forget their beloved Sava, for at the annual commemoration in Belgrade of the Burning of the Relics of St. Sava, a young theologian and professor, Nikola Ruzicich (later known as Bishop Nikanor of Nish) proposed the idea of a memorial church in honor of St. Sava. The church was to be erected on Savinac Hill in the district of Vrachar, where Sava's relics were burned. The following day many pious Serbs of Belgrade gathered to formulate plans and to select a committee for the construction of such a church. Plans and meetings continued into the 1880's and 1890's; and on the 300th Anniversary of the Burning of Relics of St. Sava, in 1895, a call to begin working on the church was issued to all parties involved. Construction began just after the Feast of the Annunciation in 1896, when a small temporary chapel was built. However, due to internal political problems, plans for a larger memorial cathedral were halted until after World War I when, from October 21, 1926 to May 31, 1927, the Board of Construction under the leadership of Patriarch Varnava posted a competition for the architectural designs of the memorial church of St. Sava on Vrachar.

With the architects selected and the plans made, in 1935 construction of the Cathedral in Belgrade began. Work was halted again during World War II due to the governmental takeover by the atheistic Communist regime. This stumbling-block was not about to stop the pious Serbs, inspired by the ideal of St. Sava, for they knew quite well the treacheries of adverse religious and political oppression. Five hundred years of Turkish oppression did not stop them, and they would not succumb to a similar situation now. The project ideals continued to gain spiritual strength throughout the 1950's and 1960's. In 1968, His Grace Bishop Lavrentius of West Germany wrote to the President of the Republic of Serbia, imploring him to remove from the partially built Cathedral the trucks, trailers, and supplies that had been stored there since World War II. Finally, in 1984, His Holiness Patriarch German, by forceful petitions to the government, was able to secure approval to resume work on the Cathedral. On May 12, 1985, the cornerstone was laid, signifying the zealous continuation of this project to the glory of St. Sava; and the first hierarchical Divine Liturgy, led by His Holiness Patriarch German, was held on Sunday, June 25, 1989.[1] Over 150,000 faithful Christians attended this first Divine Liturgy! And the spiritual project continues....

What is unique about the memorial church on Vrachar is that God Himself chose this site as a most fitting way to honor Orthodox belief in our Lord Jesus Christ through His servant, St. Sava. Little did Sinan Pasha realize that by burning St. Sava's relics on Vrachar this vicious

---

1. Due to illness, Patriarch German was forced to retire in December, 1990. The Holy Spirit, working through the Holy Synod of Bishops in Belgrade, selected His Grace Bishop Paul of Prizren as the 44th Patriarch of the Serbian Orthodox Church, succeeding the ailing Patriarch German.

crime would change the future of Belgrade, then only a strategic place, into a religious/spiritual center, and as if following some precedent, the city was to be chosen later as the nation's capital. Vrachar hill turned out to be the best topographical site for the memorial church, for it lies exactly at the axis of the main Belgrade spine which starts from Kalemegdan and runs through Terazije and Slavija Squares to the present location, ensuring the Cathedral's entrance into the silhouette of Belgrade as a permanent feature of the city. This Serbo-Byzantine style Cathedral will be the crowning point of the capital city and, due to its enormous size, will dominate the skyline of Belgrade. The image, memory, and spirit of God's faithful servant Sava will be etched into the scenery and atmosphere of Belgrade and, of course, in the hearts, minds, and souls of all pious Christians who venerate St. Sava in faith, hope, and love. Truly the famous Serbian saying will forever ring loud and clear: "Sinan Pasha vatru pali, telo Svetog Sava spali; al' ne spali slave, niti spomen Sava!" (Sinan Pasha lighted the flames, the body of Sava burned; but the glory did not burn, neither the memory of Sava!) And the words of the Psalmist will forever inspire and comfort the followers of St. Sava: *The Lord is my helper, and I will not fear what man shall do unto me. The Lord is my helper, and I shall look down upon mine enemies (Psalm 117:6-7).*

Holy Father Sava, we praise thee:
Thy life inspires us.
Thy death inspires us.
Thy love inspires us.
Thy martyrdom inspires us.
Thy glory inspires us.
Thy calling inspires us.
Thy spirit inspires us.
Thy immortality inspires us.
Holy Father Sava, we glorify thee.

St. Sava Memorial Church, Vrachar Mound, Belgrade, 1989.

KONTAKION

Tone 8

Mileshevo radiates brilliantly today,* for the holy Sava comes to Belgrade to reveal the triumph of the Lord God.* By the Great Martyrdom of Christ's servant, Sava the God-bearer,* the everlasting glory of the Kingdom of Heaven shines forth,* granting great mercy to all who venerate Sava's memory in faith, hope, and love.

St. Basil of Ostrog

TROPARION, Tone 4

From thy youth thou gavest thyself entirely unto the
Lord,* O God-bearing Father,* as thou didst remain in
prayer, labor, and fasting,* being an example of virtue to thy
flock.* Because of this, God, seeing thy blessed will,* established thee as a pastor and good hierarch of His Church,*
and after thy repose, He kept thy body incorrupt,
O holy Basil.* Therefore, with boldness* pray to
Christ God to save our souls.

April 29th

LIFE OF OUR HOLY AND
GOD-BEARING FATHER

BASIL

MIRACLE-WORKER OF OSTROG AND
METROPOLITAN OF ZAHUMLJE
(†1671)

A monk is an angel, and his work is mercy,
peace and the sacrifice of praise.
St. Nilus of Rossano

Our miracle-working Holy Father Basil, Bishop of Zahumlje, was born to pious and God-fearing Serbian Orthodox parents, Peter and Anastasia Jovanovich, on December 28, 1610, in the village of Mrkonjich in Popova Polje ("Field of Priests"), Herzegovina (Zeta). At baptism, he was given the name Stojan; and from his early childhood he exhibited a gentle and meek spirit which would later guide him during the many trials in his life. Young Stojan also manifested from the very beginning a penetrating mind, along with an extremely great love and zeal for the Church, especially the Divine Services and the dynamic teachings of the great Fathers of the Church. His humble parents sent Stojan to the nearby Zavala Monastery, dedicated to the Feast of the Entrance of the Most Holy Theotokos into the Temple, where he began his education in both secular and religious subjects, under the tutelage of his uncle Seraphim, abbot of the Monastery.

311

Upon finishing grammar school, Stojan, full of love for Christ, decided to petition for full entrance into the monastic ranks in Zava Monastery. He spent a short period of time there and then traveled to the town of Tvrdosh, the seat of the Diocese of Trebinje, entering the Monastery of the Dormition of the Theotokos. He led a strict ascetic life, keeping vigil and taming the passions by the use of the Jesus Prayer. Within a short period of time Stojan was tonsured a monk and given the name Basil, after the great Hierarch and pillar of Orthodoxy, St. Basil the Great of Caesarea, Cappadocia (honored January 1st and 30th). In Trebinje, Basil was ordained deacon and then priest. After a short stay in Zava Monastery, he was called to Montenegro, where he served as a priest under Metropolitan Mardarius of Cetinje. However, this relationship soon led to a theological and pastoral dispute which resulted simultaneously in the persecution of young hieromonk Basil.

In the early seventeenth century, especially in the southwestern Serbian territories of Primore, Hercegovina, and Montenegro, a proliferation of Uniate propaganda was disseminated by the Jesuits of Rome who hoped to convert the Serbs there to the Latin faith. Basil, then a priest at the diocesan residence of Metropolitan Mardarius in Cetinje, vehemently denounced this assault on the Orthodox faithful of these areas, all the while petitioning the Metropolitan to warn the people and to protect the faith. Mardarius, however, did nothing to combat these heretical propagandists. Furthermore, he ordered Basil back to the Monastery of the Dormition in Tvrdosh. Basil complied with this episcopal decree; yet, during his return to Trvdosh, he secretly visited many Orthodox churches and families, exhorting them "to guard the most precious deposit"—Orthodoxy—which had been entrusted to them by the great St. Sava. Thus Basil, although persecuted by his own bishop, was nevertheless considered by the pious Serbs of these areas as a glorious defender of Orthodoxy.

Living in Tvrdosh, Basil resumed his ascetic labors as Archimandrite of the Monastery of the Dormition of the Theotokos; and like St. Sava

ST. BASIL OF OSTROG
Ancient icon of the Saint in his monastery. Small prints of this
icon are given to multitudes of pilgrims today.

before him, he traveled to all parts of the diocese to strengthen the faithful. He began a great biblical, spiritual, and liturgical renewal movement based upon increased participation in the liturgical and ascetical life of the Church. He was often seen going from house to house in Hercegovina preaching the Gospel of Christ to the Serbs. News of his evangelical activities also reached the Turks at this time. Called by the Turks the *Rajina Bogomolca* (the non-Muslim Christian slave dear to God), Basil was considered both a political and religious enemy to the authorities, and thus his life was in constant danger. Hence, by the advice of his own people, Basil fled to the great Orthodox country of Russia.

Basil spent a little more than a year in Russia, visiting many dignitaries as well as spending time in small towns and villages where he learned of and experienced the passionate Russian spirit and the common people's love for Orthodoxy. Upon his return to Tvrdosh, he brought with him many holy vessels, books, and money which he distributed to churches and families throughout Hercegovina. Venerable Basil was able to open an elementary school in Tvrdosh as well as build a new church next to it within the walls of the courtyard. Yet these apostolic works did not go unchecked, as his enemies—both the agents of the Latin unia and the vicious Turks—came with full force searching for this divine preacher and defender of the true Christian faith. Hence Basil fled again, this time not to Russia, but to the Holy Mountain of Athos.

On his way to the Holy Mountain, our father Basil stopped at the monasteries of Moracha in Nikshich and Djurdjevi Stubofi (the "Pillars of St. George") near Ivangrad, and finally arrived in Pech to receive the blessing of His Holiness Patriarch Paisius Janjevac (1614-1647). Basil told him in detail of the difficulties the Serbs were now encountering with the Latins and Turks, and of his desire to flee to the Serbian bastion of spirituality, Hilandar Monastery on the Holy Mountain of Athos. The wise Patriarch granted venerable Father Basil his blessing to go to the Holy Mountain, but advised him not to stay there long; Patriarch

The 15th-century Monastery of Cetinje.

The 16th-century Monastery of Tvrdosh.

Paisius, seeing the devout, evangelical, and pious character of Hieromonk Basil, had another thought in mind—to consecrate Basil as the Bishop of Zahumlje (Hercegovina).

Basil spent a year on the Holy Mountain, residing in Hilandar Monastery. He also visited the many sketes and cells of the virtuous ascetics and hesychasts living throughout the Holy Mountain. He learned much concerning the spiritual life in Christ which strengthened him and later came to his aid in facing his new challenge in life. Upon his return, Basil visited the Patriarch, and this time Paisius had an honor to bestow upon him: Basil was selected for consecration on the Feast of the Transfiguration as the Metropolitan of Trebinje, with his residence in Tvrdosh. He succeeded Metropolitan Simeon of Hercegovina on the episcopal throne in Tvrdosh. Basil was consecrated on August 6, 1638, when he was not yet thirty years old. Although young in age, he was nevertheless deemed most wise in spirit and character, one who would be able to stem the tide of the difficulties in the southwestern territories of the Church of Serbia.

From Pech, Basil traveled to Tvrdosh where he immediately assumed his episcopal duties. He fearlessly traveled to all parts of the Diocese of Trebinje, strengthening the people against the enemies of the Church. His spiritual flock came to love and venerate him as a Saint on earth, as many miracles were recorded as a result of his touch, words, or prayers. These were some of the most terrible times of persecution for the Serbian Orthodox Church. For example, Metropolitan Paisius Trebjeshanin of eastern Hercegovina, whose episcopal throne was in Nikshich, was murdered by the Turks; also, Patriarch Gabriel (Rajich) of Pech (1648-1656) was persecuted and martyred for the faith. As a result of this terrorizing and persecution, believed to be worse than the Hebrews suffered while captive in Egypt,[1] venerable Bishop Basil had to take under his episcopal om-

---

1. On the persecution of the Serbs during this era, the mid-seventeenth century, one can read firsthand testimony in the writings of Monk Gabriel of the Monastery of the Holy Trinity in Plevalje, 1649.

Ostrog Monastery (upper), showing two churches of the 17th and 18th centuries. A white cross overlooks the whole mountain.

ophor² the dioceses of Trebinje, eastern Hercegovina, Zahumlje, and Onogoshka (Nikshich)—practically all of the southwestern Serbian lands. Furthermore, the fearless Archpastor had no place to lay his head, as his residence and monastery in Tvrdosh were completely destroyed only a few months after he assumed his episcopal duties. His life was literally in danger at all times. Yet this did not discourage the brave warrior for Christ, for Basil believed and carried out the words of the Lord, Who said, *Destroy this temple and I will build it up in three days* (John 2:19), as well as the words of the Psalmist: *The Lord is my light and my saviour; whom then shall I fear? The Lord is the defender of my life; of whom then shall I be afraid?* (Psalm 26:1).

Having no diocesan seat, Bishop Basil, after much prayer, deliberation, and advice from elders in the faith, decided to transfer his episcopal seat to the Monastery of Ostrog. Having arrived in Ostrog, Basil lived at first in the "Donji Monastir" (Lower Monastery), but then moved to the Upper Monastery and restored and renewed the cell of St. Isaiah. It was from this cell that Bishop Basil pastored his diocese, residing there for more than fifteen years.

The ascetic Basil spent his nights and days in prayer, fasting, and vigil, fortifying his soul with countless bows and full-body metanoias.³ He did this in order to acquire the Holy Spirit of God Who led him and worked through him to perform virtuous deeds and miracles. Even

---

2. The omophor is the distinguishing vestment worn by the Bishop while serving Divine Liturgy. A "small omophor" is also worn by the bishop while serving other Divine Services. This vestment is a symbol of the human nature that the Word of God assumed as Savior of the entire universe, in order to identify with us, and heal and deify us. The short prayer said by the deacon while the bishop is vested with this holy garment explains its deep theological meaning: "When thou didst take upon thy shoulders human nature which had gone astray, O Christ, Thou didst offer it to Heaven, unto Thy God and Father, now and ever and unto ages of ages. Amen."

3. A full-body prostration. *Metanoein* is the Greek word for repentance, meaning literally "to change the mind," and thus metanoias are performed liturgically in the Church during penitential periods, especially during Great Lent. They are also performed as part of daily personal prayer and are an integral part of monastic worship.

Ostrog Monastery (upper), built in a cave where St. Basil lived, died, and is buried; a beloved site of pilgrimage.

though under Turkish oppression, during his episcopacy he was able to restore and renew the Church of the Entrance of the Theotokos into the Temple on the Monastery grounds, as well as build a beautiful chapel dedicated to the Elevation of the Life-giving Cross, located on the rocky cliff of Ostrog.[4] In sum, Basil's cell in Ostrog blossomed into a holy place, the spiritual center of Serbian Orthodoxy in the mid-seventeenth century.

Although he spent much time at the Monastery, working and carrying the bricks to rebuild the walls and construct the new chapels, Basil nevertheless did not forget the flock the Lord had entrusted to him. He traveled throughout his dioceses and even went from house to house, as always, preaching the Word of God, healing the sick, setting free the spiritually captive, and fortifying the Orthodox in true worship and correct belief in the Lord Jesus Christ. Many miracles were performed by his hands, as mothers received their sick children back to wholeness, the lame were made to walk and the blind were made to see. Above all, Basil's greatest gift to his people was his glorious and luminous presence, as his dedication and commitment to the Lord was a supreme treasury of blessings and example of comfort and strength to these suffering and oppressed Serbs.[5] In sum, Basil's life and work became a living testament of commitment and dedicated service to the Lord and His faithful people.

Our holy and God-bearing Father Basil of Ostrog, after many years of prayer, fasting, and physical labor for the glory of the Kingdom of Christ, peacefully fell asleep in the Lord in his cell in Ostrog on April 29, 1671. He was sixty years old, and had faithfully and fearlessly pastored his people for over thirty years. Upon his death, his cell was flooded with an amazingly bright mystical light and was filled with a

---

4. Also during this time, St. Basil restored the Chapel of holy Great Martyr George in the Hilandar Monastery on the Holy Mountain, sending monks there to renew both the liturgical and ascetical life.

5. Ostrog was also at this time the center for the cause of political freedom lead by the "Hajduci," freedom-fighters, of Montenegro and Herzegovina.

sweet aroma which fragranced the entire area. From the solid rock beneath his cell, a grapevine grew inexplicably and has healed many who have partaken thereof.

St. Basil was honorably buried in a crypt in the Chapel of the Entrance of the Theotokos into the Temple, which he had previously restored. Immediately after his death many visitors came to venerate his life-giving relics, and miracles have been recorded there from that time until this very hour. In 1678, seven years after his passing on to the Mansions of the Righteous, his crypt was opened by the order of St. Basil himself, who appeared in a dream to the abbot of the Monastery of St. Luke in Nikshich, Raphael Kosijeravac. Upon opening the casket, Basil's body was found completely intact, aglow, very warm and soft and smelling like *Bosiljak* (the herb basil). Though he was treated as a saint while he walked among his people, nonetheless this event officially marked his canonization, as the entire Serbian Church honored him as a true Archpastor, miracle-worker, and defender of the faith in Christ the Lord.

Among the most fervent disciples of St. Basil was the last Serbian Patriarch in Pech,[6] Basil Brkich-Jovanovich (1763-1765; †1772), who, being exiled by the Turks, fled to Montenegro. In Ostrog he spent six months in incessant prayer to St. Basil, after which he wrote the Divine Services and Life of the Saint. And in 1947, the priest Basil Ivoshevich from Boka Kotorska, Professor at the Seminary of Karlovac, Srem, wrote the Akathist Service[7] glorifying St. Basil. This text is now found in Ostrog Monastery.

There are numerous days of the Church year on which St. Basil is glorified, remembered and celebrated. Of course the first are his

6. The Patriarchate of Pech was abolished in 1766. It was fully restored in Belgrade in 1920 after World War I.

7. An akathist is a liturgical service in magnification of a saint or an event. There are several akathists written in honor of the Theotokos. As this Greek word indicates, the service is done while all remain standing—"akathist" means not to sit—as all worshippers stand and magnify that holy person or event.

namedays, January 1st and 30th, the feastdays commemorating his patron saint, St. Basil the Great. There is also a week of fasting—"the Week of Holy Father Basil"—kept prior to April 29th each year in preparation for his feast. Besides these, the faithful gather at Ostrog Monastery on the Feasts of Pentecost, St. Elias, and the Dormition of the Theotokos. On Pentecost, especially, there have been gatherings of over 20,000 pious believers.

There have also been a number of churches and hospitals named after St. Basil. The most noteworthy are the Church of St. Basil in Nikshich and the hospital, opened in 1935, in Belgrade, named after St. Basil the Miracle-worker of Ostrog. Also, in the Church of Sts. Constantine and Helena in Vozhdovac, the miracle-working omophor of St. Basil is preserved to this day, granting healing to all those who venerate him in faith, hope, and love.[8]

"Holy Father Basil, thy divine life and holiness are a loving testament to the superabundant love our Heavenly Father has for all of us. Pray to Christ our God, O wonderworker, for us most needy and infirm sinners, that His healing and divine grace may enkindle and arouse within our hearts a love for the true Orthodox faith and grant us right minds, right bodies, and right spirits, so that we may also be witnesses to His everlasting glory and Kingdom, to Whom belongs glory, honor, and worship, together with His Unoriginate Father, and Life-giving Spirit, now and ever and unto ages of ages. Amen."

---

8. There exists a whole fascinating book on St. Basil: *Cv. Vasilije Ostroshki Chudotvorac*, Beograd 1971, 240pp.

ST. BASIL OF OSTROG
A contemporary Byzantine icon, distributed as a blessing
from Metropolitan Amphilocius (Radovic) to
pilgrims to Ostrog.

ANOTHER TROPARION
Tone 4

Thy glorification has been witnessed by many,* as thou hast healed pious followers* while being both in this world and in the world to come,* O miracle-working Basil.* As thou hast healed pious followers while being both in this world* and in the world to come, O miracle-working Basil.* Therefore, come to the aid of those who call upon thee in faith, hope, and love.

KONTAKION
Tone 8

Since thou didst serve the Lord from thy youth, O wise one.* And belabored thy body with prayer and vigil,* thou wast proven to be a precious vessel of the Most Holy Spirit.* Because of this He established thee as a pastor of His Church which thou didst tend well.* Therefore, thou hast departed to the Lord Whom thou didst love.* We pray to thee to remember us who keep thy memory with faith,* that all may shout unto thee: Rejoice, O most honorable Father Basil.

ANOTHER KONTAKION
Tone 8

Thou didst fearlessly guard the deposit of faith given to thee, O most wise Basil,* as thy spiritual weapons were the Gospel of Christ and the Tradition of God's Holy Church.* Therefore thou hast held three stars: being a virtuous ascetic thou didst become a star to monastics,* defending the faith, thou didst become a pillar to confessors.* Divinely pastoring thy flock, thou didst become an archshepherd of Christ.* Therefore, O divinely-inspired Basil, we call upon thy name before the throne of grace.

ST. SAVA I
A fresco of 1413, in the monastery of Kalenic.

INDEX

326

INDEX

327

INDEX

INDEX